MW01069505

The End of Early Music

The End of Early Music

*A Period Performer's History of Music
for the Twenty-First Century*

Bruce Haynes

OXFORD

UNIVERSITY PRESS

2007

OXFORD
UNIVERSITY PRESS

Oxford University Press, Inc., publishes works that further
Oxford University's objective of excellence
in research, scholarship, and education.

Oxford   New York
Auckland   Cape Town   Dar es Salaam   Hong Kong   Karachi
Kuala Lumpur   Madrid   Melbourne   Mexico City   Nairobi
New Delhi   Shanghai   Taipei   Toronto

With offices in
Argentina   Austria   Brazil   Chile   Czech Republic   France   Greece
Guatemala   Hungary   Italy   Japan   Poland   Portugal   Singapore
South Korea   Switzerland   Thailand   Turkey   Ukraine   Vietnam

Published by Oxford University Press, Inc.
198 Madison Avenue, New York, New York 10016

www.oup.com

Oxford is a registered trademark of Oxford University Press

Library of Congress Cataloging-in-Publication Data
Haynes, Bruce, 1942–
The end of early music: a period performer's history
of music for the 21st century /
Bruce Haynes.
p.   cm.
Includes bibliographical references and index.
ISBN 978-0-19-518987-2
1. Performance practice (Music)—History.   2. Music—Interpretation
(Phrasing, dynamics, etc.)—Philosophy and aesthetics.   I. Title.
ML457.H38   2007
781.4′309—dc22   2006023594

Canada Council   Conseil des Arts
for the Arts   du Canada

3 5 7 9 8 6 4

Printed in the United States of America
on acid-free paper

This book is dedicated to
Erato, muse of lyric and love poetry,
Euterpe, muse of music, and
Joni M., Honored and Honorary Doctor of broken-hearted harmony,
whom I humbly invite to be its patronesses

We're captive on the carousel of time,
We can't return, we can only look
behind from where we came.

(Dr. Joni Mitchell, "The Circle Game," 1966)

Preface

Filling a book full of words about music, I am conscious of John Hawkins's remark in his book on music history of 1776: "Tradition only whispers, for a short time, the name and abilities of a mere Performer, however exquisite the delight which his talents afforded to those who heard him; whereas, a theory once committed to paper and established, lives, at least in libraries, as long as the language in which it was written."[1]

Music moves on, while words remain behind. But even when first written, words have difficulty capturing the essence of a subject as evanescent as music. "Grant that a man read all the books of musick that ever were wrote," writes Roger North (that inexhaustible font of musical wisdom), "I shall not allow that musick is or can be understood out of them, no more than the taste of meats out of cookish receipt books."[2]

A subject like music beckons us on, inviting us to keep trying, though we know we will end up with more questions than answers. Hokusai, great artist that he was, caught just the right spirit of reconciling the vastness of our imaginations with the tininess of the accomplishments of our short lives.

> I have been in love with painting ever since I became conscious of it at the age of six. I drew some pictures I thought fairly good when I was fifty, but really nothing I did before the age of seventy was of any value at all. At seventy-three I have at last caught every aspect of nature—birds, fish, animals, insects, trees, grasses, all. When I am eighty I shall have developed still further, and I will really master the secrets of art at ninety. When I reach a hundred

my work will be truly sublime, and my final goal will be attained around the age of one hundred and ten, when every line and dot I draw will be imbued with life. To all of you who are going to live as long as I do, I promise to keep my word.[3]

"Ars longa, vita brevis." Hokusai only lived to the age of 89 [!], so he was unable to keep his extravagant promise. I doubt he was surprised, or even disappointed. We humans do what we can do, and if we are lucky, we take pleasure from it. As Okakura Kakuzo summed it up,

> The heaven of modern humanity is indeed shattered in the Cyclopean struggle for wealth and power. The world is groping in the shadow of egotism and vulgarity. Knowledge is bought through a bad conscience, benevolence practiced for the sake of utility. The East and West, like two dragons tossed in a sea of ferment, in vain strive to regain the jewel of life. We need a Niuka again to repair the grand devastation; we await the great Avatar.
>
> Meanwhile, let us have a sip of tea. The afternoon glow is brightening the bamboos, the fountains are bubbling with delight, the soughing of the pines is heard in our kettle. Let us dream of evanescence, and linger in the beautiful foolishness of things.[4]

The opinions written here about matters of style, performance, the communication of emotion, and other ephemera do not always rest on criteria that are provable. They are merely personal reflections on the present state of the historically inspired performance movement (known as HIP) seen from the point of view of someone who has been involved in it since the early 1960s. Roger North in 1728 speaks for me—perhaps for us all—when he remarks, "I have ever found I did not well know my owne thoughts, till I had wrote and reviewed them; and then for the most part, mists fell away, and fondness and failings appeared in a clear light."[5] I am delighted to share these thoughts with you. With luck they may inspire you, too, to write down your own.

Acknowledgments

Mattheson cites Sartorius as using a pair of shoes to make the point that *Voto non vivitur uno*, "It is not done with one."[1]

So many people have given me ideas, I will surely forget to name some of them.

Three years ago, the Canada Council for the Arts generously offered me the Senior Fellowship for 2003 to "write and review my owne thoughts," which constitute this book. What you cannot see, holding it in your hands, is the great pleasure I have had in devoting most of my waking hours to this project, and the tremendous learning curve it represents for me. I begin, then, by thanking the Council for its support of this and many other projects.

I promised the Canada Council this would not be a book of musicological research, and I've kept that promise (even if I have read a ton of books, many of them by musicologists, in preparing it). For a while I thought I might even avoid the need for citations, but my debt to many thinkers before me is much too great for that.

As always, for my abiding love of music and the part of it I understand, I have my parents to thank, who introduced me to it early on and shared its joys with me all through their lives. I also take pleasure and pride in naming five outstanding musicians who were kind enough at various times to have acted as my musical mentors: Ross Taylor, Alan Curtis, Frans Brüggen, Sigiswald Kuijken, and Gustav Leonhardt. I have also learned much and had major help in formulating ideas from my contact with an extraordinary musician, Susie Napper (with whom I have the good fortune to share life and the parentage of three children). The ideas in this book are not necessarily theirs, though I hope they would enjoy considering some of them, or the spin I have put on them.

For advice and encouragement with this book I would like to warmly thank Nicholas Avery, Cecil Adkins, Tom Beghin, Alfredo Bernardini, Jay Bernfeld, Tamara Bernstein, John Black, Josep Boras, Jeanne Bovet, José Bowen, Geoffrey Burgess, John Butt, Michael Collver, Lucy van Dael, Sand Dalton, Ross Duffin, Uri Golomb, Pat Grant, Peggy Gries, Arthur Haas, Steve Hammer, Stevan Harnad, Anaïs Haynes, Keith Hill, Robert Hill, Peter Holman, Alan J. Howlett, Roland Jackson, Mary Kirkpatrick, Bart Kuijken, Angèle Laberge, Jean Lamon, Marc-Olivier Lamontagne, Brad Lehman, Matthias Maute, Washington McClain, Bill Metcalfe, Scott Metcalfe, Winfried Michel, Catherine Motuz, Kate van Orden, Richard Ostrofsky, Samantha Owens, Tim Paradise, Meg Partridge, Matthew Peaceman, Jesse Read, Joshua Rifkin, Noel Salmond, Julien Saulgrain, Skip Sempé, Steve Stubbs, Teri Noel Towe, Peter Walls, Nat Watson, Jed Wentz, Jon Wild, the students of my six very interesting graduate seminars at McGill University in 2005–2007, those who listened to my lectures at the ESMUC in Barcelona in 2003 and 2005 and at the Amsterdam Conservatory in 2005, and a number of others who I hope will forgive me for temporary loss of memory.

Finally, I would like to say a word for the quiet but important support that Oxford University Press has been offering to the historically oriented musical world. Two of the five most important books that this one leans on are published by OUP, as is the indispensable journal *Early Music*. I'm personally grateful for the support and assistance of a number of the editors of this book, including Suzanne Ryan, Norman Hirschy, Robert Milks, and Lynn Childress.

Credits

I thank the following publishers for permission to use excerpts from these sources: The Circle Game, Words and Music by JONI MITCHELL, © 1966 (Renewed), CRAZY CROW MUSIC (BMI). All Rights Reserved. Used by Permission. Christopher Small, selections from pages 2, 164, 220, 267, 272, 464, 426, and 421 of *Musicking: The Meanings of Performing and Listening* © 1998 by Christopher Small and reprinted with the permission of Wesleyan University Press. Nikolaus Harnoncourt, *Musik als Klangrede*, © 1982 Residenz Verlag, Salzburg. From *Classical and Romantic Performing Practice* by Brown, C. (1999). By permission of Oxford University Press. From *Text and Act: Essays on Music and Performance* by Taruskin, R. (1996). By permission of Oxford University Press.

Contents

List of Recorded Excerpts

The recorded excerpts are available on the companion website www.oup
.com/us/earlymusic. Excerpts are marked in the text with the following
symbol: ◉

1. Amsterdam Baroque Orchestra, Koopman, 1996. Bach: Cantata
   207a/1. Erato. Track 1. 0–0:27
2. Musica Antiqua Köln, Goebel, 1996. Bach: Cantata 207/1. Archiv.
   Track 1. 0–0:38
3. Unnamed Orchestra, Stokowski, 1957. Bach: Geistliche lied
   "Komm, süsser Tod," BWV 478, arr. Stokowski. EMI Classics,
   7243 5 66385 2 5. Track 2. 2:02–2:50
4. Sarah Brightman, 2001. Handel: "Lascia ch'io pianga." Angel,
   7243 5 33257 2 5. Track 6. 0–0:51
5. Suzie LeBlanc, 2002. Handel: "Lascia ch'io pianga." Atma ACD 2
   2260. Track 4. 0–0:52
6. Concentus Musicus, Harnoncourt, 1981/83. Bach: Brandenburg
   2/2. Ultima, LC 6019. Track 1:2. 0–0:27
7. Bath Festival Orchestra, Menuhin, (? early 1960s). Bach: Brandenburg 2/2. EMI Classics, 7243 5 68516 2 7.[1] Track 6. 0–0:33
8. Philadelphia Orchestra, Stokowski, 1928. Bach: Brandenburg 2/2.
   Andante (orig. Victor), ISBN 0-9712764-6-3. Track 2:11. 0–0:44
9. Adelina Patti, 1905. Mozart: "Voi che sapete." Nimbus, NI
   7840/41. Track 2:1. 2:20–end

10. Concertgebouw Orchestra, Amsterdam Toonkunst Choir, Mengelberg, 1939. Bach: "Wir setzen uns mit Tränen nieder," St. Matthew Passion. Naxos 8.110880–82. Track 3:11. 6:55–7:50

11. Gabrieli Consort & Players, McCreesh, 2002. Bach: "Wir setzen uns mit Tränen nieder," St. Matthew Passion. Archiv 474 200–2. Track 2:33. 5:00–5:31

12. Unnamed Orchestra, Stokowski, 1957. Bach: Air, Suite 3, BWV 1068 ("Air on the G string"). EMI Classics, 7243 5 66385 2 5. Track 8. 1:10–2:10

13. Akademie für Alte Musik, 1995. Bach: Air, Suite 3, BWV 1068 ("Air on the G string"). Harmonia Mundi, HMX 2908074.77. Track 2. 0:42–1:24

14. Alessandro Moreschi, 1904. Bach/Gounod: "Ave Maria." DG, 4590652. Track 2. 0:53–1:43

15. Wanda Landowska, 1933. Bach: Goldberg Variations, theme. EMI Classics, 7243 5 67200 2 2. Track 1. 2–1:14. 0–0:31

16. Wanda Landowska, 1933. Bach: Goldberg Variations, #13. EMI Classics, 7243 5 67200 2 2. 0:38–1:23

17. Gustav Leonhardt, 1965. Bach: Goldberg Variations, #13. Teldec, LC 6019. Track 14. 0:35–1:19

18. Pierre Hantaï, 2003. Bach: Goldberg Variations, #13. Mirare, MIR 9945. Track 14. 0:34–1:19

19. Robert Hill, 2004. Bach: Goldberg Variations, #13. Private recording. Track 34. 0:32–1:11

20. Frans Brüggen and Frans Vester, ca. 1963. Telemann: Concerto, e-minor, Rec and Trv. Teldec, ASIN: B000000SII. Track 8. 0–0:46

21. Brüggen, Bijlsma, Leonhardt, 1962. Handel: HWV 365, 3d mvmt. Telefunken: 6.35359. 2. 0–0:48

22. Brüggen, Bijlsma, Leonhardt, 1973, Handel: HWV 365, 3d mvmt. ABC Classics, ABCL-67005/3. 3. 0–0:49

23. Brüggen, Bijlsma, Leonhardt, 1962. Handel: HWV 360, 3d mvmt. Telefunken: 6.35359. 4. 0–0:38

24. Brüggen, Bijlsma, Leonhardt, 1973/74. Handel: HWV 360, 3d mvmt. Track 5. 0–0:38

25. Unnamed Orchestra, Stokowski, 1957. Bach: BWV 565, arr. Stokowski. EMI Classics, 7243 5 66385 2 5. Track 11. 0–0:46

26. Los Angeles Philharmonic, Salonen, 1999. Bach: BWV 565, arr. Stokowski. Sony Classical SK89012. Track 1. 0–0:50

27. Berlin Philharmonic, Karajan, 1952. Bach: Mass in B-Minor, First Kyrie, bars 30–34. EMI-Angel 3500 C (35015-6-7); later reissues EMI Références CHS 7 63505-2, EMI Classics 5 67207 2 5. 0–0:32

28. Amsterdam Baroque Orchestra, Koopman, 1994. Bach: Mass in B-Minor, First Kyrie, bars 30–36. Erato 4509–98478–2. 0–0:31

29. Joseph Joachim, 1903. Bach: Adagio from g-minor solo violin sonata. Opal, CD 9851. Track 2. 0–0:40

30. Yehudi Menuhin, 1935. Bach: Adagio from g-minor solo violin sonata. EMI Classics, 7243 5 67198 2 8. Track 1:1. 0–0:49

31. Lucy van Dael, 1996. Bach: Adagio from g-minor solo violin sonata. Naxos. Track 1:1. 0–0:34

32. Vienna Philharmonic, Höffgen, Furtwängler, 1954. Bach: "Erbarme dich," St. Matthew Passion. EMI Classics. Track 2:9. 1:16–1:53

33. H. Koch, Romantic oboe, M. Friesenhausen, H. Rilling. Bach: Cantata 187/5. Hänssler, CD 92.056. Track 22. 0–0:49

34. B. Haynes, hautboy, M. Emmermann, G. Leonhardt, 1989. Bach: Cantata 187/5. Teldec 8.35836 ZL, 244179–2. Track 2:5. 0–0:58

35. Fritz Kreisler, 1911. Kreisler: *Liebeslied*. DG, 4590652. Track 13. 0–0:56

36. Joshua Bell, 1996. Kreisler: *Liebeslied*. Decca, 44409. Track 7. 0–0:59

37. M. Petri and G. Malcolm, 1984. Marcello: Largo, Sonata, F. Philips, 412 632–2.Track 21. 0:29–1:23

38. Stevie Wonder and Take 6, 1992. "O thou that tellest good tidings to Zion,"*Handel's Messiah: A Soulful Celebration*, set by Mervyn Warren. Reprise 9 26980-2. Track 8. 0–0:55

39. Leonhardt Consort, Equiluz, Leonhardt, 1987. Bach: "Jesu, meines Todes Tod" in BWV 165. Teldec, Das Kantatenwerk, vol. 39. 0–0:31

40. Bach Collegium Japan, Sakurada, Suzuki, 1996.Bach: "Jesu, meines Todes Tod" in BWV 165. BIS, CD-801. Track 13. 0–0:26

41. Leonhardt Consort, M. Kweksilber, D. Smithers, G. Leonhardt, 1976. Bach: BWV 51/5. Teldec Kantatenwerk vol.14, Track 5. 0–0:19

42. Bach Ensemble, Baird, Holmgren, Rifkin, 1986. Bach: BWV 51/5. Florilegium 417 616 2. Track 12. 0–0:21

43. Bach Ensemble, Schopper, Rifkin, 1995–96. Bach: "Starkes Lieben," BWV 182. Dorian DOR 93231, Track 4. 0–0:51

44. Amsterdam Baroque Orchestra, Mertens Koopman, 1995. Bach: "Starkes Lieben," BWV 182/4. Erato 0630-12598-2. Track 4. 0–0:46

45. Henry's Eight, 1997. Clemens non Papa: Ego flos campi. Etcetera, KTC 1214. Track 1. CD 16596. 0–0:48

46. Concerto Italiano, 1994. Monteverdi: Secondo Libro, "Non si levava ancor l'alba novella." Opus 111, OPS 30–111. Track 1. CD 10376. 0–0:46

47. Complesso Barocco, Curtis, 1996. Monteverdi: Lamento della ninfa. Virgin Classics, 7243 5 45302 2 7. Track 8. CD 12778. 2:29–3:20

48. Complesso Barocco, Curtis, 1996. Monteverdi: "Or che 'l ciel." Virgin Classics, 7243 5 45302 2 7. Track 17. CD 12778. 1:00–1:59

49. Joshua Bell, 1996. Kreisler: La Précieuse (alleged to be by Louis Couperin). *Decca*, 44409. Track 5. 0–0:52
50. Gabrieli Consort & Players, McCreesh, 2002. Bach: "O Mensch, bewein dein Sünde groβ," *St. Matthew Passion.* Archiv 474 200–2. Track 1:29. 5:18–6:00
51. Balbastre: *Romance* (1779), from LP produced to accompany a reprint of Fuller 1979. Musical Box Society. 0–0:58
52. Eddie South, Stéphane Grappelly (!), Django Reinhardt, Paul Cordonnier, Paris, 1937. Bach: Double Violin Concerto (swing version). The Chronological Eddie South, Classics Records, 737, ASIN: B000001NOI. Track 2. 0:50–1:48
53. Skip Sempé, 2004. Louis Couperin: Pavanne in f#. Alpha 066. Track 8. 0–1:05
54. Glenn Gould (harpsichord). Handel: HWV 426. Sony Classical, SMK 52 590. Track 1. 0–0:48
55. Glenn Gould (harpsichord). Handel: HWV 428. Sony Classical, SMK 52 590. Track 9. 0–0:57
56. Gustav Leonhardt, 1991. Forqueray: La Morangis. Sony Vivarte, SK 48 080. Track 5. Uses Skowroneck signed "Nicholas Lefébure, Rouen, 1755." 0–0:51
57. Rev C. L. Franklin. Legendary sermon, [early 1950s]. Universal Music Special, MCAD-21145. Tracks 1–2. 6:49–7:48
58. Il Giardino Armonico, Cecilia Bartoli, 1999. Vivaldi: "Qual favellar?" Decca, 289 466 569-2. Track 4. 1:02–1:52
59. Les Arts Florissants, Corréas, Christie, 1992. Rameau: *Castor et Pollux:* Act II, Scenes 1 and 2. Pollux's aire "Nature, Amour." Track 2:1. 0:21–1:20
60. Concentus Musicus, Souzay, Harnoncourt, 1972. Rameau: *Castor et Pollux:* Act II, Scene 1: Pollux's aire "Nature, Amour." Teldec, 8.35048. 0:20–1:16
61. Concentus Musicus, Souzay, Harnoncourt, 1972. Rameau: *Castor et Pollux:* Act II, Scene 2: Pollux's recit. Teldec, 8.35048. 0–0:29
62. Amsterdam Baroque Orchestra, Mertens, Koopman, 2001., Bach: Cantata 13/5. *Antoine Marchand.* 2:36–3:22
63. Concertgebouw Orchestra, Durigo, Mengelberg, 1939. Bach: "Erbarme dich," St. Matthew Passion Naxos 8.110880–82. Track 2:14. 0–1:11
64. Amsterdam Baroque Orchestra, Prégardien, Koopman, 1995. Bach: Cantata 172/4. A. Marchand. Track 23. 0–0:23
65. Leonhardt Consort, v.Altena, Leonhardt, 1987. Bach: Cantata 172/4. Teldec. Track 11. 0–0:56
66. Haynes, Napper, Haas, 1998. F. Couperin, Septième Concert, 1st movement. Atma, ACD 2 2168. Track 2. Complete
67. Haynes, Taylor, Napper, Poirier, 1998. Bach: Cantata 116/2. Atma, ACD 2 2158. Track 5. 0–1:01

68. Susie Napper, 2005. Corrette: 3d movement from the Sonata in d minor from *Les délices de la solitude*. Atma ACD 2 2307. Complete
69. Nadina Mackie Jackson, 2005. Corrette: 3d movement from the Sonata in d minor from *Les délices de la solitude*. MSR Classics MS 1171. Complete
70. C. Huntgeburth and W. Michel, 1982–85. Simonetti: Adagio ma non tanto, Sonata II/3. Mieroprint, EM 5000. Track 13. 0:47–1:35
71. Ludger Rémy, 1992. Tomesini: Andante in D, 2d Clavierstuck. Mieroprint EM 5005. Track 2. 0:51–1:52
72. Ensemble Caprice, Rebel, 2001. Maute: 3d movement, Concerto detta la Sammartini. Atma, ACD2 2273. Track 10. 0–1:06

The End of Early Music

Introduction

*In matters of Antiquity, there are two extreames, 1. a totall
neglect, and 2. perpetuall guessing . . .*

(Roger North, 1728)

Literacy

In music, we give the highest status to our "art" musicians in formal dress
who perform the kind of music to which we give the name "Classical."
But because our society is exceedingly literate, these Classical musicians
have evolved in a curious way: they're so good now at reading music that
their natural ability to improvise has atrophied. Most of them have no
choice but to perform from written pages (in the memory or on the
stand).

Literacy has created a preoccupation with the "repertoire" or Canon
of great works, and a text-fetishism that does not allow performers to
change any detail of the "masterpieces" of the past. There are many re-
searchers who devote their lives to finding out the "intentions" of composers. So it's not surprising that Classical musicians don't improvise
much. In fact, few of us can improvise at all. We even write out our graces
and cadenzas (which were originally developed as fenced-off areas reserved for improvization).

Please don't misunderstand me: as musicians, we are as good today
as the musicians of the past. But our training has become overspecialized,
directed as it is toward playing written music. Derek Bailey puts our current situation in a nutshell:

> One reason why the standard Western instrumental training produces
> non-improvisors (and it doesn't just produce violinists, pianists, cellists,

3

etcetera; it produces specifically non-improvisors, musicians rendered incapable of attempting improvisation) is that not only does it teach how to play
an instrument, it teaches that the creation of music is a separate activity from
playing that instrument. Learning how to create music is a separate study totally divorced from playing an instrument.[1]

This separation between composing and performing hasn't always existed. Before the rise of Romanticism, improvisation and composition were
normal activities for any musician. In a time when new pieces were in
constant demand, being a composer was nothing special, just part of the
process of producing music. But even if a musician didn't always write
their improvisations down, they had to know how to make up music on
the spot. Without that ability, they couldn't play the music of the time.

Baroque notation is like shorthand, a quality known in the trade as
"thin" writing. Baroque composers rarely included marks to indicate
phrasing gestures, for instance, or dynamics, note-shaping, flexibility of
tempo, and subtlety of rhythm. Variables of that kind are implied in the
playing style, however, so performers supplied them as a matter of course.
Thin writing was not thin because "thick" writing hadn't been invented
yet; it was deliberate. It accommodated spontaneous input from the performers. To play or sing only what was written would not have been sufficient or have pleased the listeners—least of all the composer. It would
have been like a jazz saxophonist playing only the tune, and straight at
that! In the Baroque period, a musician needed less written information,
because they were like a combination of an improvising jazzman and a
reading Classical player. In any case, neither the essential graces (the *agréments*) or the more elaborate passaggi could be accurately notated, and
when they were improvised it left room for some aspects of a piece to be
different each time it was performed. This created an ad hoc environment
that was reinforced by other elements: rehearsal was minimal, the leader
played in the group, and the media (such as playing styles and instruments) were constantly changing.

The Romantic Revolution

What hangs like a veil between the musicians of today and those of pre-
Romantic times are the changes in ideals and mentality, the paradigm
shifts that are symbolized by the Industrial Revolution that took place between about 1760 and 1840, and more specifically the French Revolution
that began in 1789.

To make the story of nineteenth-century culture start in the year of the
French Revolution is at once convenient and accurate, even though nothing
in history "starts" at a precise moment. For although the revolution itself had

its beginnings in ideas and conditions preceding that date, it is clear that the events of 1789 brought together and crystallized a multitude of hopes, fears, and desires into something visible, potent, and irreversible. . . . There are so many evidences of a new direction in thought and culture.[2]

The musical revolution does not seem to have been gradual. It was truly a break in history. The major change in the designs and techniques of every kind of musical instrument at the beginning of the Romantic period, for instance, was no slow evolution; it was a rupture with the past that took place in less than two generations. But new kinds of instruments were symptomatic of something bigger. Everything, it seems, was changing.

Canonism and Classicism

For centuries the ideals and standards of quality of literature, architecture, and the graphic arts had been set by examples that originated in Classical antiquity. Artists and writers had done their utmost to emulate these "Classic" models. But in music, no such examples had survived; very little evidence of the nature of ancient Greek and Roman music has ever been found. The Romantics decided to create their own Classical models, using the exquisite conceit that music was an "autonomous," "absolute" medium. Music could at last move up from craft to art; could become "Classical." Composers became the heroes, promoted to the status of geniuses. Musical pantheons were erected, and plaster factories geared up to create busts of composers, like so many ancient Roman emperors, the resemblances to the actual composers a matter of chance.

A Canon of Classical works began to be built up, with Beethoven's symphonies as its base. This way of thinking, called *Canonism*, was the cornerstone of the Romantic movement from its beginnings, and represented a fundamental shift in Western musical culture. An expression of the present-day Canonic attitude is the survival of many musical institutions founded in the nineteenth century: publishing houses, journals, orchestras, opera houses, and conservatories. Canonism is symbolized by nineteenth-century concert halls with the names of "great" composers immortalized in friezes around the walls.

The Classical Canon is the repertoire we all know from the nineteenth century, undeniably beautiful music to which most musicians of the present day still dedicate their talents. In such a context, a composer's works came to be seen almost as scripture. The "paradigm of music as consisting in works written by the great of the past, transmitted in writing and accepted by the current generation through its enactment, supported by written programs, by basically non-innovatory performers"[3] pretty well describes the Classical music scene of today. And Canonism is selective;

admission to the god-like domain of great composers has been virtually impossible since about the time of the First World War.

Despite Canonism's continuing widespread authority, most musicians nowadays are scarcely conscious of it as a concept. Yet it is so pervasive and familiar that not only does it form the core of the repertoire for symphony auditions, but any good young instrumentalist knows how each piece is expected to be played, right down to bowings, dynamic marks, and places to breathe.

The Canonic ideology leads to a number of corollaries that form the basic assumptions of Classically oriented musicians. They include:

- great respect for composers, represented by the cults of genius and originality,
- the almost scriptural awe of musical "works,"
- an obsession with the original intentions of the composer,
- the practice of listening to music as ritual,
- the custom of repeated hearings of a limited number of works.

Canonism is strictly a "Classical" thing. Jazz doesn't worry about the "intentions" of a composer, rock doesn't give much weight to who "composed" a piece, pop music doesn't get hung up on a prescribed and immovable repertoire. Nor were they an issue for our ancestors before about 1800 either. Baroque composers weren't artists, after all. They were clever craftsmen, rather like building contractors or horse-race jockeys today, more interested in competence than greatness. Nor did the scores in which their compositions were written (or more commonly, the unscored parts) have any importance beyond facilitating their real work, which was performing concerts. In any case, the pages of notes they handed out were incomplete and quite useless without the musicians who knew how to convert them into music.

Modern HIP musicians are under the Canonic spell too. Usually Classically trained, they sometimes find themselves confusing fidelity to a style with fidelity to particular hero-composers. Against their own logic, they sometimes treat scores as untouchable (that is, unchangeable). They tend to ignore 90% of the historical repertoires of their instruments, gathering dust on library shelves, while listening and playing over again and again the same works (like Messiahs and Christmas oratorios) much more often than they were ever meant to be heard. Without thinking, they also tend to lump Period performance with "Classical" music (as witnessed by their adoption of the Victorian dress suit and frock, the uniforms—Period, actually—of both the Romantic and Modernist symphony musician), and they perform in anachronistic environments (purpose-built concert halls filled with silently respectful audiences). These are all creations of Canonism; none of them had been considered necessary before the "modern age."

Progress or Adaptation

One of the basic messages of HIP is the rejection of the idea of progress that still holds many of us—unconsciously—in thrall. The history of music, HIP is saying, is not a story of gradual improvement; or, as Collingwood put it, "Bach was not trying to write like Beethoven and failing; Athens was not a relatively unsuccessful attempt to produce Rome."[4] The history of art can be seen as a kind of Darwinian evolution only if we remember one essential condition: evolution depends on the principle of appropriate adaptation to environment. The goals of a Vivaldi concerto are quite different from those of Mozart, Beethoven, or Paganini; and to compare them is rewarding only in the context of their differing artistic aims. Most important of all, the evolutionary theory breaks down when it is associated with value judgments. A common assumption among musicians is that art evolves in a continuous line to the perfection of the present. This implies that the world of art today must be the best of all possible worlds—a conclusion most people would find difficult to agree with.[5]

Serendipity

To appreciate the full implications of the fundamental differences between Romantic and pre-Romantic music takes time. One could even say the work of modern HIP musicians consists of the slow realization of how different a pre-Romantic piece can sound from anything they have heard before. And this realization often comes along with an effect known as "Serendipity." Serendipity is the joyful phenomenon of making happy and agreeable discoveries unintentionally.[6] Like Columbus setting out to find a route to the Indies and accidentally discovering America instead.

The Serendipity effect is directly tied to the pursuit of Authenticity. It addresses the question—not an unreasonable one—whether it really matters if we perform details as they were done in their own period. My experience has been pretty consistent: the reason for incomprehensible practices does not often become evident until we actually do it that way ourselves, sometimes for a long time. Stated as a principle of musicking, we could say that if you attempt to be historically consistent, persistence will eventually show a logic that was not immediately obvious. Although it doesn't guarantee them, Serendipity promises rewards for experiment.

Taruskin himself finds that the effect of the historically oriented frame of mind may open performers'

> minds and ears to new experiences, and enable them to transcend their habitual, and therefore unconsidered, ways of hearing and thinking about the music. . . . The object is not to duplicate the sounds of the past, for if that were our aim we should never know whether we had succeeded. What we are

aiming at, rather, is the startling shock of newness, of immediacy, the sense of rightness that occurs when after countless frustrating experiments we feel as though we have achieved the identification of performance style with the demands of the music.[7]

Musical Rhetoric

Prior to the Romantic Revolution, music and the arts in general were based on values and practices that seem fundamentally different from those we call "modern." The magnitude of the gap is difficult to appreciate and often difficult to see. These differences are discussed more thoroughly in the chapters that follow, but I want to give here some idea of what they are, in order to suggest that, seen dimly through the veils of Romanticism that hang between them and us, there was an alternate system, another ethos. It was an ethos that once worked, and while we do not need all of it, any more than we need the economies and governments of the period, we can learn from it and draw on it for inspiration for our own present time. At the very least, a knowledge of an alternate value system will help us better understand our own.

To quote Walter Ong, "until the modern technological age, which effectively began with the Industrial Revolution and Romanticism, Western culture in its intellectual and academic manifestations can be meaningfully described as rhetorical culture."[8] Rhetoric, a system of public communication and persuasion invented by the ancient Greeks, developed by the Romans, and enthusiastically revived in the Renaissance, was mentioned or discussed by virtually everyone who wrote about music until about 1800.

Rhetorical music had as its main aim to evoke and provoke emotions—the Affections, or Passions—that were shared by everyone, audience and performers alike. Canonic music, by contrast, was usually autobiographical in some sense, often describing an extreme experience of the artist-composer: cathartic or enlightening, but above all solitary and individual. Another difference is that in a performance, the Baroque composer was better off alive, because in that way, they could help make their music work well by playing along. The Romantic artist-composer, on the other hand, was best dead, because that seemed to make it easier to appreciate their genius. Another difference was that while Rhetorical music was temporary, like today's films—appreciated, then forgotten—Canonic music was eternal and enduring. Rhetorical music was transient, disposable, its repertoire constantly changing. Canonic music was by definition stable, repeatable, and orthodox.

With the rise of Canonism, Rhetoric found itself marginalized and eventually demoted to little more than a negative vibe; "Rhetoric" nowadays usually means something like "bombast." The compelling force of the idea of musical Canon makes it hard for us now to imagine how basic the principles of Rhetoric once were to musicians.

Authenticity as a Statement of Intent

We don't think about it much, but in fact those old pieces were not written for us. Nobody back then knew what we would be like, what kinds of instruments we would be playing, or what we would expect from our music. In fact, they didn't even know we would be playing their pieces. So, a little adaptation is called for to fit their music to us.

Here's where we get onto the subject of Authenticity because there's a choice of approaches. One way is like "Chinese-Canadian" restaurants, where the inspiration is from China (and perhaps the cook as well), but the end result does not surprise the palette of a Canadian who "knows what they like." This is how a symphony orchestra plays Vivaldi's *Seasons,* for instance, using the inspiration of a culture nearly 300 years removed from us and adapting it to the familiar sounds of the symphony orchestra. (I won't say "modern orchestra" because the instruments being played aren't modern in any sense; we'll get to that later.)

There is another approach to eating Chinese food outside of China. Some people look for food not adapted to some other taste; what we might call "authentic" Chinese. Menus are written in Chinese only. Some of the tastes may take time to learn to appreciate, but the experience is "expanding," perhaps in more ways than one (!).

For modern symphony musicians, "music of the past belongs to the present as music, not as documentary evidence,"[9] as Dahlhaus put it. James Parakilas called this "music as tradition":

> Classical performers present music as tradition by making the past continuous with the present. . . . Listeners hearing music as tradition hear it as something belonging to them. . . . Classical composers, however warmly personified, speak a timeless, universal message. They speak to modern listeners because they have spoken to generations of listeners.[10]

Time, in this chronocentric paradigm, stands still. The symphonies of a German born in 1770 become contemporary. And because his symphonies have never stopped being played, we assume that we are dealing with an unchanged performing style. And yet, even a casual exposure to early twentieth-century recordings indicates that preserving a performing style is like trying to hold water in your hand. It is a lovely illusion to think of modern symphony concerts as part of an unbroken tradition, but historically speaking there isn't much difference between symphony orchestras and "Early music" concerts. Both are working with lost traditions, the difference being how they think of them.

At first glance, a movement like HIP (the Historically Inspired Performance movement), which actively tries to join historical awareness to historical music, seems like the perfect example of Canonism: honoring dead composers. But it is the paradox of HIP that it uses the past as inspiration but does not, like Canonism, pretend to be a continuation of it. HIP starts in the present and ends in the present. As Collingwood put it, "The revolutionary can only regard his revolution as a progress in so far as he is also an historian, genuinely re-enacting in his own historical thought the life he nevertheless rejects."[11] HIP highlights the historical dimension; it draws attention to the profound differences of music before and after 1800 in ideology, values, and performing practices. And as HIP gradually succeeds in embracing pre-Canonic, Rhetorical practices, it is conscious of taking distance from the values and customs of Canonism. The symphony musician playing Brahms and the Early musician playing Bach are both playing in styles whose oral traditions have been lost, but the difference between them is "between a blink and a wink," their own perception of what they are doing in relation to history.

More than anything else, Authenticity seems to be a statement of intent. Totally accurate historical performance is probably impossible to achieve. To know it has been achieved is certainly impossible. But that isn't the goal. What produces interesting results is the *attempt* to be historically accurate, that is, authentic.

There was a time when "AUTHENTIC" sold records like "ORGANIC" sells tomatoes. Musicians didn't usually make up the liner notes that went with their recordings, and if they were described as "authentic" when they were really "an *attempt* to be authentic," it seemed like quibbling.

Before the 1980s, HIP was not well enough established to attract much attention or sympathetic criticism. But in that decade, Richard Taruskin began publishing his critical articles and reviews. Taruskin brilliantly articulated the nature of Modernism and its threat to HIP, and in doing so did a great service to music.[12] Eloquently and wittily, Taruskin also stuck a good many holes in HIP's balloon in his articles, questioning the ultimate reliability of historical information in general and the motives of performers. His writings, unfortunately, had the effect of embedding Authenticity in "scare-quotes," which is the way it usually appears these days. "Authenticity" has even been called "the movement's ominous theory" and an "arrogant claim." Authenticity became a hexed word and served for a while as a kind of lightening rod for anybody who was dissatisfied with some aspect of the Movement.

Despite this, the idea that the word represents refuses to go away. The reason is clear: Authenticity is simple, it's logical, and (as we have seen) it's central and essential to the concept called HIP.

"Scare-Quotes" for Authenticity

Taruskin objected to the moral and ethical overtones of the claim by HIP musicians to use "instruments or styles of playing that are historically appropriate to the music being performed," which devalues other approaches to performance. He invoked the "invidious comparison": who, he asked, would want to use inauthentic instruments or styles of playing?[13]

I don't see a problem here. Who indeed? A value judgment it certainly is, but nobody's forcing anybody else to change their instruments or styles of playing. Whatever word we use for the concept of historically appropriate actions, I can't see why noticing and acknowledging historical changes of style and instrument needs defending.

It seems to me that what does need defending, and what is logically and æsthetically questionable, is the old traditional attitude, the chronocentrism described in chapter 1 that insists on using a single performing style for the music of all periods and blithely ignores differences of style and instruments. A colleague of mine, in a moment of levity, wondered whether there were any convenient terms or acronyms for various forms of "non-HIP." He suggested

> Historically Clueless Performance? Wild Guesswork Performance? Whatever Feels Right Performance? Whatever My Personal Hero Did Must Be Right Performance? Didn't Do My Homework So I'll Wing It Performance? Anything Goes Performance? History Is Irrelevant Performance? Whatever They Did On My Favorite Recording That's What I Must Imitate Performance? Just The Facts Ma'am Performance? What My Teacher's Teacher's Teacher's Teacher Did Because He Was Beethoven Performance? OK, I'm getting carried away here, but all those types of performance *do* exist, even if there aren't convenient labels for them.[14]

Even if tongue-in-cheek, this list is a pretty good summary of the rationales for not playing HIP.

Let's reverse the anachronism, and imagine one of Brahms's piano concertos played on a harpsichord. Absurd idea—but is it any more absurd than Bach's harpsichord concertos played on the modern grand?[15]

The End of Early Music

As has been clear for a generation now, the one thing our music is not is "Early." There was once a reason for that name: "Early music" was once a different kind of music from the norm, often deliberately different. We describe the unknown by comparing it to the known. To take one instance, there was the normal Boehm flute; then there were the historical flutes, which were variants, like the "Baroque flute," the "Renaissance flute," and so on. The same with the "modern" bassoon and the "Baroque" bassoon, "Baroque" drums—and this is quite incredible if you think about it—even the "Baroque violin"! The violin, the archetypical object and symbol of the seventeenth century, was given a name that implied that the altered string setups used in the symphony orchestras of today were supposed to represent the real norm, the plain "violin." Then there was the harpsichord, which, if it hadn't had a separate name, would have been the "Baroque piano." In the same way, historical performing styles were looked on as exceptions and taught in a special class called "Performance Practice," where one learned about whatchamacallit ornaments and other curious ways of performing, out of the traditional mainstream.

But the mainstream is always changing, and these "Early" instruments and their "Early" playing styles now no longer seem so exceptional or exotic. They're more like "Late" than "Early." There is a tradition, young as it is, that gives logic to them. An indication of this is that as recently as the 1980s, recordings were often advertised as using "historical instruments"; you rarely see that on CDs nowadays. It has become normal and unremarkable.

So, if "Early music" is no longer Early, let's call it by a more accurate name. That name should be "Modern music," since it is a relatively recent phenomenon. But this term is already taken. In fact the idea that really captures the spirit of the period we've been calling "Early," the principle that motivated artists, intellectuals, and musicians of the time, was Rhetoric, the art of communication. As I will discuss in the coming chapters, music was such an eminent example of applied Rhetoric, it would be logical to call it by this, its principal paradigm, its operating system. Rhetoric is particularly appropriate because it was a system the Romantics despised and marginalized. *Rhetorical music* thus expresses the essence of the musical spirit prior to the Romantic Revolution.

Here we are, then, at the beginning of this book, witnessing one small end of "Early music." From now on, I'll call it by this new name, *Rhetorical music.*

Musicking

"Musicking" is a word coined by a very interesting author, Christopher Small. By "musicking," Small means to imply that music is not a thing, but an activity, and includes "all musical activity from composing to performing to listening to a Walkman to singing in the shower—even cleaning up after a concert is a kind of musicking."

Taking Small's meaning, I think of musicking as a kind of "multi-disciplinary" term that helps me frame my own concept of a nexus of Rhetorical musical activities that includes performing, instrument making, editing music or making it available to musicians, teaching musical performance and music history, studying music history, composing new pieces and analyzing existing ones, and so on. All of these are forms of historical musicking, and the dynamic that joins them is a sense of style. The same principles and values frequently apply more or less consistently over all these activities.

Terminology and Concepts

Speaking of names for things, Confucius pointed out that when terms are not well defined, discussion is not smooth. So it's probably worthwhile to take a little time for this.

There is no way to know if our modern restorations accurately recall the original repertoire and practices of music before 1800, try as we might. So we can't in all honesty give the same names to the original and the restoration. Thus a modern copy of an old *original* instrument is a *Period* instrument. A modern musician whose sense of style is based on an old original style is a "Period performer" or a "historical performer." I use "Period style" in a generic sense for an infinite number of styles, united only by the fact that they all must be restored from lost originals.

There are two aspects of style: Romanticism, for instance, as compared with Romantic performing protocol. The latter is the performing techniques and conventions, the manner or protocol in which a piece is executed that uniquely distinguishes it as a style. The other aspect of style is a general attitude or stance that applies to all the arts, music included; these are the ideas that are taken for granted: the philosophy, artistic assumptions, and motives of a style, its *ideology*, in other words. Classical musicians play in Modern style, for instance, without the faintest clues about Modernism, or how it differs from Romanticism. I will normally call these two aspects *ideologies* and *performing protocol*. It seems strange that these two aspects of any given style are not directly related. There is no causal connection between Portamento and Romanticism, for instance.

Within the Rhetorical era, my focus is primarily music from about 1600 to 1800, for two reasons. One is that it is the period in which I have worked as a performer. The other is that the motivating principles of the music of this period, the Baroque, were revolutionary when they appeared and were largely obliterated when they were supplanted, so in their revival they seem once again revolutionary.

Here are some other terms I use frequently:

Affection: Passion; Affect; Humour; mental state; feeling; emotion

agogics: taking rhythmic freedoms in order to distinguish the relative melodic importance of notes

agréments: essential graces; small ornaments like appoggiaturas, trills, and mordents, usually marked with coded signs. *Compare* passaggi

authentic: historically accurate and credible

beat hierarchy: difference of stress on the beats of the bar; Good and Bad Notes

Canonic music = Romantic music

chronocentrism: the attitude that one's own time or period is superior; the equivalent in time of the spatial concept of ethnocentrism.
Contrasted here with pluralism

Classical period: roughly 1770–1800

climax phrase = long-line phrase

delivery: effective performance; *compare* declamation

declamation (*Vortrag*): playing or singing in an impassioned oratorical
manner; expressing strong feelings addressed to the passions of the
listeners. *See also* Eloquent style

Early music: *see* HIP, Period style, and Rhetorical music (all valid
simultaneously)

eloquence: vividly or movingly expressive public discourse; good Delivery, marked by force and persuasiveness; being effective at
touching an audience and moving their hearts

Eloquent style: a Baroque performing style that is vividly and movingly expressive; playing or singing in an impassioned oratorical
manner. Based on declamation and gestural phrasing. Contrasted
here with: Strait style

essential graces: *see* agréments

figure : a specific, recognised motif or gesture

gestural phrasing: phrasing based on gestures and figures rather than
on the overarching long-line

gesture: a physical movement that has meaning

gesture, musical: a generic figure; a short sequence of notes; a musical
building block; a segment or subdivision of a phrase; the smallest
unit of musical meaning into which a melodic line can be divided

HIP (historically-inspired performance; historically-informed performance): a movement in reaction to the Romantic and Modernist movements. Also called Authenticity Movement; Early music
Movement; Period Performance Movement; Second Practice. Contrasted here with: original performance

historical performer = Period performer

ideology: the philosophy, artistic assumptions, and motives of a style
rather than its performing protocol (the manner, techniques, and
conventions by which a piece is executed)

invention: the composer's essential thematic idea, whether of an entire
composition or the smallest gesture within it; the first stage of an
oration or composition: the inspiration and argument

Klang-rede: musical discourse

long-line phrase: phrase developed in the early nineteenth century,
often taken in one breath or bow, starting softly, building to a
"goal" or "climax," then diminishing = climax phrase

musicking: coined by Christopher Small. Implies that music is not a
thing, but an activity. Musicking includes "all musical activity

from composing to performing to listening to a Walkman to singing in the shower—even cleaning up after a concert is a kind of musicking."[16]

OVPP: one voice per part in Bach's vocal pieces

passaggi: elaborate improvisations or diminutions; free ornamentation; Coloraturen; optional variations; Passages (Galliard), variations (Neumann); extempore variations (Quantz)

performance practice: Common Practice; evidence of what and how music was performed; practical stylistic conventions of historical performance

Period: activity produced in the present in imitation of one from a particular historical period (as in "Period furniture" or "Period costumes"). In this book it normally means the musical style of the seventeenth and eighteenth centuries. Contrasted here with: "original"; Ancient

Period composition: a modern composition convincingly in the style of a past period

Period instrument: an instrument that is contemporaneous with the time the music was written

Period style: style no longer performed through an oral tradition but needing to be acquired through written sources

pluralism: the awareness of the historical development of music and the changes of style that have taken place in it. Contrasted here with: chronocentrism

replica: a copy exact in all details; a clone

Rhetorical music: music made when musical Rhetoric was valued and used, beginning with the Renaissance and including the late eighteenth century; rejected by the Romantic Revolution

Romantic Revolution: the Æsthetic Revolution; Great Divide or Cultural Hinge framed by the Industrial Revolution, roughly concurrent with the French revolution (1789) and Beethoven's Third Symphony (1803)

Romantic music: music from about 1800 onward (including most contemporary music)

Romantic period: the period from about 1800 onward, dominated by the aesthetic values of Romanticism

Romanticism: the musical ideology of the nineteenth and twentieth centuries; not Romantic style

rubato / *tempo rubato*: expressive alteration of tempo

Serendipity: making happy and agreeable discoveries unexpectedly

Strait style: a form of Period style characterised by emotional detachment and a lack of expressiveness; Modernist Period style

I

PERFORMING STYLES

1

When You Say Something Differently, You Say Something Different

It is possible, through different kinds of delivery, to make [musical] passages sound so different that they are scarcely recognizable.

(Emanuel Bach, *Versuch*)

"Style Is That Which Becomes Unstylish"

Coco Chanel was once quoted as saying, "La mode, c'est ce qui se démode." Style changes are easy to see in clothes. Every year has its new ideas, and the years lump themselves into "periods." In men's fashions, for instance, there is the ultra-conservative white-tie-and-tails at one end, a style that is literally identical to formal wear a hundred years ago. Further along the gamut is the business suit, which changes in details but has remained relatively stable in basic identity for at least the last century. On the other end are the highly variable casual fashions like weekend garb, which change seasonally. Music has parallel categories: on the conservative end are wedding, funeral, and most religious repertoire, in the middle is the relatively unchanging "Canonic" music, and on the informal side is popular music, highly variable and constantly shifting.

Christopher Small writes about a similar case in the theater and films:

I recently saw again Lawrence Olivier's 1943 film of Shakespeare's *Henry V*. To those of us who saw it the first time around, it seemed that Olivier had found a way of speaking Shakespeare that flowed and resonated with the sounds and rhythms of everyday speech and of acting with bodily gestures that appeared utterly natural and spontaneous. But on seeing it again fifty years later, it seemed as extravagantly theatrical—as fruity, almost— as those ancient recordings of famous Victorian actors which we in our time found so hilarious. It was not Olivier's fault; it is just that the conventions of representation have changed over the fifty years. There *is* no natural way to speak Shakespeare.[1]

It used to be, back in pre–World War II days, that performing style in Romantic music would "demode" very slowly. In those days there was only a single performing protocol, one style that "fit all" and was used for music of many different kinds of composition. It was only in popular music that musical styles developed and atrophied in the space of a year or less.

But it wasn't always like that. Before the Romantic Revolution, concert music was much less stable.

Innovation

The Baroque period has been called "a celebration of ephemera"[2] because, like modern clothes designers, eighteenth-century performer-composers were required to be constantly producing new creations.

- In the 1770s, for example, Burney wrote that "musical compositions are so short-lived in Italy, such is the rage for novelty, that for the few copies wanted, it is not worth while to be at the expence of engraving, and of the rolling-press."[3]
- Von Uffenbach wondered in 1716 how Lully's operas could still be so effective, considering how old they were (Lully had died in 1687, scarcely twenty-nine years before—that would have been a bit like wearing bell-bottoms and a tie-died shirt nowadays).
- Sebastian Bach wrote in his memorandum to the Leipzig City Council in 1730 that "the state of music is quite different from what it was, since our artistry has increased very much, and taste has changed astonishingly, so that the former style of music no longer seems to please our ears."
- Johann Mattheson couldn't understand how in his time (1739) Corelli's music was still admired, since most of it had originally been published back in the 1680s and 90s, a half-century before.[4]
- Mattheson also notes, after describing many kinds of essential graces, that "in the past our learned musicians have compiled whole books . . . on nothing but vocal ornaments . . . which however have no relationship with the above-mentioned and must not be confused with them. . . . Things change almost yearly and the old graces are out of style, are changed, or even make room for the more recent fashions."[5]
- There is even documentation of dismissal proceedings against a cantor in Flensburg in 1687, who "had performed the same pieces repeatedly without introducing anything new."[6]

Roger North's comments in 1728 on "one Mr John Jenkins, whose musicall works are more voluminous, and in the time more esteemed than all the rest, and now lye in utmost contempt. I shall adventure to give a short account of this particular master, with whom it was my good chance to have had an intimate acquaintance and friendship [!]."[7]

By the 1730s, people listening to Purcell (who had died in 1695) were liable to consider it a kind of "Church-Musick," and Handel's music seemed too erudite to some people in the late eighteenth century—two generations after his heyday—and was only presented in excerpts.[8]

Charles Avison gives us a clue what mid-eighteenth-century English musicians thought of the music of Elizabethan times, when, according to him, "plodding Geniusses" encumbered "the Art with a *Confusion of Parts,* which, like the numerous and trifling Ornaments in the *Gothic Architecture,* was productive of no other Pleasure, than that of wondering at the Patience and Minuteness of the Artist."[9]

To us, it is surprising to realize how interested people were in novelty, in music they had never heard before. Listeners expressed joy and approval when a composer succeeded in some particularly effective statement, much like a rock audience today. Spontaneous applause between the movements, or even while the musicians were still playing, was common. It seems to have been exactly the reverse of today's Classical audience. Then, the interest was in innovation; now, it seems to be conservation.[10]

People today think of Stravinsky's *Sacre du printemps* as "modern," for instance, though it was premiered in . . . 1913. The present concept of contemporary music can thus include music nearly a century old. By contrast, in England in the late eighteenth century, music that had been around for twenty years was performed in a series known as "antient music."

It is revealing to observe Charles Burney's view of Sebastian Bach, who had been dead less than a generation when he wrote in 1773. To Burney, old Bach seemed to be a figure from the distant past, from "the Gothic period of the grey contrapuntists."[11] Burney held Bach's son Emanuel in high esteem, and commented:

> How he formed his style, where he acquired all his taste and refinement, would be difficult to trace; he certainly neither inherited nor adopted them from his father, who was his only master; for that venerable musician, though unequalled in learning and contrivance, thought it so necessary to crowd into both hands all the harmony he could grasp, that he must inevitably have sacrificed melody and expression.[12]

These examples suggest how quickly style was changing in the eighteenth century.

As for performing styles, all this instability came to a halt, relatively speaking, in the early nineteenth century, when there was a major shift in aesthetic. Since that time, musicians have deliberately tried to use the same general style of performing—Romantic style. At least, they have meant to, and think they have been. It is as if people now at the beginning of the twenty-first century were still wearing the styles of clothes that were popular two centuries ago (in fact, the clothes—and the instruments—are not quite the same, though they are close). This very strong historical tradition is reinforced by a sense of pedagogical lineage, as musician's CVs and conservatory course-catalogues attest: musicians frequently identify not only their teachers but, if they are eminent enough, the performing "school" to which they belong. It is from this heritage, often going back into the nineteenth century, that they derive their authority and influence as performers and teachers.

Another shift occurred in the 1960s: music started being performed in deliberately different styles. On the space axis were the discoveries in ethnomusicology, offering us insights into other musical cultures that exist now, as well as something to which to compare ourselves. On the time axis, styles and instruments appeared that claimed to be copies of historical types. The shift in the 1960s was so basic that even the musicians who chose to ignore it found themselves automatically classified as playing in a style—by default—the one we call "Modern."

Eating the Cookbook

A few years back, on a walk on the Kloveniersburgwal, I found a beautiful portal leading into one of the buildings at the University of Amsterdam. Over the top was an inscription that read, "Wie hetzelfde anders zegt, zegt iets anders," which means "To say something differently is to say something different." This idea could be understood in musical terms as "a piece performed differently is a different piece," or, going further, "performing style can sometimes take precedence over notes." This idea is arguably the basis of twentieth-century Period style in music.

An example of the idea that "a piece performed differently is a different piece" is the effect a simple change of tempo produces:

🔊 AUDIO SAMPLE: 1. Amsterdam Baroque Orchestra, Koopman, 1996. Bach: Cantata 207a/1

🔊 AUDIO SAMPLE: 2. Musica Antiqua Köln, Goebel, 1996. Bach: Cantata 207/1

As Christopher Small and other musical thinkers have pointed out, music is not a thing: it is an act, something people do.[13] We normally like to think of the work as the written object because it has a fixed, stable form. We talk about the "music" on the stand. But the notes on the page aren't a work; in fact, they aren't music at all. They are merely a recipe for performers to follow—a cookbook. It's like trying to eat a cookbook; there is a missing step in-between. Theoreticians of various kinds like to argue this point, but to people who actually musick, who listen or perform, it is self-evident that a work takes on its definition in performance. Musical meaning doesn't exist until the moment of "reception," the moment a piece is performed and heard.

Harnoncourt describes the experience of going to listen to a performance of Monteverdi and hearing Wagner instead. During Monteverdi's lifetime, the repertoire that could be heard was what was written by contemporaries—there was no Canon of older repertoire. Now, we have many more styles in our ears—the music dramas of Wagner and the operas of Puccini, for instance. So it is possible today, unlike 350 years ago, to turn a Monteverdi opera into a nineteenth or twentieth century work by arrangement or instrumentation.[14] There are other ways Monteverdi operas can get "modernized" through phrasing, articulation, vibrato, or the modern vocal style that neglects to deliver the meaning of the text.

But even without past music at their backs, Baroque musicians could draw on many performing styles, and thus give the music quite different characters. If a piece is different each time it's performed, its identity depends on how it's played. It's like jokes, which can be different depending on who's telling them. Put in other words, the *how* of musical events is in fact their *what* as well. Geminiani in 1751 wrote in his *Art of Playing on the Violin,* "Even in common Speech a Difference of Tone gives the same Word a different Meaning." A simple example of this is how the same words uttered with different emphasis can change meaning in these three questions: "What is this thing called love?" "What? Is this thing called *love?*" and "What is *this* thing called, Love?"[15]

For me, I remember there used to be a time when if I heard a recording without knowing what it was, I could usually identify it—that is, I could say who had written it. But a few years ago, I found I'd lost that ability. Now, it is the performance I hear first; a *Messiah* can sound like Mozart or Mahler because it is being performed in a style I associate with those composers. To demonstrate this idea, I suggest you listen to the following track without checking what it is, and guess the composer.

 AUDIO SAMPLE: 3.

Sounds like Sibelius, but not quite. Would you ever guess Bach?[16]

"Handel in early-music performance," observes James Parakilas, "sounds more like the heir of Purcell than like the forerunner of Mendelssohn. Traditional music [i.e., performing style], by contrast, draws the earliest works in its tradition toward the later ones."[17]

With the passage of time, then, the identity of a piece is gradually altered through its performances. José Bowen has shown how Mahler's Sixth Symphony is gradually getting longer, based on some thirty recordings made during the second half of the twentieth century. Performances of this piece have evidently gotten slower. This is a simple example of how performing tradition has altered our conception of a work's identity. "Tradition is enforced through reproduction: notes which are no longer played are no longer part of the tune (as portamento is no longer essential to the Brahms Violin Concerto)."[18]

That a piece performed differently is a different piece is no doubt truer for some pieces than others. Beethoven symphonies, for instance, are so well known that differences are on a pretty superficial level. But a Marais gamba suite could sound quite different depending on the player. Marais himself thought that "the most beautiful pieces [lose] all their savour when not played in their proper style."[19]

Mattheson commented in 1739:

> Those who have never discovered how the composer himself wished to have the work performed will hardly be able to play it well. Indeed, they will often rob the thing of its true vigour and grace, so much so, in fact, that the composer, should he himself be among the listeners, would find it difficult to recognize his own work.[20]

One of the contributors to Diderot's *Encyclopédie,* Frédéric de Castillon, who lived in Germany, reported that Johann Hasse "could hardly recognize his airs when they were performed by Frenchmen at Paris."[21] Castillon concluded that it is musical emphasis that causes a piece of music that is expressive for a German to be inexpressive for a Frenchman. I suspect there were other factors that differed as well.

Quantz observed that "the success of a piece of music depends almost as much on the players as the composers. The best of compositions can be wrecked by a bad expression, and a mediocre composition improved by a good expression."[22]

Harnoncourt writes of the old traditional instrumentation of the *St. Matthew Passion*: "The string section spreads a tapestry of sound over everything, so overwhelming that the meticulous instrumentation of the first chorus is drowned out. It seems that we are listening to Brahms."[23]

The idea is now in the air that Bach didn't even use a chorus and that OVPP (one voice per part) lets the orchestra's parts be better heard without forcing. Obviously, our vision of this piece has changed radically since the 1960s, and what people now hear is effectively a different piece.

The *NG 2* (the Grove *Dictionary of Music*) suggests that one definition of improvisation is "the creation of the final form of a musical work as it is being performed." But there is no music I can think of that does not fit this definition. I would guess that whoever wrote these words believed, like a number of theorists these days, that a piece could reach its final form without being performed. It is amazing that anyone could mistake a piece of paper for music, but that's what happens when you get super-literate. Of course a score is an important component of the process of arriving at music, but its role is merely the encoding of potential performed versions of the work. And as I'll discuss later, scores are not exact, since not all performing parameters can be specified.

In New music concerts, as Parakilas points out, it is often difficult to sort out the performance from the work. "The difficulty is made visible in the typical ritual at the conclusion of a performance: performer onstage and Artist-composer somewhere in the audience graciously attempt by outstretched or clapping hands to deflect the audience's applause toward each other."[24] This ambiguity is, of course, due to not knowing a piece. Another example he gives is a work performed by only one musician:

> Listeners who go to hear a Beethoven symphony can compare the performance they hear to many others in their memories. . . . In the years when John Kirkpatrick was the only pianist playing [Charles Ives's] Concord Sonata, there was nothing special about his version; it had no style. Now that other performers play it, listeners can compare performances and so distinguish the style of the work from the style of any one performance. . . . In other words, the work is now classic.[25]

Wanda Landowska tells the story of how Chopin, who had just listened to Liszt play one of his—Chopin's—nocturnes, asked him in all seriousness "Whose piece is this?"[26] And Diderot wrote of Voltaire's astonishment at seeing *La Clairon*, the famous actress, playing a role in one of his plays, and asking "Am I really the one who wrote that?" *La Clairon* had succeeded in creating dimensions of the scene beyond those that Voltaire himself had been able to imagine.[27]

Here's another example of how a performance defines a piece. Sarah Brightman's recording of Handel's famous aria "Lascia ch'io pianga" is still unquestionably in popular style on her CD *Classics:*

🔊 AUDIO SAMPLE: 4. Sarah Brightman, 2001. Handel: "Lascia ch'io pianga"

Among the tags that transmit the pop style are the orchestra sound (reminiscent of Montovani), playing a simplified accompaniment. None of the depth of tragic feeling is even hinted at in this superficial, juvenile vision of Handel, nor would that have been appropriate, considering the listeners. I was impressed with Brightman's interesting gracing in the third verse until somebody told me it was lifted from the version in the movie *Farinelli*. By comparison, here is a version of "Lascia" with Suzie LeBlanc, as we think it would have been done at the time:

🔊 AUDIO SAMPLE: 5. Suzie LeBlanc, 2001. Handel: "Lascia ch'io pianga"

Chronocentrism: "Music as Tradition"

According to Carl Dalhaus, "The fact that today's public treats the music of the 18th and 19th centuries as its own is so taken for granted that we scarcely notice just how strange and paradoxical this situation actually is."[28]

It has been traditional throughout the history of Western music to regard earlier compositions with respect, but as old-fashioned and in need of updating to fit current style.[29]

> During most of history men scarcely differentiated past from present, referring even to remote events, if at all, as though they were then occurring. . . . Even when ennobled by nostalgia or depreciated by partisans of progress, the past seemed not a foreign country but part of their own. And chroniclers portrayed bygone times with an immediacy and intimacy that reflected the supposed likeness.[30]

To musicians of the traditional school, there is only one performing style: their own. Fashions, and knowledge of fashions, do not extend backward beyond a couple of generations, to their teacher's teacher. This used to be the way everybody related to the past. Bach's music, it was believed, could be understood on the same æsthetic terms as Beethoven's or Wagner's. "Our predecessors tended to think that no problem existed; one simply played the music according to inherited custom, and if in the process we refashioned it, that was our right."[31]

This is a *chronocentric* position, assuming that one's own time or period represents the reference point; the equivalent in time of the spatial concept of ethnocentrism. I'll talk more about this in part III.

Chronocentrism was the norm until well into the twentieth century (and still is in many conservatories), musicians honoring their historical lineage and believing they were preserving a style of interpretation that formed an unbroken chain of authority and orthodoxy. Despite their occasional interest in the music of the past,[32] when Romantic musicians performed earlier repertoire, as far as we know, the idea of deliberately changing their performing style to correspond to the music simply did not occur to them.

While there are clear national differences within this style, a Russian musician would have had no trouble performing with an Italian, a Frenchman, or an American; they had a basic agreement about what music was and what it was supposed to accomplish.

This style was of course Romantic. Nowadays we tend to associate it with the music of the nineteenth and early twentieth centuries, but until the

1930s it was the standard for performing Baroque, Renaissance, and Medieval repertoire as well. As Taruskin put it, "Our performances of Tchaikovsky are of a piece with our performances of Bach."[33] Peter Walls described the single style as "an assumption that music of whatever period . . . is best served by the range of expressive devices that have been accepted as standard over the past fifty years or so."[34] An example of this attitude is Andreas Moser's *Violinschule*, written with Joseph Joachim in 1905. The book was meant to deal with stylistic issues in the performance of music of the past. But Moser too was captive on the "carousel of time," as we can see from this distance. Clive Brown remarks that Moser's ideas have more to do with the late nineteenth century than with those of earlier times.[35]

Wanda Landowska, who knew Romantic style only too well (and loved and hated it in a way we can only imagine), called it simply *the style*, and associated it "with that wan, formal indifference which, heavy, dull and monotonous, gives us the impression of attending an unknown person's funeral: it is indecent to appear interested, yet we cannot cry either, since the ceremony does not move us."[36] She was looking at "the" style from very close, whereas we have the luxury of distance and comparison.

Throughout the nineteenth century, there were instances of HIP (the historically inspired performance movement). Mendelssohn, for example, organized a number of Bach revivals, including the famous *St. Matthew Passion* performances in 1829, and historical concerts in Leipzig (where he held the title of municipal music director, as had Bach).

With the supreme confidence that comes with a view of the past as a part of their own present, Mendelssohn and his contemporaries "looked upon early music not as a body of historical artefacts to be painstakingly preserved in their original state but as a repository of living art that each generation could—indeed should—reinterpret in its own stylistic idiom."[37] The Berlin Singakademie performed parts of the Mass in B Minor in the 1820s and 30s. They were performances in heavily edited form, with additional introductions and different instrumentation. "Bach dressed in the musical garb of Carl Maria von Weber!"[38] This was the period when "the intoxicating sound of mixed mass choirs had just been discovered and the overpowering, large Romantic symphony orchestra had just been created." Mendelssohn led a massive chorus and orchestra totaling 170–200 performers and made extensive cuts in the *St. Matthew Passion*. The same approach led Wagner to "correct"—in a spirit of total sympathy—certain problems he perceived in Beethoven's works, including the Ninth Symphony.[39] This was the attitude of the majority of performers until the 1960s. As Taruskin put it,

A performer schooled in the mainstream (any mainstream) receives his basic training before he has reached the age of consent, . . . therefore his musical responses and tastes will have been formed at a preconscious level—will be vested, so to speak, in his spinal column. And there would be nothing wrong with that if our musical culture were the kind of homogeneous thing it remained, say, until World War I. In fact it would be the best possible thing.

James Parakilas called this "music as tradition":

> Classical performers present music as tradition by making the past continuous with the present. . . . Listeners hearing music as tradition hear it as something belonging to them. . . . Classical composers, however warmly personified, speak a timeless, universal message. They speak to modern listeners because they have spoken to generations of listeners.[40]

Carl Dahlhaus wrote, "Music of the past belongs to the present as music, not as documentary evidence."[41]

Orthodox symphony musicians work within a received tradition, so although the repertoire they play may have been written centuries ago, they think of it as "present" repertoire and as a contemporary art form. The date of a piece's writing, and the way it was performed then, are mere technicalities in their minds. The philosopher and historian R. G. Collingwood pointed out that

> To re-enact another's thought does not make historical knowledge; we must also know that we are re-enacting it . . . unless [a historian] knows that he is thinking historically, he is not thinking historically. . . . The revolutionary can only regard his revolution as a progress in so far as he is also an historian, genuinely re-enacting in his own historical thought the life he nevertheless rejects.[42]

By Collingwood's reasoning, because these musicians are not conscious of thinking historically about their performing, they are not in fact doing so. (The same repertoire performed by Period players is looked at differently: within a "historical" frame. Whether it is authentic is beside the point. What is important is the "historical" mentality, making the attempt, being aware—as historians also are—of thinking historically.)

A characteristic of chronocentrism is that one is not normally aware of it. José Bowen compares performing protocols to accents in speaking languages. Our own accent is of course the most difficult one to hear: "Intellectually we realize that [interpreting a score] is highly conditioned and operates by the use of a large number of conventions; we recognize that to other people we speak with an accent. To our ears, however, our style of speech or performance seems natural, and it appears that it is everyone else who speaks with the accent."[43] Chronocentrism was easier to achieve because of the Romantic principle of Autonomy, or Absolute Music. I'll talk more about this in chapter 4; I'll just quote here an enlightening passage from Lydia Goehr's *Imaginary Museum*: "One way to bring music of the past into the present, and then into the sphere of timelessness, was to strip it of its original, local, and extra-musical meanings. By severing all such connections, it was possible to think of it now as functionless. All one had to do next was impose upon the music meanings appropriate for the new aesthetic."[44] This brings to mind the standard approach among music analysts today, which is clearly articulated in the very first sentence of the 63-page article on analysis in *NG 2:* "Analysis. . . . [is] that part of the study of music that takes as its starting-point the music itself, rather than external factors." Here, in an encyclopedia published in 2001, is a standpoint that could not exist without the background of the beautiful Romantic concept of a timeless, Absolute Music. This concept is implicitly rejected by HIP.

There are two obvious physical symbols of this Romantic sense of chronocentrism: the instruments played in symphony orchestras and the uniforms the players wear.

Musicians nowadays often speak of "contemporary instruments" or "modern instruments," by which they mean the instruments played in symphony orchestras today. This is a Classic example of chronocentrism. In fact, orchestras use instruments whose basic designs were developed long ago: the winds during the nineteenth century and the strings before that. The last major changes occurred well over a century ago. They are Romantic instruments in every sense, and they would be "Period instruments" if their players were not in denial. The absence of any significant change in instruments over the last 180 years is "particularly striking if we consider that in previous centuries, almost all instruments were significantly modified every few years, or at least once in each generation."[45] The oboe used in symphony orchestras today, for instance, has scarcely changed since 1881; it has changed less since then than the hautboy changed in any twenty-year period during the eighteenth century.[46]

By 1820 the fundamentals of the Romantic instrument types had been achieved. Most oboes made in 1820, for instance, will play fairly well (if not ideally) using the reeds of today. As Harnoncourt observes, the distinction that is often made between so-called "modern instruments" and the "historical instruments" of Beethoven's time is pretty academic. "In one case, the instrumentarium of 1850 is used, in the other case, that of 1820."[47]

This is why in this book I use the term "Romantic instruments" for the instruments of the symphony orchestra instead of "modern instruments." Modern instruments exist, like the Moog synthesizer, the electronic music studio, and the DJ's kit (plus, of course, if one chooses to look at them in this light, Renaissance and Baroque instruments, since they have appeared in the last generation). But there is no logical reason for calling a valved brass instrument or a key-system woodwind "modern"—even a saxophone, an instrument invented in the late 1830s.

About the clothes musicians wear in concerts, it's not surprising that Classical musicians wear uniforms at concerts (and that they can get fined for wearing the wrong colored socks); what is interesting is that the uniforms they wear are precisely the ones the Costume Department of the Victoria & Albert Museum display as formal evening dress for the year 1900 (men in white tie and tails, women in pastel frocks). The symbolism of this is striking. It is as if the musicians of today are wearing Period costumes, the period in question being the late Romantic.

A received performing style has elements that cannot be written down; it is passed on not only by example and word, but in more subtle ways. Music students acquire it from their teachers and fellow students; they spend a considerable part of their energies trying to grasp it (it is sometimes transmitted by body language, sometimes by anecdote, sometimes by a teacher's reaction to the student's performing, etc.).

A hint of the way Bruno Walter in the 1950s thought about received traditional performing style is his comment on interpreting the *St. Matthew Passion.* He wrote, "I knew I was in agreement with tradition in this." What could he have meant by "tradition" in a case like Bach? The twentieth-century tradition of performing Bach's choral works must have descended from the general approach to Bach's larger choral works that began in the early nineteenth century in Vienna with R. G. Kiesewetter and at Berlin and Leipzig with Mendelssohn. No doubt there had been major changes before it reached Walter. But this was what he called "tradition," and what some people still today cling to with nostalgia. Rather a different idea from Rifkin's OVPP (one voice per part).

Robert P. Morgan, surprisingly, sees a society that accepts multiple simultaneous styles as one whose sense of the present is missing.[48] "Only when the current moment loses an essential character and personality of its own, and thus loses its ability to cast its own peculiar colouration on the past, is one able to look upon the past with such detachment and objectivity." Morgan sees this as a danger: "Our sense of the musical present, and thereby of our own musical selves, is fatally threatened, dissolving into a patchwork of disconnected fragments snatched from here, there, and everywhere." I agree with his vision but not with his conclusion.

What Morgan is looking at is a culture with a heightened awareness of time and history, one so confident of itself it can sample alternate worlds without fear of losing touch with the present real one. Consider North American "cuisine," which can be excellent or awful, but has no original identity. It is always "quoted," as it were, from Mexico, France, Japan, India, and so on. Personally, I am very comfortable with this situation. Period style too can be excellent or awful. We can understand and even appreciate contemporary Ozarks Bluegrass, even a Balinese gamelan.[49] Other present-day manifestations of this same eclecticism and open-mindedness that show an extraordinary ability for self-orientation and the ability to shift styles, are the shock and disorientation of coming out of a movie theater, of taking a plane trip to a different continent, of talking to people by telephone half a world away, and especially of reading science fiction (which, like Period style, starts with the question "What if . . . ?").

All these potentially disorienting practices arose, like HIP, in the twentieth century, in an atmosphere of pluralism. It can be very enlightening to step outside one's traditional received culture, to take distance from one's own normal artistic imperatives, however tentatively and however small the step. That is what HIP has begun to achieve.

The Rise of Pluralism: Matching Style to Period

It was not chance that the development of ethnomusicology in the twentieth century paralleled that of HIP, with its pioneers around the turn into the twentieth century, and its new developments after World War II. Pluralism is part of a general social trend, the development of sensitivity to other cultures and their art forms, the reverse of ethnocentrism. The gesture extends chronologically as well as geographically, so that the past also becomes a "foreign country."

Pluralism seems to be an age-old issue with musicians. Although Monteverdi had no problem writing in both Prima and Seconda Pratica, some of his contemporaries felt obliged to choose between one or the other.[50] Morgan's attitude described above reflects the same conservatism in the twentieth century, caused by an assumption, usually unarticulated, that there can be only one performing style at a time. It seems a pity to pull the shades.

2

Mind the Gap

Current Styles

And for this reason, in every age, the musick of that time seems best, and they say, Are wee not wonderfully improved? And so comparing what they doe know, with what they doe not know, they are as clear of opinion, as they that doubdt nothing.

(Roger North, *Notes of comparison*, ca. 1726)

Three Abstractions: Romantic, Modern, and Period Styles

In his famous singing book published in 1723, Pier Francesco Tosi wrote that "Musick in my Time has chang'd its Stile three times."[1] That seems like a lot of change, but then, we could say the same about our own time. For us, too, there were three broad currents in the century we just left. I'm thinking of the three approaches to performing music from the Rhetorical period.

There is, as far as I know, no general vocabulary for describing these styles.[2] Most of us are familiar with two of them: Period style and Modern style. The other one, Romantic style, was in full sway at the beginning of the twentieth century but is heard now only on recordings. Romantic style began to mutate after the Great War (World War I) toward the accuracy and precision of Modern style, to a degree that eventually changed its identity. Modern style is thus the direct descendent of Romantic style;[3] being the product of its time, it shows the typical attributes of Modernism, following written scores quite literally and being tightfisted with personal expression. As I will elaborate throughout this book, I consider the Modernist spirit to have been a disastrous blight on the music of the latter part of the twentieth century.

I'm using the word "style" here in a general sense, and my descriptions are approximate, lumping tendencies together in three broad categories, and looking at them in their extreme, polarized forms. Within these three general types, there are many variants.

As for Period style, since the 1960s, it has gradually taken charge of the earlier repertoire. Period style questions many of the basic premises and axioms of Modern style. The most obvious difference is the use of instruments that match the period when the music was conceived. But the style of playing is revolutionary as well.

Let's listen to the three styles applied to the same piece. This is the second movement of the Second Brandenburg Concerto. First is a Period recording from the early 1980s conducted by Nikolaus Harnoncourt, followed by an earlier example in mainstream Modern style, led by Yehudi Menuhin.

AUDIO SAMPLE: 6. Concentus Musicus, Harnoncourt, 1981/83. Bach: Brandenburg 2/2

AUDIO SAMPLE: 7. Bath Festival Orchestra, Menuhin, (? early 1960s). Bach: Brandenburg 2/2

Next is a performance by Leopold Stokowski and the Philadelphia Orchestra recorded sixty years earlier in 1928, in which the conception is so different that we might think we were hearing a different composition.

AUDIO SAMPLE: 8. Philadelphia Orchestra, Stokowski, 1928. Bach: Brandenburg 2/2

Which is the "real" Bach? Of course, it is doubtful that audiences in 1928 would have accepted either of the other two later versions. Not serious enough!

Recordings of the Brandenburg Concertos can serve as a measure of how the three general styles (Romantic, Modern, and Period) are used today for performing historical repertoire. Of the commercial recordings of the Brandenburgs made in the last fifteen years, just over half—eleven— are in Period style. The rest are in Modern style, except for the re-release of the Stokowski.

Romantic Style: An Absolute

The easiest of these styles to recognize is the old Romantic one because no one nowadays dares to play in it. But the great Romantic tradition, with its portamentos, fluctuating tempos, and unrelenting earnestness, was once as established as cruise steamships and telegrams. Romantic style was what was heard aboard the Titanic, for instance, and no one dreamed it would one day be as obscure and inaccessible as that famous ship. Romantic style is now extinct, and therefore an example of music with a lost tradition. But it differs from other lost traditions in being documented in sound recordings, including recordings of the music that interests us here, pieces composed before 1800. It can thus be understood in a way other extinct styles cannot. Here's an example, made in 1905, seven years before the Titanic's maiden voyage. This is Adelina Patti, one of the finest opera divas of the time.

 **AUDIO SAMPLE:** 9. Adelina Patti, 1905. Mozart: "Voi che sapete"

It's clear that the way people perform now and the way they did a century ago are different. Opera singing, full of traditions and conventions, is the most conservative style of Classical music we have, and yet this recording shows what a difference a century makes; Patti became rich and famous for singing like this, but today she would be laughed off the stage of the Met. Her conception of the music is interesting; vibrato is rare and subtle, and phrasing is by smaller units that could be called gestures (the idea discussed in chapter 11). Musicians today could no more get away with using that old style—if they knew how—than actors can produce melodrama.

The examples I'm using of Romantic style, it should be noted, are all from the tail-end of the period, because music recording did not get started until the end of the 1890s. An example is the Concertgebouw recording of the *Matthew Passion,* recorded in 1939 and conducted by Willem Mengelberg. This performance has clear roots in the nineteenth century, as Mengelberg was trained in the 1880s, and conducted a particularly sensitive and devoted *St. Matthew* at the Concertgebouw every Palm Sunday beginning in 1899. Everyone listening to the 1939 recording knew this might well be the last one, with the Germans at the Dutch doorstep. Here is part of the final chorus.

AUDIO SAMPLE: 10. Concertgebouw Orchestra, Amsterdam Toonkunst Choir, Mengelberg, 1939. Bach: " Wir setzen uns mit Tränen nieder," *Matthew Passion*

To us, there is something truly strange about this performance. Not so long ago, most people would have said that the main difference between Period and Romantic styles was the instruments. But when we get as far away from our own familiar style as this, the differences between instruments pale compared to other issues.

For orientation, we can contrast Mengelberg's recording with a new one conducted by Paul McCreesh in 2002. Mengelberg's recording represents a tradition from the early part of the twentieth century; McCreesh's, one from a century later. They form together an effective comparison of Romantic and Period style.

🔊 **AUDIO SAMPLE:** 11. Gabrieli Consort & Players, McCreesh, 2002. Bach: "Wir setzen uns mit Tränen nieder," *Matthew Passion*

Listening to recordings of Romantic style like those we have just heard, we immediately notice the rhythmic freedom and concern for expression. And, being good Modernists, the lack of precision will catch our attention. But at its best, Romantic style is awe-inspiring. Michelle Dulak characterizes it as "heavily inflected, free, perhaps 'sentimentalized.'"[4] This is the plush, opulent, symphonic sound we associate with Brahms and Mahler; so much so that at times it is difficult for modern ears to hear it as Bach. All in all, Mengelberg's is an approach to Bach that ignores what is known of how he himself played, and turns him into a contemporary of Wagner. This is, of course, exactly what it intended to do.

It is enlightening to confront this history, so close to us in time. Its æsthetic is less distant than we think. Whether we recognize it or not, Romantic ideologies still hold most of us in thrall (like, for instance, composer-intention, *Werktreue,* the work concept, the transparent performer, the suppression of gracing and improvisation, Absolute music, the musical Canon, and repeatability). We are generally unaware of these ideas, they are simply unconscious assumptions we have grown up with. Nor, if we articulate them, do we usually know where they come from. But they affect the way we react to music—even Rhetorical music (that is, music from before about 1800). I'll discuss all these ideas in part II on Romanticism. For now, we'll concentrate on the sound of Romantic style.

The Romantics (and therefore most of us) were obsessed with melody. Like a chocolate addiction, Wagner wrote of "what unique importance it is to every musical message, that the melody shall hold us without cease."[5] Baroque Basses—I'm talking "continuo" here—are not one part among equals; the Bass is like the trunk of a tree. As exercises, Baroque students had to write different top parts over good Basses—upper parts like summer leaves blowing in the wind! That the melodic gestures in the treble parts simply mimic and confirm the events taking part in the Bass is not intuitively obvious to us because of our obsession with melody. Here's an example: in Bach's "Air on the G string" it is the Bass line that is probably the most interesting part, but listen to what Stokowski and "Symphony Orchestra" do to it.

AUDIO SAMPLE: 12. Unnamed Orchestra, Stokowski, 1957. Bach: Air, Suite 3, BWV 1068 ("Air on the G string")

I have to say I find Stokowski's transcriptions irresistible in sheer expressive energy, even if they are clueless in relation to what Bach had in mind.[6] Stokowski turns the upper voice into a melody characterized by complex (what is now often called "mannered") dynamic nuance. This "cantabile" mode (the "beautiful" stop is on) uses dynamic shapes based on technical situations in the upper part, or sheer intuition, not on the information so clearly revealed by the Bass. High and long notes often get emphasis for no other reason than that they are high and long, whereas real harmonic events that could act as cues for nuance, like suspensions and dissonances, are ignored. Many Period players phrase "from the top" like this as well, having inherited a melody-based bias from Romantic tradition. Meanwhile the players of Stokowski's Bass line plod along note by note like horses pulling a heavy carriage, playing as if they were the "accompaniment" (a concept that is destructive in itself), offering no hint of the harmonic implications in the Bass (that could be conveyed by differences in length or dynamic). Far from taking command, they are subservient to the arbitrary tricks and trivial melodic extravagances taken by the upper parts. Compare this with a recent Period style recording that "puts out" less but gets good mileage from what Bach actually wrote. (Here too, the Bass could have done more.)

AUDIO SAMPLE: 13. Akademie für Alte Musik, 1995. Bach: Air, Suite 3, BWV 1068 ("Air on the G string")

Recordings That Document the Heart of Romantic Practice

Romantic style can be heard in recordings going back to 1903.[7] The roots of those early twentieth-century performances extend, of course, far back into the nineteenth century. The earliest recordings document the styles of famous performers who were in their primes—or beyond them—in about 1900. Since anyone recording in that decade would have been born a good generation before that, and often much more, these recordings give us a window into the heart of Romanticism, allowing us to hear what it was really like. In a few rare cases, we can even hear what Baroque music sounded like in the ears of the nineteenth century.

As Timothy Day observes, there are sound-cylinders of well-known singers born as early as 1819:

> there are recordings of seven singers born in the 1830s and twenty-four born in the 1840s, four hundred sides or cylinders in total, all of them artists

formed before the stylistic transformations wrought by Wagner and the Italian *verismo* school, and some of them collaborators of Brahms and Verdi and Wagner and Grieg and Sullivan. . . . There are recordings by Joachim, who played Mendelssohn's Concerto under the composer's direction in the 1840s and for whom Brahms wrote his Violin Concerto, whose style was completely free from the continuous vibrato that Kreisler introduced.[8]

Joseph Joachim made recordings in 1903 when he was 72 (we will listen to one of them at the end of this chapter). Joachim was one of the great violinists of the nineteenth century; he made his début in 1839 and was closely associated with Mendelssohn, Liszt, the Schumanns, and Brahms. His intermittent use of a subtle vibrato and portamento show "remarkable similarities" to the violin practice documented by Spohr in 1832 and David a generation later. Joachim's recording of his own Romance in C does indeed show, as Clive Brown says, a great nineteenth-century musician's sense of the important and the subsidiary. Joachim took considerable freedom with rhythm and embellished extensively. Brown finds "disparities" between Joachim's performance and the text as published.[9]

"Disparities" is of course a relative term; by his own lights, Joachim was probably just playing what was indicated. In any case, his style may well be representative of the period of his formation in the mid-nineteenth-century. While the major stylistic change of the latter part of that century—and the one often heard on the early twentieth-century recordings—was the Wagner revolution, Joachim was quite vocally opposed to Wagner (and later rejected Liszt as well).

Joachim's playing is also reminiscent in many respects of the singing of Alessandro Moreschi (1858–1922), the "last castrato," who recorded in Rome in 1904 and 1906. This is one of the most arresting recordings I've heard. Moreschi was conductor of the Sistine Choir and also sang at St. Peter's. Castrati were rare by Moreschi's time (he was an exact contemporary of Puccini). They had started to disappear from the time the French (who never accepted the tradition) invaded Italy in 1796. Moreschi began his training in 1871. It is not only his quite amazing vocal quality that one notices, but his style; the *New Grove* comments that to twenty-first-century ears "such obvious emotion is a little embarrassing."[10] Robert Hill remarks that "Moreschi's 'heart on his sleeve' rendition [can be seen] as a craftsmanlike handling of a range of ornamental devices without which his audience would probably have felt deprived."[11]

🔊 AUDIO SAMPLE: 14. Alessandro Moreschi, 1904. Bach/Gounod: "Ave Maria"

Hill suggests that to say that Moreschi is performing in bad taste (which is our immediate reaction) would be as appropriate as judging the Peking

Opera using Modernist European standards. Clive Brown makes an interesting speculation about Moreschi, pointing out similarities in his style to the instructions in Domenico Corri's *Select Collection* (ca. 1782) and *Singer's Preceptor* (1810). Since for most of the nineteenth century castrati were isolated and excluded from mainstream singing, such as opera, Moreschi's performing style may have been artificially preserved, and represent a style that scarcely mutated after about 1810.[12]

Many of these early recordings are moving and unforgettable. To our ears, conditioned as they are by Modernism, the most striking difference between then and now is the delivery: these musicians declaim, and they are serious about it. Recordings made at the turn of the century or just afterwards sound strangely overstated. Glenn Gould, the paragon of a Modernist, commented:

> When we listen to the early phonograph recordings by artists reared in the latter half of the 19th century, we are struck not by the felicities or the gaucheries of their artistry but by how very different the performing premise seems to have been from that to which we are now accustomed—how very high the level of whimsicality and caprice, how very flirtatious and extravagant the range of dynamics . . . to what a very large extent they must have depended on the visual connection, on the supplemental choreography of movement and gesture.[13]

Gould's observation is perceptive. But what he heard was conditioned by his time. Whimsy and caprice, flirtation and extravagance were noticeable to Gould because they were so foreign to the remarkably serious conception of Classical music of a half-century ago. For us nowadays, these are qualities we could profitably put back in to our recorded performances, as they would be understood and appreciated by many listeners.

Prophets of the Revolution: Dolmetsch and Landowska

It is paradoxical and somewhat poignant that Wanda Landowska and Arnold Dolmetsch,[14] the two original cultivators of "stylistic nostalgia,"[15] are unknown to most of the younger musicians active in HIP at the beginning of the twenty-first century.

Landowska and Dolmetsch were the first "star" performers of the Movement: teachers, activists, prophets of the revolution that was to come. Their books are still interesting from a historical perspective, especially for the philosophies they propose. The performing tradition against which they were reacting was the tail-end of the Romantic. There was interest in original instruments, although at that time the interest was in types of instrument for which there were then no modern equivalents: the harpsichord, viola da gamba, lute, and recorder. The bigger Period instrument revolution had to wait for the 1960s.

Landowska was a fine pianist who began playing harpsichord in about 1905 and toured regularly, playing with major orchestras and well-known musicians. World War I stopped her teaching in Berlin and World War II kept her from living in her house and compound in Paris; she finally settled in the United States. Her technique and flair were impressive, and she played well-known repertoire, like Bach, that until then was known only on the piano.

Landowska laid out eloquent arguments for reviving historical repertoire and performing styles in a beautifully printed little book called *La Musique ancienne*. It was revolutionary at the time, and it is a measure of her success that its ideas have now become familiar; reading it, I find many of my own ideas there, often better articulated. Landowska was very serious about honoring the spirit of the past but was not interested in literal re-creation. Her philosophy was symbolized by the iron-framed, high-tension harpsichord she used, the design of which she developed together with Pleyel.

It is interesting to listen now to recordings of Landowska's playing, conceived as it was in reaction to the predominant Romantic style of her time.

🔊 AUDIO SAMPLE: 15. Wanda Landowska, 1933. Bach: Goldberg Variations, theme

Her style was of course the product of the taste of a century ago, a time that seems infinitely farther from the Baroque period than the present does. Her recordings have never appealed much to me, though I admire her authoritative self-assurance, her strong personality, and decisive ideas. It is mostly the sound of the instrument that turns me off: tinny, nasal, a "bucket of bolts"; the opposite of voluptuous, a sound that sustains for what seems an artificially long time yet with little development, and of course the special tone quality produced by tuning in equal temperament.

🔊 AUDIO SAMPLE: 16. Wanda Landowska, 1933. Bach: Goldberg Variations, Variatio 13

Pleyels are difficult to appreciate after the revolution in harpsichord making by Skowroneck, Hubbard, and Dowd around 1960. The overwhelming impression of Landowska's approach is that it is what pianists do when they play harpsichord: the touch is heavy, her *agréments* are played without spontaneity and self-consciously—as if they were in bold print in the score, not organic parts of the piece. Landowska plays with the didactic exaggeration of someone educating her listeners.

The other early prophet, Arnold Dolmetsch, was active in promoting HIP in England from the 1890s. The contents of Dolmetsch's book, published in 1915, show how much more committed he was to accurate historical performing style and instruments than Landowska. He not only performed and taught but was one of the first builders of copies (not yet replicas) of historical instruments. His playing on all kinds of instruments was erratic ("soul, but no chops"), and he prided himself on not practicing. But as Haskell has pointed out, he has to be called the "seminal figure" in HIP; "it was he who set the agenda for and defined the issues addressed by the revival."[16] That his work has never been adequately appreciated or acknowledged is probably due, as Haskell says, to the disruption created by World War II, which "threw up a barrier between him and his successors. Musicians and scholars who picked up the thread in the late forties and fifties found it easy to believe they were starting afresh."

It is also true that two swallows do not by themselves make a Spring, and as great as these two figures were, and although others were involved,[17] it was impossible to create the kind of movement that developed in the later part of the century.

If the æsthetic spirit of Landowska had much in common with the disciplined idealism of Rudolf Steiner, Dolmetsch's matrix was the irresistible style of William Morris.[18] "For most people the early Haslemere festival performances conjure up visions of aesthetic young men and elderly ladies in Liberty smocks and sandals."[19]

No doubt a part of Period style was fixed by these two eccentric pioneers. Both of them were evidently difficult and proud. In *Musique ancienne,* Landowska never once mentioned Dolmetsch. "Landowska held court, a diminutive but authoritarian figure who expected her word to be taken as gospel. Students quickly learned that, as one of them put it, 'she never explained anything and one could not question her.'"[20] Dolmetsch was described in 1932 as "in some respects decidedly warped, to the point of craziness[; he] said many foolish things, but he does know a great deal . . . he is conceited to the utmost and will tolerate no disagreement."[21]

Dolmetsch and Landowska could scarcely be described as warm friends. In her biography of Dolmetsch, Campbell writes of a purported meeting between the two, during which Landowska fell at Dolmetsch's feet and called him "Maestro," asking him to make her a harpsichord "for nothing—as did Pleyel—because she was a great artist. Dolmetsch is reputed to have refused saying she knew nothing about harpsichord playing."[22]

The Authenticity Revolution of the 1960s

The success that HIP enjoys today was scarcely imaginable in the generation following World War II, when it was little more than a fringe movement, reacting against the established style (by then, mostly Modern).

HIP's rise in the 1960s was so unlikely that it was not possible to foresee. Ever since then, its imminent demise has been confidently predicted. Meanwhile, it continues to thrive and grow.

In the 1960s, it is doubtful whether a movement could have had credibility if it did not have an element of protest and revolution about it. A mainspring of HIP in the 1960s was a rejection of the status quo. Musicians like me, just getting started then, defined our movement in opposition to the Classical establishment; we forced our conservatories to change (my little battle as a student in Amsterdam was to be allowed to study harpsichord as a keyboard minor instead of piano). The mainstream at the time had long since moved away from Romanticism. These were Modernists we were battling.

Dolmetsch had died in 1940, but by the 1960s his arguments were making more and more sense. By good fortune, Britain provided two books of critical importance to the Movement at this juncture. Thurston Dart's classic *Interpretation of Music* (1954) provided the rationale, and Robert Donington's *Interpretation of Early Music* (1963, dedicated to Dolmetsch) offered methods of realizing style just when we needed them. Donington's book was built on a very effective principle: it quoted the hearts of the most useful sources on every imaginable subject relating to performance practice. Donington provided only minimal commentary— just enough, I think—letting the sources speak for themselves. His book served as a handy source in the 1960s and 70s. Unsung as it is now, it was a key element in the development of HIP.

Indications of performance practice, as documented in books, notation, and other sources, were available in two forms: an ever-growing number of reprints of primary sources in their original forms and in a large and flourishing modern secondary literature (of which Donington's book was a shining example).

As for the instrument issue, most of the activities of HIP before the 1960s were based on the revival of pre-nineteenth-century organs and the then virtually obsolete instruments like the harpsichord and recorder. But a more radical concept was about to emerge—the revival of earlier forms of the familiar instruments of the orchestra: the "Baroque" violin, the "Baroque" flute, etc.

Appearing so early, it is not likely that Paul Hindemith knew what ramifications his bold and progressive speech, "Johann Sebastian Bach, a Compelling Legacy" was eventually to have. In 1950, it was a manifesto for revolution. "We can be sure," he wrote,

> that Bach felt quite comfortable with the vocal and instrumental types that were available to him, and if we care about performing his music as he himself imagined it, then we ought to restore the performance conditions of his time. And in that case it is not enough that we use a harpsichord as continuo instrument. We must string our string instruments differently; we must construct our wind instruments with the scalings of the time; and we must even

recreate the relationship between *Chorton* and *Kammerton* in the tuning of our instruments.[23]

From the vantage point of today, it isn't easy to appreciate how revolutionary these ideas were in 1950.

One of the great conductors of Bach in those days—when Bach was still a "contemporary" composer—was Bruno Walter. Deeply earnest in his approach to the *St. Matthew Passion,* Walter wrote in 1957 that "we can no longer be guided by the number of executants [!] that were under Bach's direction in St. Thomas's Church, Leipzig; we must make allowance for the musical and emotional requirements of the work and the acoustic properties of our large concert-halls or churches."[24] Walter also uses this argument to justify his opinion that "Concerning the number of strings employed, we may feel quite independent of Bach's Leipzig orchestra." Deeply imbued with the traditional chronocentric approach, Walter simply assumed that Bach's situation was not as good as his own. He wrote, "The fanatical outcry, 'Barabbas', manifests a dramatic boldness and dynamic vigour in Bach's invention such as the choral resources of his day certainly could not have afforded him." (What would Walter have thought of OVPP—one voice per part? By the way, the effect of "Barabbas" in McCreesh's OVPP recording just might have satisfied him.)

Walter's approach was not challenged until the later 1960s (and though embattled, continues to this day). But Hindemith's very different sentiments were shared by others, and within a few years, things had changed dramatically. The basic issue, the Replication Principle, the "exact copy," was applied more or less to all the Period musicking activities of HIP. I talk about replication in chapter 8; it was part of a wave of literacy that swept our culture in the 1960s. Replication affected instrument making, editions and copies of music, and research, which was constantly turning up more information to help performers become ever more stylish. On the leading edge of the Movement, "copies" became "exact" duplicates of originals, as near as could be achieved, with no conscious historical compromises. String instruments were set up as they had been when they were made (we thought), and historical bows began to appear, along with the first serious copies of wind instruments.

Performers changed as well. Before the shift, a historical player like Ralph Kirkpatrick considered Baroque playing techniques "disadvantageous," and Thurston Dart thought it "ridiculous" to employ the original fingerings of the Baroque.[25] Harpsichordists like Walcha, Richter, Malcolm, and Kirkpatrick, using pianistic ideals, were playing "long legato phrases, unsupportive Bass lines, [with] a lack of pulse and rhythmic character."[26] This kind of playing became harder to find by the 1970s. Sigiswald Kuyken and Lucy van Dael were playing the violin "chin off" by 1974–75.

I remember attending a course given by Gustav Leonhardt on the Goldberg Variations in 1965, just when his second recording of them was released. Here is his Variatio 13 from that recording; above it, my note of his comment in my score reads "Written-out ornaments, thus *free*" (i.e., imitating improvised passaggi).

🔊 **AUDIO SAMPLE:** 17. Gustav Leonhardt, 1965. Bach: Goldberg Variations, Variatio 13

It is interesting to see where later harpsichordists have gone with this idea of playing "big notes" (i.e., notes that look like the plain melody) as written-out graces. Pierre Hantaï in 2003 is considerably freer with the rhythm than Leonhardt, his teacher.

🔊 **AUDIO SAMPLE:** 18. Pierre Hantaï, 2003. Bach: Goldberg Variations, Variatio 13

Robert Hill's 2004 live recording is still freer with the rhythm, especially this variation, which projects a spontaneity that comes from playing it as an encore.

🔊 **AUDIO SAMPLE:** 19. Robert Hill, 2004. Bach: Goldberg Variations, Variatio 13

And so for a brief period in the 1960s and 70s, a wave of pro-replication sympathy washed over HIP, and everyone involved with it seemed for a while to be considering—if not buying—the idea. It didn't last, but by the early 1970s, the word "authentic" was being regularly used for recordings; authentic interpretation, authentic instruments; the implication was that this was something new, exotic, more up to date and correct, the musical equivalent of organic vegetables. Dorottya Fabian writes of "the confidence and optimism of the period," and writers at the time, like Babitz and Mertin, began publishing their encouragements.[27]

The Advent of Period Instruments and "Low Pitch": "Strange and Irregular Colors"

HIP entered the 1960s with concerns for stylistic performing, but Period instruments were not yet a priority. By the end of the 60s, the new instruments were established as standard for Period performing. We have documentation of this development in the form of recordings. A good example of state-of-the-art Period style in 1962 is a recording of Telemann's e-minor concerto for recorder and traverso made by Frans Brüggen and Frans Vester, who in the next decade were to become icons and gurus on their instruments. In 1962, the ensemble plays at A-440 on Romantic instruments; strings are set up in modern style, Brüggen plays on a modern design of recorder (not a copy of an old original), and Vester on what he was later to call the "iron flute."

🔊 AUDIO SAMPLE: 20. Frans Brüggen and Frans Vester, ca. 1963. Telemann: Concerto, e-minor, Recorder and Traverso

For me personally, the switch to Period instruments occurred while I was studying recorder with Brüggen in the mid-1960s. I began my lessons using the latest hardware at the time at A-440 (Dolmetsch, later Coolsma). These were not copies, but free impressions inspired by the general design of Baroque recorders.[28] But by the time I had finished my studies three years later, I was looking for a very different kind of instrument: one that replicated exactly the dimensions of an original, was voiced in a similar way, and was tuned to what was then quaintly called "old pitch," or A-415. I had played several originals by that time, as well as the copies of Martin Skowroneck, and seen how different they sounded and felt to play. I was lucky to find Friedrich von Huene, a maker who was willing to hire me as an apprentice with a view to collaborating on a pilot project to make such instruments. We produced copies of the Copenhagen Denner alto in 1969, and in the same year Hans Coolsma, working with Brüggen, began making Bressan copies; both were at A-415, which at the time was unusual.[29] The first serious copies of traversos and hautboys at 415 quickly followed.[30]

The difference between Baroque instruments and Romantic ones was underlined by the adoption of Hindemith's imperative that we "even recreate the relationship between *Chorton* and *Kammerton* in the tuning of our instruments." The adoption of A-415 as the pitch standard of copies affected the sound quality of both instruments and voices, especially to the ears of people brought up hearing only instruments at 440. Using a different pitch in Period style had another effect as well: it made it virtually impossible to mix Romantic and Baroque instruments in the same ensemble. This in turn forced musicians to choose between the two, defining themselves as "modern" or "historical"; there was a symbolic barrier, thrown up by the mundane reality of pitch. Once an emblem of innovative practice, A-415 has itself now become a symbol of conservatism in its own right, sometimes blocking experiments with other historical pitch levels.

The 1960s were thus concerned with physical resources: instruments, their pitches, sizes of ensemble, and unfamiliar playing techniques. Adopting Period instruments was a major undertaking. Musicians are "traditional"; they do not easily adopt changes in their instruments, and in this case they were virtually learning new instruments, most of them without a teacher or even a hope of outside help. Musicians found themselves willy-nilly becoming scholars and readers in libraries, as well as craftsmen making instruments.

It wasn't until the 1960s, and then only occasionally, that questions of performing style began to be discussed. Those were the days when performances that got expressive or detailed (in the ways indicated in primary sources) were still unfamiliar and were often perceived as "mannered."

Chain Reaction

An important moment in the development of HIP was the appearance in 1967 of the recording of Bach's *St. John Passion* on original instruments by Nikolaus Harnoncourt and his orchestra, the Concentus Musicus of Vienna. This recording was one of a series of relatively well-known large Bach pieces that the Concentus produced in this period. The *St. John* was a good choice for experiment; it "was less culturally encoded or 'owned' than the *Matthew Passion*."[31] It appeared at a time when there was much talk of political revolution, and in the late 1960s the educational systems all over Europe were transformed in response to a general unrest and dissatisfaction with the status quo. The Concentus's releases using original instruments were indeed revolutionary for the time and represented the first serious attempts at a Period orchestra. Harnoncourt's words in the liner notes take Hindemith's manifesto a step further:

> One day we shall have to recognize the fact that the wish to hear old music in an unedited form, as close to the original as possible, sets off a chain reaction (tempi—numbers of performers—acoustics of halls—sound and sound-blending of instruments) which cannot be halted, and at the end of which stands a performance corresponding to the circumstances at the time of composition in every respect.[32]

Here is the idealism that characterized 60s HIP, the sense of logic and justice that was common at the time. The *St. John* was a pivotal performance, as it achieved for the first time most of the elements of the new Period style in which HIP still performs. It is interesting that Harnoncourt, who started the whole thing, is still known today for his "strongly disruptive, interventionist [performing] style."[33]

At about the same time, Harnoncourt wrote in more aggressive language about performances of Monteverdi's *L'Orfeo*:

> It is, I think, interesting that virtually none of the arrangers project the work into the present time by radically modernizing it, but rather offer it in a

"new" packaging at least 100 years old, *i.e.* in the style and sound of the last century, the age of Wagner. I cannot, as the reader has learned, be objective about such juxtapositions. Whoever will concern himself with the music of Monteverdi and his age must necessarily take a stand and become a believer. The listener must also be called upon to listen critically and not just for enjoyment, and then choose the approach he finds more convincing. He should take a position, he should justify to himself why he accepts one approach and rejects the others.[34]

The phrases "take a stand and become a believer" and "The listener . . . should take a position," may sound overdone nowadays, but they reflect some of the zeal of what is sometimes called a "revival" (the religious overtone is not inappropriate) or "movement" (with a suggestion of political protest). The "vehemence and self-righteousness" of these players was shared by composers of the same generation; New music and "Early music" were the twin movements for truth and change.

The rise of HIP in the mid-1960s created a "fork in the road" that required musicians to choose a direction when they performed historical music. It meant that those who chose to stick with tradition and Modern style did so either out of a sense of conviction—or by finding a rationale for rejecting Period musicking. Modern style is also a statement of intent: when it is applied to Rhetorical repertoire, it deliberately uses anachronistic instruments and ignores major elements of original style, even when they are available.

Guru Style: Rhetoric without the Name

Fabian writes that when Brüggen, Leonhardt, and Harnoncourt started playing in Period style they "shocked many contemporary listeners" who considered their playing "mannerist exaggerations or fashionable trends."[35] She compares the recordings by Leonhardt, Harnoncourt, and (surprisingly) Casals, where Bach's *Manieren* and *Auszierungen* are treated as graces, and offer "less intense tone production, flexible, lightly slurred rhythmic groups, contrametric rubato, detailed dynamic nuances, shorter than written values in case of longer notes, varied types of trills, obvious cadences and clarity of structure."[36]

As she points out, the earliest recordings of the Concentus Musicus using original instruments, when listened to today, don't seem to be projecting a performing protocol substantially different from Modern style.[37] The differences seemed larger then, of course, and there was no question that a new style was developing.

A striking comparison of Modern and Period styles can be heard on the two recordings of the Handel recorder sonatas by Frans Brüggen—the same pieces, with the same continuo players, Gustav Leonhardt and Anner Bijlsma—made in 1962 and a decade later. Like all performers in the early 1960s, these musicians were products of Modern-style education. The later recording made in the 1970s is in a style that they had in the meantime virtually invented. These recordings document the process through which the Dutch version of Period style (now practiced around the world) was developed during the 1960s.[38] Bijlsma commented, "If you compare old recordings by Frans Brüggen with his later ones, you can hear the enormous change that has taken place in his ideas about music. It makes you wonder. Was he wrong then? Or is he wrong now? Where's the mistake? There is no mistake. Truly great music travels along with you, just as the moon travels along with a train."[39]

🔊 AUDIO SAMPLE: 21. Brüggen, Bijlsma, Leonhardt, 1962. Handel: HWV 365, 3d mvmt

🔊 AUDIO SAMPLE: 22. Brüggen, Bijlsma, Leonhardt, 1973, Handel: HWV 365, 3d mvmt

🔊 AUDIO SAMPLE: 23. Brüggen, Bijlsma, Leonhardt, 1962. Handel: HWV 360, 3d mvmt

🔊 AUDIO SAMPLE: 24. Brüggen, Bijlsma, Leonhardt, 1973/74. Handel: HWV 360, 3d mvmt

An interesting insight into how performing styles develop is offered by José Bowen, who describes in some detail the history of a jazz tune (*'Round Midnight*), showing how the performing is both example and definition, and that

> every musical performance makes us reconsider our concept of the musical work. The effect of each performance, however, grows smaller as the tune develops a tradition. The initial performances have the ability to shift the "center of gravity" farther than can later versions, which literally have more tradition to move. The new bossa nova version by Jessica Williams will probably inspire a few similar performances, but it is not going to be able to shift the central style of rendering the tune as the Dizzy Gillespie and Miles Davis versions did thirty years ago.[40]

In the same way, the style gurus of the decade 1965–75 began with a good deal of leeway, but the longer they played, the more their innovations became "standard," and the less variation became possible. Now, with Period style established as a recognized norm used by musicians everywhere, a rationale to explain it is beginning to present itself. As I will discuss in part IV, this style appears to be the logical outcome of the application of principles of Rhetoric, although in the 1960s little was known about it.

3

Mainstream Style
"Chops, but No Soul"

Imagine you turn on the radio and hear the second movement of Brandenburg 2. After two bars, if you're an experienced listener, you know it's a Modern ensemble playing, not a Period one. What do you hear that tips you off? Perhaps it's the pitch and sound of the instruments. For me, it's a mixture of details that add up to a very different general style; things like

- "seamless" legato,
- continuous and strong vibrato,
- long-line phrasing,
- lack of beat hierarchy,
- unyielding tempos,
- unstressed dissonances,
- rigidly equal 16th notes.

There was a time, after World War II, when this was the only style. This was the way it was done, except for a few outdated codgers, still holding out for the old Romantic sentimentalism.

Modern style, you may have noticed, is not one I enjoy much, at least when it's used for performing Rhetorical music. It has its place, and for a very limited repertoire of Stravinsky and the Neoclassicists, it's the most appropriate style around. The problem is that it has spread to musics where it acts as a restraint and a damper, since its practices are so different from either Eloquent or Romantic styles.

Modernism and Modern Style

"The way we play today directly reflects a polemical struggle that transpired three-quarters of a century ago."[1] Modern style, which became the norm in the 1930s, owes its existence to its role as a reaction to Romanticism.

> An austere, explicitly anti-sentimental . . . approach to performance evolved at mid-century and came to dominate; examples include the conducting of Arturo Toscanini, George Szell, Hermann Scherchen and Fritz Reiner, . . . the pianism of Artur Schnabel, Rudolf Serkin and Glenn Gould and the refined approach to the violin displayed by Joseph Szigeti and Jascha Heifetz.[2]

Modern style is the principal performing protocol presently taught in conservatories all over the world. Its spirit is summarized by a succinct piece of graffiti found in the bathroom of an American conservatory: "Chops, but no soul."

Robert Hill describes the appearance of Modernism like this:

> In the period immediately following the First World War, a new spirit seized the imagination of the Western mind. A profound cultural paradigm shift, one that had been gathering momentum for many decades, finally achieved critical mass. . . . Essays, concert and recording reviews, memoirs, textbooks, reference-work entries all mirror the change in attitude. Partisans for both the late-Romantic and the modernist viewpoint engaged in polemical attacks. Actually, on most issues—espousal of fidelity to the text, eschewal of self-aggrandizing performance behaviour, condemnation of expressive exaggeration—the two schools of thought differed only in degree. They differed fundamentally in their attitudes with regard to the acceptable range of interpretive prerogative, and very specifically in their attitudes towards modifications of tempo and agogic accent.[3]

The traits that distinguish Modern style appear to us to be almost all negative compared with Romantic style—essentially restrictions: unyielding tempo, literal reading of dotting and other rhythmic details, and dissonances left unstressed. Modern style is prudish, the musical equivalent of "political correctness."

If Romantic protocol was heavy, personal, organic, free, spontaneous, impulsive, irregular, disorganized, and inexact, Modern style is the reverse: light, impersonal, mechanical, literal, correct, deliberate, consistent, metronomic, and regular. Modernists look for discipline and line, while they disparage Romantic performance for its excessive rubato, its bluster, its self-indulgent posturing, and its sentimentality. Taruskin calls Modernism "refuge in order and precision, hostility to subjectivity, to the vagaries of personality." It is characterized by formal clarity, emotional detachment, order, and precision.

As the arch-Modernist, Stravinsky is often blamed for this twentieth-century "objective performance style." Arturo Toscanini was also a strong influence in creating the Modernist concert atmosphere that is still current. Toscanini has been called a "New Puritan," a believer in playing nothing more and nothing less than what the artist-composer wrote on a page, "Com' è scritto." Modernism's concerns are accuracy and good intonation, literalism in reading scores, automatic (i.e., predictable) tempos, and limited personal expression. Music reduced to audible mathematics, functioning like an automaton.

All these traits lend themselves well to the new twentieth-century factor in performance: recording. (Accuracy and good intonation are needed when recordings are listened to—as they are—repeatedly. Literalism and limited expression are useful if one has to combine many takes; the less individuality each take has, the more interchangeable it is). But as values to apply to repertoires from before the modernist era, they are of dubious appeal. As Robert Hill suggests, Modernist principles "probably seriously distort the countenance and the 'message' of earlier repertories and consequently their effect on the listener."[4]

In one respect, Modern style is unique. That is in its prominent use of continuous vibrato. We think of continuous vibrato as a legacy of Romantic style, but vibrato did not become continuous on strings until the 1920s, when Modern style was taking over. On winds, it appeared around the turn of century in France, in the 1930s in England (except for Goosens, who started using it in the 1910s), but not in Austria/Germany until after 1945(!).[5]

Modern style has wrought a significant transformation in how the "Classics" sound. A rare and interesting comparison of Romantic style and Modern style is offered by two recordings. Stokowski's arrangement of Bach's Toccata and Fugue, BWV 565, which he recorded in 1957–58, was recently re-recorded by Salonen and the Los Angeles Philharmonic.[6] Here is a double stylistic overlay: Stokowski in (more or less) Romantic style over Bach and Salonen in Modern style over Stokowski.

🔊 AUDIO SAMPLE: 25. Unnamed Orchestra, Stokowski, 1957. Bach: BWV 565, arr. Stokowski

🔊 AUDIO SAMPLE: 26. Los Angeles Philharmonic, Salonen, 1999. Bach: BWV 565, arr. Stokowski

To judge from these two recordings, we have lost much in substituting Modern style for Romantic style. Listeners hearing the Salonen version can easily imagine the music written down, it is read so literally. Stokowski's effects are less clear, more impressionistic. Stokowski's version is quite moving, and his players play as if they are committed to the music. Salonen is icy by comparison; the musicians do not seem to be involved and tend to play mechanically but with great precision. In its vehemence,

Stokowski's performance is almost out of control at times (a bow slaps the strings occasionally). He also changes tempo, speeding up and slowing down, inspired by the music, presumably; Salonen keeps a steady, controlled tempo, changing only slightly at sections, never within a section. Ritards at new sections are much less marked in Salonen than Stokowski.

The intensity of the Modernist distaste for Romantic style can be glimpsed by comparing our own attitudes towards Romantic style. Most musicians nowadays regard it patronizingly as in "bad taste," and it is considered *sentimental,* a word often used in the 1920s when the Modernists were attacking Romanticism. Other words that describe Romantic style are "schmalzy" and "on the sleeve." Modernist values, by comparison, are generally seen by musicians as "good musicianship."

Uri Golomb recounts how Bach's large-scale vocal works, which earlier in the century had been performed in monumental Romantic mode, came under Modernist control. He cites a "piercing attack on romantic Bach performance" by Wilibald Gurlitt in 1951 that was symbolic of the turning tide toward a positivist, expressively restrained Bach who never knew "vulgar crescendos or decrescendos or gaudy rubato."[7] Gurlitt's comments resemble those of Stravinsky; "the two writers share a disdain towards romanticism in Bach performance."

Fabian notes that recordings of the Brandenburgs from the 1950s and 1960s seem

> to strive for a sustained line with hardly any caesuras, breathing, or lifting of the bow. Intense tone production, dynamically shaped long phrases, strict metre and rhythm, lack of pulse [= meaning here the beat hierarchy], playing all notes with equal importance and slurring them all together in a continuous legato characterize most of the versions [she lists fourteen different recordings].[8]

This is a good description of Modern style. This is where we all came from, directly as performers, or through our teachers, who all played that way.

The Performance Practices of Romantic Style and Modern Style Compared

Let's begin by describing Romantic style, afterwards considering how Modern style differs from it. The main attributes of Romantic style are:

- portamento (on string instruments an audible change of position, or slide),
- extreme legato,
- lack of precision (not deliberate),
- tempos that are usually slower than anyone would use today,
- lack of distinction between important and unimportant beats, due to an unrelenting heaviness and a surfeit of emphasis,

- melody-based phrasing,
- exaggerated solemnity,
- concern for expression,
- controlled use of vibrato,
- agogic accents (emphatic lingering),
- rubato.

Portamento is probably the most easily recognizable trait of Romantic style. It is frequently and beautifully used in both Furtwängler's and Mengelberg's *St. Matthew* recordings. Portamento tends to lend emphasis and tenderness to a passage. It seems to have become prominent among some violinists in the last quarter of the eighteenth century; traditionally it was thought to have originated with singers. Salieri claimed in 1811 that it had been "recently" introduced.[9] Recordings that use it are identifiable now as "old"; old-style recordings are of course Romantic.

In an interview made in 1977 when he was 88, Sir Adrian Boult described to Peter Wadland the demise in the 1930s of the portamento, a symbol of Romanticism:

> AB: It just seemed to go out of fashion. Quite suddenly. People didn't talk about it, you know. It just happened. And one suddenly realized after a few years that the string playing was much cleaner and, uh, . . . musical than it had been, and this sloppy portamento just disappeared.
>
> PW: Why was it actually used? It surely wasn't sloppy. I mean, it was for expressive effect, wasn't it?
>
> AB: I think it was. I think it . . . like vibrating, it was, it was a way of, of conjuring up, putting, bringing tears to the eyes of the young ladies.[10]

Bringing tears to anyone's eyes is not a priority of Modernism.

An obvious difference between Period and Romantic styles is the amount of legato. By the beginning of the nineteenth century an increase in the use of legato is indicated in sources ("gluing" the notes together "like a hurdy gurdy,"[11] as Quantz described an amount of legato that he considered excessive). An instance is Clementi's "best rule" for pianists in 1801. When articulation was not indicated in a piece, Clementi suggested "to adhere chiefly to the LEGATO; reserving the STACCATO to give SPIRIT occasionally to certain passages and to set off the HIGHER BEAUTIES of the LEGATO."[12] (Romantics really talked like this.) The long-line, by its nature, implies a legato approach. The most connected possible way of playing separate bow strokes on violin was the "*grand détaché*," developed in the late eighteenth and early nineteenth century. The new designs of keyed woodwinds that were coming into vogue at this time take more pressure to play, so players are reluctant to stop and start again; this matches their use of the long-line phrase. The standard Baroque instruments, using much less pressure in embouchure, breath, touch, or bow, can be stopped and started more easily.

Legato is a legacy of Romantic style, and it had become so pervasive that Hermann Keller, in his influential book *Phrasing and Articulation* (1955), compared it to religion: "Just as Schleiermacher defined religion as the absolute dependency upon and connection of the individual to God, so too is legato in music the symbol of connectedness, of preservation, indeed of completeness, or of humility before music."[13] Twentieth-century musicians were probably unaware of the "hurdy gurdy"[14] effect of the "seamless" legato in Modern style, as undetectable as our own accents. A comparison was not possible until the appearance of Period style.

Another easy trait to hear in both Romantic and Modern styles is the phrasing. Phrases profile structural divisions in the music, helping to clarify its meaning and musical grammar. The Romantic era developed a new kind of super-legato phrase known as the *climax* or *long-line* phrase.[15] It is often taken in one breath or bow, starts softly and builds to a "goal" or "climax" and then diminishes. The long-line phrase was already being thought about in the 1770s, was developed in the early nineteenth century, and had become dominant at least a decade before 1850.[16] This kind of phrase necessarily results in regular crescendos and diminuendos that are out of proportion to the brief figures or gestures that make up a Baroque melodic line. Applied to Baroque pieces, the long-line phrase comes across as a gratuitous and meaningless crescendo or diminuendo. Long-line phrases, vibrato, and a general legato sound are ubiquitous in Romantic and Modern performance, and together create the famous "patina" that blankets and often obscures recordings of Bach made in the early twentieth century.

Related to the long-line phrase is the *expressive crescendo*, an added crescendo that has no relation to the grammar[17] of the piece. The expressive crescendo is gratuitous and arbitrary. It is frequently used by Period ensembles for dynamic variety or to indicate "emotion."[18]

The early recordings I've heard are generally scruffy: not together and not always in tune. It sounds as if they were thinking of the bigger motion; one has a general impression of a different attitude toward precision and consistency. Mistakes were tolerated (perhaps because of the way recordings were made back then). Robert Philip describes early twentieth-century rhythm as sounding "somewhat chaotic . . . [but] there is an informality, an improvisational quality about it . . . There is an impression that it could all be different at the next performance."[19] He notes the comment of a musician who played with Joachim, "To play with the 'Old Man' is damned difficult. Always a different tempo, a different accent."[20]

Compared to the consistency of Modern style, I find this self-indulgence endearing. Brown comments on the same subject,

> Throughout the [nineteenth] century [there was an expectation] that performers would modify the written notation in a multitude of less obtrusive ways [than elaborate gracing], which, although they involved departures from or additions to the strict meaning of the notation, were probably not seen as

significant alterations to the composer's text any more than a modern performer regards continuous vibrato as an embellishment.[21]

Furtwängler, the arch-Romantic, had a reputation for being spontaneous, impulsive, never the same way twice. Speaking from personal experience, this is not a manner that is looked on with approval among
musicians today. Inconsistency is equated with a lack of professionalism.

Tempos in Romantic style are usually slower than anyone would consider using today. In the case of dances, they are so slow and "cantabile"
that their characteristic rhythms are difficult to perceive, and they become
unrecognizable as dances.

The usual impression given by Romantic music is of an unrelenting
heaviness due to too many accents. The beat hierarchy, so important in
Baroque style, and which continued to be preached until the late nineteenth century, had clearly waned: while good beats are emphasized, so
are bad beats, and every other kind. Pickups are often played loudly into
their downbeats.[22] Here is an extreme example made in 1952, followed
by a recent recording of the same passage in Period style.

🔊 AUDIO SAMPLE: 27. Berlin Philharmonic, Karajan, 1952. Bach:
Mass in B-Minor, First Kyrie, bars 30–34

🔊 AUDIO SAMPLE: 28. Amsterdam Baroque Orchestra, Koopman,
1994. Bach: Mass in B-Minor, First Kyrie, bars 30–36

The exaggerated solemnity of Romantic style is palpable; it takes its
responsibilities very seriously, and nothing is ever tossed off or delivered
with nonchalance: this is monumental, imperative music. To many Romantics, music was transcendent revelation, a rapturous contemplation
of the Beautiful.

Duffin comments, "There is a measured gravity about the performance as if the performers were showing a great respect for the music."[23]
As an earnest of its seriousness, last notes in Romantic style are often
played two or three times longer than they are played today and begin
with shimmering vibrato.[24] Occasional trills are tolerated (out of a sense
of duty, it sounds like), but once out of the way, the "real" note with its
melodic shape begins (graces in general are treated as aberrations, as disturbances to the general system).

Related to that is the strange impression one has of being small in a
giant land. This is the effect I think Landowska meant when she wrote of
"Enlargements that make everything appear great and sublime, as though
they were seen through a magnifying glass."[25] "It was also said," she
wrote, "that Bach's music, even in its least important theme, is immense,

powerful, and colossal." "Why perform one of his gigues," she asked, "as if it were a prayer?"[26]

Vibrato, the MSG of Music

In Period style vibrato is used selectively rather than constantly (to draw attention to important notes), with varied speed and intensity depending on expressive context, and often associated with *messe di voce*, expressive dynamic swells.[27] In Modern style, vibrato is an integrated element of tone quality, used continuously and aggressively, resulting in a constant feeling of activity and nervousness. Related to the effect of constant vibrato is that of the modern tuning system known as equal temperament. The tuning of chords in equal temperament gives a similar adrenalin rush, as it is very active, in contrast to the stability and calm of the pure thirds of meantone.

The more we experiment with temperaments, by the way, the more their significance appears to be in their expressivity. We begin to realize that they exert a serene but enveloping influence on the character of the music. Equal temperament, the tuning of necessity among modern players, was known by Bach's and Vivaldi's contemporaries, but was neither necessary nor popular.[28]

Coming back to vibrato, in the interview cited above, Sir Adrien Boult commented on the rise of continuous vibrato, which he had witnessed. Peter Wadland asked him, "I gather that at certain stages [in] the orchestras, some of the old members used the [unclear] straight playing, and the younger members used the more modern vibrato playing." Sir Adrian's reply was, "Yes, I suppose that happened. It seemed to blend pretty well in the end [last 3 words unclear], but I wasn't really conscious that the thing was changing very much." It is curious that the change was not abrupt, one day to the next, so that few seem to have been aware of a difference until everyone was doing it, and lots of it.

> Vibrato has come to impose a uniform heightened expression on most playing (and singing). The effect is to deny that any passages are 'unexpressive' or 'neutral'. The idea that 'the steady tone' should predominate, and that vibrato should be used only to intensify carefully selected notes or phrases, as Joachim, Auer, and others insisted less than a century ago, is quite alien to most late 20th-century string-players and many woodwind-players.[29]

Brown calls this usage "patently unhistorical," underscoring a basic difference between Romantic and Modern styles. Vibrato was used with discretion and selectively in Romantic style. Of course, there will no doubt come a day when constant vibrato is also "historical," and associated with the period after 1950.

By the early twentieth century, Ysaÿe and Kreisler were known for their vibrato. It doesn't sound so strong to me, but there is definitely less in Joachim's 1903 recording. Joachim began performing in 1839. An interesting comparison is Joachim's Adagio from Bach's g-minor solo sonata next to Menuhin's in 1935, and van Dael's in 1996. These three recordings show different uses of vibrato in styles about 135 years apart.

🔊 AUDIO SAMPLE: 29. Joseph Joachim, 1903. Bach: Adagio from g-minor solo violin sonata

🔊 AUDIO SAMPLE: 30. Yehudi Menuhin, 1935. Bach: Adagio from g-minor solo violin sonata

🔊 AUDIO SAMPLE: 31. Lucy van Dael, 1996. Bach: Adagio from g-minor solo violin sonata

Notice Menuhin's prominent and constant vibrato, his way of featuring 16th notes, giving each one an emphasis, and his unwillingness to leave the silences one hears in Joachim's Romantic and van Dael's Period (Eloquent) style playing. Menuhin's intensity and vehemence are typical of Modern style and are in contrast to the lighter, gentler Affection created by Joachim and especially van Dael. Some of these differences are personal, of course, but they must also reflect the ambient ideas of the time.

Vibrato remains today a contentious subject, particularly with singers. By the 1950s, the "wobbly singer" had become the norm. An example of the use of Modern style vibrato in the context of a general Romantic style is the alto soloist in Furtwängler's "Erbarme dich," recorded in 1954.[30]

🔊 AUDIO SAMPLE: 32. Vienna Philharmonic, Höffgen, Furtwängler, 1954. Bach: "Erbarme dich," St. Matthew Passion

Her vibrato is extreme, as if she is singing a Wagner opera at the Met today. The same aria in Mengelberg's Romantic recording of 1939 uses vibrato somewhat more discreetly.

Period style is not totally at odds with Romantic style. Some eighteenth-century practices were carried over until somewhere around 1850, and a few even longer. Brown points out that while æsthetic ideas went through a dramatic change in the first quarter of the nineteenth century, performing protocols mutated more slowly. According to him, beat hierarchy and overdotting survived through the nineteenth century and into the twentieth.[31] Dissonances, like appoggiaturas and chromatic notes, continued to be stressed in the nineteenth century. Modern style has abolished these traits.

I've mentioned the *agogic accent,* also known as "emphatic lingering." It involves prolonging the first of a group of four notes in faster passages and making it stronger. It is a technique that clarifies metric groups and delineates figuration.[32] Quantz advised this practice for unslurred passages that are too fast for pointing in pairs *(notes inégales).*[33] Clive Brown describes the agogic accent, or what seems very similar, in the nineteenth century. It is a rare occurance in Modern style, of course, where every 16th note is emphasized.

Robert Hill argues that time is the basic performing parameter that divides Modern style from previous ones because "when the player organizes time subjectively rather than adhering to an external, regular beat, timing decisions must be genuinely intuitive. They must be improvised, even if according to some kind of schematic plan; they cannot be 'reproduced.'"[34] Hill sees tempo and beat modification as the most important target of the Modernists. But there were others.

The *Stilkommission* that was set up at the Vienna Conservatory in the early 1960s included among its goals the elimination of "the virtuoso transcription and agogic freedom of the Liszt-school [which] have surrendered to the original version and to metrical rigor."[35] Hill observes that the basic unspoken message of the "Style Commission" was "that late Romantic interpretation itself was a kind of monstrosity, an aberration in music history, a shameful descent into depths of vulgar excess." This "Commission" might be considered the symbol of Modernism's rejection of Romantic style and a return to "correct" performing style. Most other noteworthy differences between the two styles are questions of degree. Modern style does not share with Romantic style its tendency to melodically based phrasing, its radically slow tempos, its intense solemnity, or its indifference to details of accuracy like ensemble and intonation. On the contrary, Modern style can be said to give priority to ensemble and intonation; this obsession with precision is probably due to recording.

The most obvious attributes of Modern style are inherited from Romantic style: the "seamless" legato, long-line phrasing, and a lack of beat hierarchy. But Modern style is mostly defined by the Romantic traits it suppresses. Dulak describes it as "a practice already drastically stripped down, regularized, clarified."[36] It does not usually inflect or shape notes, emphasize the second half of notes in syncopations, dot note-pairs in proportions other than exactly 3:1, use portamento or agogic accents or placement, add gracing at all generously, or use rubato (tempos are metronomic and unyielding).

Sol Babitz described it as "sewing machine" style, thinking of the rigidly mechanical rhythmic approach,[37] the four equally stressed 16ths, and the limited flexibility in tempo that often characterizes performances of historical repertoire heard in Modern style.

Children of Modernism

Modern style includes the misanthropic notions of "perfect compliance" and the "transparent" performer. Here is part of a review by Virgil Thomson of a piano recital in 1940 that is symptomatic of the disturbing mind-set in North American musical academia following World War II. Composers seem often to have been especially aggressive in advocating an "academic" non-interpretation: "Not one sectarian interpretation, not one personal fancy, not one stroke below the belt, not a sliver of ham, mars the universal acceptability of his readings. . . . And if he seems to some a little distant, let us remind ourselves that remoteness is, after all, inevitable to those who inhabit Olympus."[38]

This sounds like polemic, especially the bit about "universal acceptability." Taruskin cites Stravinsky, who had considerable influence on progressive musicians in the 1920s and 1930s and was an outspoken advocate of an "objective" style of performance, which he called "execution," defined as "the strict putting into effect of an explicit will that contains nothing beyond what it specifically commands."[39] Here is the Urtext Imperative ("If it's not commanded, it's forbidden") in all its unequivocal repulsiveness. "The point is that of scrupulous fidelity to the letter of the text, and an ascetic avoidance of unspecified nuance in the name of expression, or as Stravinsky stigmatizes it, in the name of 'an immediate and facile success that flatters the vanity of the person who obtains it and perverts the taste of those who applaud it.'"[40] Stravinsky expected the performer to act as a selfless transmitter of the musical work, adding nothing of their own character or ideas; "the highest quality in an executant . . . is 'submission.'" Timothy Day notes Stravinsky's (serious?) envy of the military band leader, "who keeps a revolver strapped in a holster by his side, and a notebook in which he marks a player's mistakes and, for each one, sends him to jail for a day."[41]

In a gentler form, Edward Elgar apparently shared this way of thinking. Elgar is said to have complained that "all his music required was to be left alone to say what it had to say in its own way: the expression was in the music, and it was not only unnecessary but harmful for the conductor to add to it an expression of his own."[42]

Period Style Compared to Modern Style

Anner Bijlsma (a modern reincarnation of Luigi Boccherini, the famous eighteenth-century cellist[43]) discusses these stylistic differences on the cello. Aside from physical modifications, playing has changed: he lists typical modern traits as constant vibrato (on consonance and dissonance alike), the avoidance of open strings (because they can't have vibrato), the desire for inaudible bow-changes (instead of using them for expression), and clearly a preponderance of slurred over separate notes. Bijlsma sees all these alterations as tending in the same direction: equality.[44]

Comparing Period style to Modern style, the overriding impression comes from the way 16th notes are treated—tossed off or etched out in rigid and disciplined equality—the difference between a note scrawled by hand in pencil and a stone tablet carved by a Roman scribe. I wonder if "inequality," famous from the specific case of "notes inégales" and "notes pointées," is not in fact a bigger concept? The attributes of Period style like phrasing by gesture, dynamic nuance, inflection (individual note-shaping), tempo rubato, agogic accents and note placing, pauses, and beat hierarchy all tend to run counter to the predictable, the automatic, the machine-like regularity of Modern style. They are wheels with a flat section, crumpled surfaces, irregular and unequal elements that demand special attention. Are we seeing here the paradigm of standardization implied in the Industrial Revolution, where a number 2 screw is supposed to be the same diameter, length, and pitch wherever one goes, which seems to lead toward simplistic systems, like Landowska's metaphor of "transforming a gothic cathedral into a skyscraper."[45] So many musical subjects seem simpler in their modern versions: equal temperament compared to extended/modified/regular meantones, a single pitch standard (albeit with "transposing" instruments as part of it), long-line phrases compared to gestures. Is it possible that the basic principle behind all the issues that separate the two styles is Bijlsma's "equality?"

Ignoring the beat hierarchy in Modern style is often combined with related characteristics:

- Unimportant notes are emphasized. Baroque music in Modern Style is often described as "clockwork-like" or "wallpaper music" because all notes—and all beats—are given equal weight and volume. Put another way, the unimportant notes like most 16ths have equal emphasis and are given as much bow stroke or tonguing as more important notes, giving an impression of over-meticulous seriousness. This way of playing also requires a lot of energy.
- Vehemence is commonly applied instead of more nuanced and varied expression. Modern performances rarely relax.

Here is an example of a piece played two ways. The first is characteristically Modern: legato even in the fast section, few pauses, constant vibrato (even on the last note), rhythm read in the exact proportions, and no nuance within notes (notice the last high note near the end of the piece). The second is essentially the reverse. Hearing the two of them side by side may help clarify the subjects I've been discussing (individual note-shaping and dynamic nuance). On the issue of literal reading, compare the rhythm of the first gesture in the hautboy part.

🔊 AUDIO SAMPLE: 33. H. Koch, Romantic oboe, M. Friesenhausen, H. Rilling. Bach: Cantata 187/5

AUDIO SAMPLE: 34. B. Haynes, hautboy, M. Emmermann, G. Leonhardt, 1989. Bach: Cantata 187/5

Click-Track Baroque

In Romantic style, there was clear and purposeful variation of tempo within a movement. Rubato was common, and precision was not. In Furtwängler's "Erbarme dich," rubato is extreme at the ends of sections (like the end of the violin's first ritornello). Mengelberg's use of rubato is more frequent (I estimate every bar the tempo either slows or quickens).

Relaxations of tempo exist in modern performances, but they are rare.[46] Rushing, which is strictly forbidden in Modern style, was apparently cultivated as an expressive device by the Romantics.

> In the view of people in the 1930s and 40s, von Bülow's rubatos were a "pernicious influence" (von Bülow died in 1894). His method of tampering with the score has created something of a tradition among German conductors which persists until today. The frequent use among so many modern German conductors of Luftpausen . . . and much of the exaggeration and overstatement that appear in so many performances of Classic symphonies can be traced directly to von Bülow. "Textual fidelity, as practiced by Toscanini, was the historic antidote."[47]

Nowadays the principle of slowing down and speeding up within a movement is not popular; in fact, it is frequently criticized by musicians and music teachers ("You're rushing," or "you're dragging"); it is usually regarded as a sign of lack of control. It is as if a "click track" (used for multi-take tapes) was keeping everything at a uniform, invariable pace. And yet, as Robert Philip has demonstrated by studying early recordings, the unchangeable tempo has emerged only since World War II.[48] There is thus a good chance that it would surprise an eighteenth-century musician to hear such predictable regularity. The difference is already clear going back to the early twentieth century, as Robert Philip observes:

> Modern rhythm has not just become more orderly. It has lost much of the informality and rhetorical unpredictability of early 20th-century performing. The relationships between notes are closer to a literal interpretation, and there is less emphasising of contrasts by tempo variation or by the various forms of rubato which used to be acceptable. Modern flexibility is much less volatile, both in detail and across whole movements. The overall result of these changes is that performances are much less characterised in their rhythm than they were earlier in the century.[49]

Here's an example. Fritz Kreisler's playing (1911) is so rhythmically subtle that it is questionable whether it could be reproduced by a modern violinist.

 AUDIO SAMPLE: 35. Fritz Kreisler, 1911. Kreisler: *Liebeslied*

Joshua Bell recorded the same piece quite beautifully and made an excellent attempt at Romantic style, including both portamento and rubato. But he couldn't (or wouldn't) catch the rhythmic nuance. Bell can't escape his ambience, his context. Never do we wonder what is notated on his page, it is regular and logical, whereas Kreisler uses rhythm to confound uniformity and consistency; by our criteria, what he plays and what is written resemble each other only approximately. Bell's teacher, Josef Gingold, born in 1909, was still playing like that in his late seventies when I heard him in Jerusalem. Captives on the carousel, we are creatures of our time.

AUDIO SAMPLE: 36. Joshua Bell, 1996. Kreisler: *Liebeslied*

Strait Style and Modernism

The Achilles' heel of Period performance is Modernism, whose root is fear of Romanticism. Let me put that more clearly, if I can. Many Period performers are so anxious to avoid Romantic style that they draw into their shells and cease to be visible at all. This is not difficult to do, because the same mechanism is normal among Modernist performers.

The writer who succeeded in drawing general attention to the presence, or even dominance of the cold hand of Modernism in Period performance was Richard Taruskin, who also broached the term "Straight style" in print. It's an appropriate word, but I think it's more accurately spelled "Strait," as in "strait jacket." From reading most of Taruskin's articles, you would not guess that HIP consisted of anything other than performances by players and singers of Straight/Strait style. But by the time his critiques started appearing, many historical performers in Europe had already spent a decade or more trying to distance themselves from Modernist playing. For some reason, Taruskin never brought that subject up; perhaps he didn't know about it. He did write with admiration about a number of historical performers he would have found difficult to call "Straight," like for instance Harnoncourt. But Taruskin never clearly acknowledged this essential element of the most interesting of the musicians performing in Period style: their anti-Modernism. His commentaries were brilliant and served a good cause, but HIP is and was more complicated than his picture suggested.

What Taruskin saw in Straightness was extraordinary transparency and precision. He missed a willingness to make irregularities, the persistent subtle fluctuations of tempo and dynamics that make performance eloquent, and which are justified only by personal feeling. "There is . . . no aspect of today's authentistic performance practice more pertinent to 20th-century aesthetics, and none harder to justify on historical grounds, than its ambience of emotional detachment, its distancing of voice from utterance."[50]

Strike Up the Bland: Strait Style Described

The best description of Strait style I know was written by Quantz, who called it poor *Vortrag:*

> [The *Vortrag* (= Delivery) is poor when] everything is sung without warmth or played at the same level without alternation of Piano and Forte, . . . one contradicts the Passions that should be expressed, or executes everything in general without sensitivity, without Passion, without being moved one's self, so the impression is given that the musician is singing or playing as an agent for someone else.[51]

Matteson, comparing "the cool Germans" (who were they?) to the more demonstrative French and Italians, writes that "they sing very decently and rigidly, as if they had no interest in the content, and are not in the least concerned with the consideration of the proper expression or meaning of the words, indeed even when seeing the words for the tenth time they hardly understand them or take them in properly."[52] And going back to 1676, Thomas Mace, in his *Musick's Monument,* bemoans the musicians who "Drudge, and take much Pains to Play their Lessons very Perfectly as they call it (that is, Fast) which, when they can do, you will perceive Little Life, or Spirit in Them, merely for want of the knowledge of this last Thing, I now mention, viz.: They do not labour to find out the Humour, Life, or Spirit of their Lessons."[53] John Mason in 1748 described the counterpart in oratory as speaking with "a flat, dull, uniform, Tone of Voice, without Emphasis or Cadence, or any Regard to Sense or Subject of what is read. ... . Such a Monotony as Attorney's Clerks read in when they examine an engrossed Deed."[54]

So I guess we have to give this approach some historical validity. Nor can we fault it for technical competence. Strait musicians are often among the best in the business. Taruskin describes them as showing "firm and dependable all-purpose technique at the service of a very meticulous professionalism, and they are very good with ensemble. You can settle down and put your feet up with them," he says, "confidant that every detail will be consistent and ready."[55] In fact, Strait musicians excel in technical detail. But the problem is that if you spend hours working on playing in tune and together, you can't expect an inspired concert—you can expect a concert that is in tune and together.

An example is this recording by Michala Petri. After Frans Brüggen, what can be done on the recorder? No one in this or the next generation is likely to approach the degree of musicality or technical control that Brüggen achieved. Petri's purpose is unclear. She manages to systematically delete Brüggen's flamboyant personal flair, and in doing so, also negates the most important aspect of his gift to the world: the new insights he offered into the music and the instrument. Gone, as if Brüggen had never been. What is left are well-played notes.

🎵 AUDIO SAMPLE: 37. M. Petri and G. Malcolm, 1984. Marcello: Largo, Sonata, F

Taruskin defined his "Straight" style a little differently than I do. For him, its principal quality is predictability and compliance to rules; tempos and phrasings "off the rack," as he put it.[56] Strait style comes across as "prim correctness," a miniaturizing spirit, mild-mannered and "light-weight, leery of the profound and the sublime."[57]

I would agree with that, but there are more basic issues, like failing to reach out to the audience and the misguided notion that it is accept-able or even desirable to perform in a "no one at home" predictable way. Strait style players probably think of this coolness as "tasteful playing," but it is the taste of Modernism, not of the Baroque period.

Among the least interesting recordings I've heard recently is a choir of doubled voices (a built-in restriction on expression) with an excellent reputation, the Tallis Scholars. They sing in a quite predictable way, with occasional vibrato; competent but boring, without message.

I am aware that there are musicians and listeners to whom this style appeals. Indeed, there is a market for "easy listening" and "feel good" music as well, to which this is related. Many people who know little about music tell me they like "Classical" because it projects a sense of order and is soothing. These are not my objectives, but there is no reason we should all be in agreement about the goals and ends of music any more than that we should all like the same movies. But, for many of us involved in Period musicking, Strait style interpretations are tedious and dull.

In the end, Strait style is a kind of "Modern style lite" or Modern style "minus" (though there is precious little left to remove from Modern style). Not the wobbly vibrato of Modern style, but usually some amount of constant vibrato, long-line phrasing, and a temperament that is differ-ent from equal only in name. It is like the pianists who play harpsichord repertoire but do it dryly and on tiptoe, thinking they are being "correct" by limiting the expressive power of the piano.

Taruskin's endearing description of the "Crooked musician" was es-sentially the Romantic genius, who gives every musical event "a unique, never-to-be-repeated shape"; the "real artist," as he calls them. But both the recordings he compares sound Strait to me. As often happens, both these groups have the kind of precise ensemble and close uniformity of sound that belongs to a Modernist orchestra; they sound conducted. You can hear, as John Butt observes, "what many performers had marked in their parts."[58]

In an era of remorseless competition for work among musicians and a demand for technical perfection, where a split note will probably cost a player their job, it is no wonder players are not inclined to take chances. This is one of the factors that helped create Strait style, together with the fact that most of the work is in orchestras, where the ambience does not invite or encourage individual initiative.

Strait style appeals to many who see it as an antidote to the vehemence of Romanticism, which rarely lets up its intensity. The problem is the tendency to make everything restrained and temperate. The missing element is the fire of Rhetoric, an expressive music that is not Romantic (see part IV).

II

HOW ROMANTIC ARE WE?

4

Classical Music's
Coarse Caress

Romanticism, we keep thinking, is over, or almost over. Already a century ago, Wanda Landowska wrote in her brilliant prose:

> If I am not mistaken, Romanticism is departing with a noisy farewell. . . . Let us not emulate those fashionable hosts, of whom Shakespeare speaks, who take leave negligently of the departing guest. Let us bow down, very low. Romanticism gave us strong emotions and unforgettable ecstasies; it awoke in us unbounded ideas and supreme flights of fancy; it flattered our palate with tart and bitter fruit, which seemed so good after an overabundance of sweetness; it brushed our skin with the coarse caress of a wild beast. May all the centuries to come look with full respect and envy upon its grandeur, which is still hovering sovereignly.[1]

"Still hovering sovereignly"; it is true that some of the old Romantic performing fashions are gone. But while Modernism has made inroads into the territories of Romanticism, the Romantic repertoire remains firmly secured, and many of the potent æsthetic axioms of the nineteenth century are very much alive and pervade modern thinking about music.

One thing we can deduce about music prior to the Romantic Revolution is that musicians in those days could not have shared our Romantic values to any noticeable degree because they hadn't been conceived or implemented yet. When Rhetorical performers made their music—"in those days averse to all romanticism," as one early Romantic recalled her childhood[2]—the ideals of Romanticism had not yet become "regulative," as philosophers sometimes say. Laurence Dreyfus writes that "Bach and his contemporaries willingly reveal the common terms of their thought. And from these common terms can be inferred a great many things, not the least of which is that certain of our (anachronistic) concerns are strikingly absent."[3]

Romanticism arose along with other values that are the foundations of modern life, like human rights, democracy, the decimal system, the universal use of family names, marriage based on love, and street addresses. No wonder it is so pervasive. As musicians, we find ourselves looking at Rhetorical repertoire through a series of veils, consisting of axioms and dogmas, usually unspoken, that are so strong in our culture that they tend to distort and obscure for us everything that pre-Romantic people thought music was meant to do, or how they went about playing it: not just how to play a trill, but something as basic as how to read the page. All of us who are involved with HIP are unconsciously imbued with Romanticism, and many of the music historians whose researches we read, even those with advanced ideas in other areas, still take some of these venerable nineteenth-century ideas for granted.

Whether we intend it or not, Romantic habits are so much a part of how we do music that they represent barriers to approaching historical styles, often unconscious ones. We are not always able to recognize (and see through) Romantic myths and legends like:

- Canonism,
- autonomous music (Absolute Music),
- belief in progress in instrument technology and technique,
- originality and the cult of genius,
- worrying about attribution,
- untouchability and text fetishism,
- expecting it all to be beautiful,
- the transparent performer and "perfect compliance" to the score,
- music as the autobiography of the artist-composer,
- ritualized and ceremonial performance,
- the Urtext Imperative,
- the interpretive conductor.

How do we deal with all this Romantic drapery? If it really is our purpose to revive repertoire from before the rise of Romanticism, if inventing new performing styles inspired by historical traditions is what we are about, or, if we simply wish to see Rhetorical music in something like the same terms as it was originally seen, we should make the effort to identify the heady influences of the nineteenth and twentieth centuries now unconsciously embedded in our culture. Robert Philip suggests one way to do that: "Examining early recordings is, one might say, rather like sending a telescope outside the earth's atmosphere; it is possible to see more clearly into the past, because of the absence of local interference."[4] Beyond the "gravity" and "lights" of Mother Earth (or Mother Romanticism), our knowledge will give us a clearer view of the distant brilliance of Rhetorical music.

It would be simple if we could just say that to perform in an original Period style, a bottom-line, minimal condition would be the absence of Romantic practices. But what about those attributes of nineteenth-century style that carried over from the eighteenth century? Baroque and Romantic styles may have been fundamentally different in philosophy, but they had a number of performing traits in common. These differences and connections need to be sorted out. We can only touch on some of them here. Both styles are intensely expressive, and Modernism, which avoids expression, tends as a result to lump them together. If we wish to develop our means of expressing the Affections, we need to make a distinction between Romantic expression and Baroque expression.

It would be interesting to know just how Romantic we are. What is "Romantic," anyway? And how do our dogmas, the legacies of Romanticism, obstruct our view of the old musicians and how they made music? Knowing what the curtains look like will probably help in seeing through them. Let's start with the thickest of all, the Canon.

The Musical Canon

A Canon is a corpus of works that is regularly heard, an authoritative list. Theodore Thomas, "founder of the modern American orchestra," called it "the great works of the great composers greatly performed, the best and profoundest art, these and these alone."[5] "Great" (which is itself a pretty Romantic idea) means in this case chosen by recognized authorities as suitable for contemplation and admiration, and respected as superior examples and benchmarks of value.

A perfect example of Canonism gone wrong is a pianist trying to choose one of Beethoven's cadenzas to one of the concertos (not only are the pieces overplayed, but cadenzas are defined as sections that are improvised). Another example is the custom in Genoa at the opera: it's said that the ultimate form of singer rejection there is for the audience to sing along with the soloist.

Nikolaus Harnoncourt sees the development of the Canonic idea as a cataclysmic event, and I have to agree. "At that time, the whole fabric of Western music, and of Western culture in general, was profoundly shaken."[6] As Jim Samson described it:

> A newly consolidated bourgeois class began to define itself artistically in the late 18th century. . . . It established its principal ceremony—the public concert . . . and began to create a repertory of Canonic music, with related concert rituals, to confirm and authenticate the new status quo. By the mid-19th century it had already established much of the core repertory of the modern Canon, in the process giving itself cultural roots, 'inventing' tradition and creating a fetishism of the great work which is still with us today.[7]

Thus, starting in the nineteenth century, an artificial "Canonic" music appeared, consisting of a Canon of so-called masterpieces destined to stand for eternity. In banal terms, works like Beethoven's symphonies have the same function as the large stone statues and monuments in city parks, enduring symbols of an established culture (which is something Beethoven would probably have been impressed to have known about). Most people pass such objects by without paying much notice of them, as long as they remain there. (Most of these monuments, interestingly, seem to come from the same period, namely the Romantic. They resemble the quasi-Greek architecture of many other ritual buildings in city centers like opera-houses, government offices, art galleries, theaters, and libraries.)

There is another way to look at Canonism that we could call the "decomposing composers" condition. This may be the seed from which the whole Romantic Movement grew: it was a shift from concert programs of contemporary music to that of past music by dead composers (white and male, of course). Weber notes, for example, that the proportion of music by living writers in concerts at the Leipzig Gewandhaus "declined from over 70% in the 1820s to little over 20% in 1870."[8] Since the nineteenth century, music has been oriented backward, to the past.

> The Great Composers who are summoned up by the conductor's gestures are not flesh-and-blood people, . . . it is abstractions of these men who are present, mythological culture heroes . . . constructed to serve the needs of present-day people from shards and fragments of biography, and by a kind of back-formation. . . . They cannot be alive in the present. They *have* to be dead in order to be immortal, and they have to be immortal to be mythic heroes.[9]

Their names and busts often line the walls of our most prestigious concert halls.

As John Spitzer points out, "the whole edifice of art criticism and taste is based on the proposition that people ought to like some art works better than others."[10] Quality control is essential in maintaining the Canon. Part of constructing a hierarchy of greater and lesser hero-composers within the Romantic Pantheon involves assessing value and establishing standards, starting with who and what to let in the front door of the Pantheon, and including a totem pole of the great works and artist-composers arranged in order of precedence. Judgment was indeed one of the important factors for Immanuel Kant, the æsthetician whose influential book *Critique of Judgement* (1790) marked music with an obsession with standards of taste and value.[11] This imperative to judge is very strong and is the stance of most informed listeners today; if they discuss a concert they have just heard, their subject will often be whether the music or its performance was æsthetically "good." Going to a restaurant, on the other hand, they would be more likely to talk about whether they liked the food, not whether it was "good" in some objective way. "Classical music" radio shows sometimes rank recordings by number, and reviews of concerts in the paper are essentially judgments rather than (like the rest of the paper) chronicle.

By the end of the nineteenth century a repertoire of reassuringly familiar Canonic pieces had been assembled, but there was still a bit of room for new ones. A typical late nineteenth-century orchestra program thus sampled the antique but made allowance for the new. Contrast that with a typical late twentieth-century orchestra program, which usually omitted the new, or slipped it in surreptitiously.

The Canon of western Romantic music is rather limited. Harnoncourt called it "this very paltry selection, which was chosen by our great-grandparents."[12] The repertoire of works that attracts a significant audience today stops at about the time of World War I. Very few pieces written after that time have more than a specialty interest for current audiences.

Listeners are ardently faithful to the works of the Canon. The vocabulary that surrounds them includes "immortal masterpieces," "works that will live forever," and "the world's greatest music." Some of this may be commercial hype, but there are many who think of them as "the best the human race has thought and done."[13] Maybe they're right; I'd just like a little variety, and a bit of lightness.

Charles Burney and the Beginnings of Musical History

A book on the history of music was still no more than an idea when Charles Avison noted in 1753: "[A] History of the Lives and Works of the best Composers; together with an Account of their several *Schools,* and the *characteristic Taste,* and *Manner* of each: —A Subject, though yet untouched, of such extensive Use, that we may reasonably hope it will be the Employment of some future Writer."[14]

To most musicians of the time, studies of that kind must have seemed superfluous. Music was by definition contemporary; what was heard, with few exceptions, had been written within the last generation. Who needed history? Speaking of "the historical sense in music," Joseph Kerman has commented that

> the assumption that music of the past is of aesthetic interest . . . is of relatively recent vintage. The historical sense in music is much newer than in literature, where Canonic texts have been handed down for millennia, or in art, where temples and cathedrals stand for centuries and galleries have been cultivated since the Renaissance. But a musical tradition is not made up of texts and artefacts. Music is evanescent, and until recently the repertory of Western art music did not extend back more than a generation or two; in the deepest sense, music history extended back no further.[15]

The first edition of *Grove's Dictionary,* published in 1878, managed to enclose the sum total of human knowledge about European music in four volumes. The present Grove's—that has just appeared (and sometimes glows in the dark, it is so full of short-term up-to-date knowledge)—is twenty-nine volumes.

As Charles Burney prepared the first volume of his history of music in 1770, he noted that "though every library is crowded with histories of painting and other arts, as well as with the lives of their most illustrious professors, music and musicians have been utterly neglected."[16] His argument was that

> The day, and hour, are carefully consigned to posterity, when towns have been sacked, and armies defeated, yet the exact time is seldom enquired, when discoveries the most useful to human nature have been made, or the greatest productions of genius conceived.
>
> He would, therefore, be thought a most contemptible biographer, who, in the life of a musician, should circumstantially relate the year, the day, the hour when, and place where, a particular *sonata* was composed, though, by its excellence, it should bid fair for delighting the lovers of music, as long as the present system of harmony shall subsist.[17]

The roots of Canonism are entwined with those of the new interest in history, and Burney himself seems to be suggesting it here. That he appears to have thought about this is implied in his observation that "there are classics in poetry, sculpture, and architecture, which every modern strives to imitate; and he is thought most to excel, who comes nearest to those models."[18] By "classics," he was thinking of the Hellenistic models, of course, most of which remain lost to this day. As William Weber writes,

> Western musical life had never had a learned, classical tradition comparable to that of literature and the fine arts. Since only fragments of Greek and Roman music had survived, there were no models for humanistic emulation or scholarly study.... The art remained oriented toward the immediate present; works were composed, enjoyed, and quickly forgotten. There were no [past] masters as we know them now.[19]

This was about to change, however, and signs had already appeared in England. To succeed, a "learned, Classical tradition" needed plausible histories of music, and musicians willing to play the old stuff. The Concert of Antient Music took care of performances. And for the history, it was to be two writers in London, Charles Burney and John Hawkins—and both in the same year, 1776—who published the first systematic histories solely on the subject of music.[20]

Since he had no usable books to consult when writing his history, Burney was forced to gather his data "in the field," like ethnomusicologists in our times. "I found the shortest and best road to such information as I wanted, was to talk with the principal professors, wherever I went," he wrote.[21] "Had the books that I have hitherto consulted, which have been very numerous, supplied me with the information I wanted, relative to a History of Music, upon which I have been long meditating; I should not have undertaken [the travels described here.]."[22] He set out on the first of his research trips in June, 1770, "attended with much fatigue, expence, and neglect of other concerns." In those days it was customary for travelers to keep a journal or diary, and by good luck, Burney decided to publish his. He was an original, penetrating, and articulate thinker, and the diaries are one of the purest examples of primary research into European art music that has ever been written. To those of us interested in the music of that period, the result is fascinating; using Burney's eyes and ears, it is as if we are in a time machine, making a musical voyage in which we are able to meet personally many of the renowned musicians, artists, and scholars of the mid-eighteenth century. Among the most interesting of these were Agricola, Emanuel Bach, Balbastre, Franz Benda, Armand-Louis Couperin, Diderot, Farinelli, Gluck, Hasse, Marpurg, Padre Martini, Metastasio, Leopold and Wolfgang Mozart, Quantz, Voltaire, and Wagenseil.[23] Of the many concerts he heard on his tour, two of the most remarkable were the *Concert Spirituel* in the great hall of the Louvre and one of the private concerts at Sans-Souci played by Frederick the Great.

Despite his involvement with history, however, Burney was clearly not an antiquarian. "Learned men and books may be more useful as to ancient music," he wrote, "but it is only *living* musicians that can explain what *living music* is."[24] While a movement to revive "ancient music" existed in London starting in the 1720s (see chapter 8), Burney's stance was probably representative of what many eighteenth-century musicians would have thought of HIP (if the idea had even occurred to them). Man of his age, Burney wrote:

> Who will venture to say, that the musician who should compose or perform like Orpheus, or Amphion, would be deservedly most applauded now? Or who will be bold enough to say, *how* these immortal bards *did* play or sing, when not a single vestige of their music, at least that is intelligible to us, remains? As far as we are able to judge, by a comparative view of the most ancient music with the modern, we should gain nothing by imitation. To copy the *canto fermo* of the Greek church, or that of the Roman ritual, the most ancient music now subsisting, would be to retreat, not to advance in the science of sound, or arts of taste and expression. It would afford but small amusement to ears acquainted with modern harmony, joined to modern melody. In short, to stop the world in its motion is no easy task; on we *must* go, and he that lags behind is but losing time, which it will cost him much labour to recover.[25]

Burney's assumption was of a continuing advance toward perfection that, in his view, reached its zenith in the music of his own day.[26] For him, "contemporary music" was by definition superior to the music of the past.[27] He believed, in fact, that "to say that music was never in such high estimation, or so well understood as it is at present, all over Europe, would be only advancing a fact as evident, as that its inhabitants are now more generally civilized and refined, than they were in any other period to be found in the history of mankind."[28]

Burney's supreme confidence in the music of his own time rings strangely in our modern ears. We do not share his confidence in progress, which seems to us naïve. To cite one recent writer:

> The whole history of art . . . can be examined profitably in terms of Darwinian theory only if one fundamental point is kept in mind: namely that the evolution of particular forms and styles continues only so long as the aesthetic aims that nourish them prevail. The history of art is the history of a succession of artistic ideas, ideals, and beliefs; and the life span of the forms and styles involved is measured by the degree of success attending the artist's aims. The tenets of the Vivaldi concertos are quite different from those of Mozart, Beethoven, or Paganini; and to trace the evolution of one from the other is rewarding only insofar as the different artistic aims are understood. Above all, the evolutionary theory of progress is faulty when confused or identified with value judgments. According to one evolutionary interpretation, art evolves in a continuous line to the perfection of the present. If this is so, the world of art today must be the best of all possible worlds—a conclusion that is palpable nonsense.[29]

Why Did the Romantics Call Music "Classical"?

In the same year that the first histories of music were published, 1776, a group of English noblemen founded the Concert of Antient [!] Music (the spelling of "Antient" was evidently deliberate to lend an "olde English" tone[30]). It was this organization that first began to use the term "Classical" to mean "the idea and practice of a Canon." By the early nineteenth century, "Classical," virtually synonymous with "Canonic," had become a common musical term.[31]

The Concert of Antient Music defined its repertoire as no younger than about twenty years; in other words, a piece was defined as "Antient" that had been written twenty-one years or more before it was performed. Today, it's an attitude we're familiar with in clothes styles, but our conception of music is very different.

Anton Webern's music still has an honored place in contemporary music circles, for instance, and he remains difficult for present-day audiences. Yet Webern began working in 1906, over a hundred years ago, and he died in 1945. Recordings of his music, or even that of his better-known contemporaries, Schoenberg and Stravinsky, are not common.

We could say that in a way modern listeners are the prisoners of Canonism, as it acts as a limitation on repertoire. Audiences are indeed impatient with the unfamiliar or anonymous. Few pieces by "Kleinmeister" are tolerated.

What Conservatories Conserve

Although conservatories existed in the eighteenth century, they were essentially a creation of Romanticism, and all the great conservatories established in the first half of the nineteenth century were modeled on the Paris Conservatoire, Romanticism's symbolic educational institution.

Wagner was a great admirer of the Paris Conservatoire. He thought a conservatory should be "an institution in which the traditions of performance established by the masters themselves are conserved."[32] Founded as a product of the French Revolution and generously funded by the government, the Conservatoire codified the new Canonic ideals. One of its original purposes was, like France's Bibliothèque nationale, to "conserve" the French national heritage. Conservatories replaced the old master/apprentice system with uniform approaches to pedagogy that emphasized technique (and often ignored musicality; the music came later, if at all). Systematic "methods" to develop technique were commissioned from all the instrumental professors, which were very different in spirit from the self-help "tutors" of bygone days. The Conservatoire was enormously influential throughout Europe, and many of its innovations are still in use today.

As an exercise in ethnomusicology, Henry Kingsbury recently studied a modern conservatory in the United States. One of the things he observed is that the conservatory's catalogue devoted many pages to describing the lines of tradition that preceded each of its teachers: "Here one sees mentioned the shades of Landowska, Cortot, Szigeti, Thibaud, Flesch, and Steuermann, as well as the still living Serkin, Rampal, Biggs, Copland, Babbitt, and Boulez. . . . [These are] indications of musical authority, and thus are potential resources for teachers in the recruitment of students."[33] It is common for musicians' CVs to name teachers. This is an indication of how important pedagogical lineage is in modern concert music. "The importance of all this name dropping, it must be emphasized, is to present each faculty member as the individual conservator of a distinct and distinguished musical heritage." Priests and guardians of the sacred flame of tradition; no wonder HIP's out-of-hand dismissal of the received playing tradition is seen as outrageous by many Canonic musicians who honor their musical predecessors!

HIP proposes the performance of a piece in the style of its original time. We can thus say that HIP is not interested in a work's "reception history" (that is, everything that happened in the performance of a work after it was first performed). In the following, Charles Rosen gives a good example of the reasoning of those who choose to play Bach in Modern style (which appears to be what Rosen calls "the real life of music"): "The original impulse behind Early Music was a desire for a thoroughgoing renewal. Nevertheless, to refuse to come to terms with the way Bach, for example, has been interpreted and misinterpreted through time, to see how his work carried the seeds of its own future, is to shut oneself off sadly from the real life of music."[34] Here are shades of the Victorian approach to history, that the past and the present are an unbroken whole and that "the seeds of the present seemed immanent in the past."[35]

Should we see "the seeds" of the piano in the harpsichord, as well? (In some sense, it's true: the same players could use the two instruments, and they often served the same function as anchor instruments in small ensembles.)

Although it is not yet obvious, there is no doubt that Rosen's Modern style itself has a shelf-life with a pull date; the way they play Bach on the grand piano nowadays—or, for that matter, on the harpsichord—will itself one day be a historical curiosity.

Tradition would thus appear to be the factor that conservatories conserve. If a musician's heritage is important to their reputation and authority, one of the roles of conservatory teachers is to act as conservators and figureheads of that heritage. Indeed, a received tradition of some kind seems to be a condition of concert music; musicians need a living tradition, a laying-on of hands.

It is true that many conservatories now include teaching in Period style. Although I taught for a number of years in a conservatory, it has always seemed to me that they are a dubious place to study Rhetorical music. Rhetorical music is (as I argue in chapter 14) profoundly anti-Classical. Institutionalizing HIP in the twentieth century has influenced us all into thinking of it as a department of Classical music rather than a bloc with distinctly different principles. The careers of many members of the Movement have been sustained through their monthly pay checks from Conservatories, which shows how the Movement's sting of protest has been drawn. Conservatories rarely encourage the kind of independent thinking that originally inspired HIP.

At the moment, conservatory students who study with modern teachers but are interested in playing Rhetorical repertoire in Period style are on their own. As I will discuss in chapter 9, Baroque style can quite convincingly be played on Romantic instruments. One of the hautboists I admire is Masashi Honma, who, as well as *hautboist,* is also solo *oboist* in the Tokyo Metropolitan Orchestra. I once asked him in a public interview to compare how he played Rhetorical music on the two kinds of oboe; his reply was that he played them exactly the same way.

That was a surprise at the time. But seen in this light, there would seem to be no reason conservatory students who study Romantic instruments shouldn't learn to play Rhetorical music in Period style. If their teachers can't show them how, Period players can.

Absolute Music (the Autonomy Principle)

In 1810, the writer E. T. A. Hoffmann articulated in his "irritated and outspoken" writings the notion of an autonomous music disdaining "every aid, every admixture of other arts."[36] Music, he wrote, "discloses to humanity an unknown domain, a world that has nothing in common with the outer world of the senses that surrounds it." In that Romantic world, music "leaves behind all feelings that can be determined through concepts, to surrender itself to the inexpressible."

The name *absolute Tonkunst,* used by many early nineteenth-century philosophers and critics, has been called "teutonic jargon," but Romantics fell in love with the concept, considering music "the art of arts, just because it is indefinite, innocent of reference to the external world, and richly, because imprecisely suggestive."[37] All the Romantic arts took up the idea of "thinking in music, thinking with sounds, the way a writer thinks with words,"[38] and expressing in notes what was inexpressible in other media.

In the Romantic æsthetic, Absolute Music was raised above speech as an intimation of the Absolute; it could say what words could not.[39] The new Romantic idea was that "words, instead of being an essential component of a piece of music, are either irrelevant to or even distracting from its meaning."[40]

Autonomous music, music unadulterated, was thus by definition instrumental, free at last of singers. A century earlier, at the beginning of the eighteenth century, Le Cerf de la Viéville had written precisely the opposite: that in operas, "the instrumental music (*symphonie*) is the least essential element of the musical event, since the music itself is only present to help express the speech and feelings of the opera, which the *symphonie* does not express [by itself]."[41]

The move away from "eloquent" music is evident in the gradual demise of the recitative toward the end of the eighteenth century. The recitative had been an attempt to blend speech and music, to imitate the natural inflections of common speech. By the late 1700s most forward-looking musicians probably agreed with Burney, who wrote in 1773 of "mere *Recitative,* with which every one is tired and disgusted!"[42] And instrumental tutors of the early nineteenth century, far from the eighteenth-century idea of considering the voice as a model of how instruments could play, scarcely referred to the voice at all, or turned it into a courtesy gesture to earlier tradition; the real interest was in purely instrumental technique.

The ultimate manifestation of Absolute music was the proposal that appeared in 1958 in an article called "Who Cares if You Listen?" by the composer Milton Babbitt. Babbitt urged a situation in which artist-composers "would be free to pursue a private life of professional achievement, as opposed to a public life of unprofessional compromise and exhibitionism [pleasing, in other words, musical 'laymen']."[43] Babbitt compared modern composing to higher math or advanced physics, fields that could only be understood by specialists. He proposed that universities and foundations pick up the tab for supporting it as a kind of "pure research" (and against all odds, this is what has happened). The implication is that musical compositions are not necessarily meant to be listened to, certainly not by the general public.

We'll have occasion to revisit the concept of Absolute music in the pages that follow.

Pachelbel's Canon Becomes Canon

For listeners in Rhetorical times, to have heard a piece of music a second time was probably like seeing a play or reading a book a second time is to us now. It is something one does only occasionally with very special works or difficult ones.

> When [music] did survive many performances, numerous changes could and usually would be made to the music in the process. Rarely did musicians think of their music as surviving past their lifetime in the form of completed and fixed works. When musicians thought about repeatability, they thought more of the multiple uses of themes and parts for various different occasions, than of one and the very same whole composition being repeated.[44]

I think the best comparison in modern times is to films, the most successful of which don't seem able to last in first-run theaters for more than a year, and where audiences are aware of the age of every film they see. In what seems much the same spirit, Quantz felt obliged to warn his readers about being overly enthusiastic about newly composed music: "The beginner . . . must not pay any attention to whether a piece is quite new or already somewhat out of date. Let it suffice them if it is simply good. For not everything new is for that reason beautiful."[45]

We are now well along the road to developing a new Canon of immortal masterpieces—but this time of Rhetorical pieces. There are already many "greatest hits." *Messiah* is the obvious one; the Brandenburgs and *Eine kleine Nachtmusic* are often heard now as background muzak. Even amongst Bach's cantatas, a few are popular and played frequently (partly because of their instrumentations), while others of equal musical interest are neglected.

Many modern musicians—players of both Romantic and Period instruments—have performed the *St. Matthew Passion,* for example, two or three dozen times (some gambists playing with symphony orchestras a good many more than this), and many listeners have heard it at least that often (and keep coming back for more); yet Bach himself apparently performed it a total of only five times: twice in 1727 and once in 1729, 1736, and 1742 (each performance a somewhat different version). And for him, or any of his contemporaries, even that many repeats was unusual. So we are industriously transforming Rhetorical music into new Canons. Is this what we want to do, or is it force of habit? Imagine what would happen to a good book if we read it twice a year for five years, and if we heard recordings of it in elevators; that is what we are doing to the Four Seasons.

Whatever Canonism has done to music, one thing is clear: it was not the normal way of thinking about music in earlier times. Canonism as we know it did not yet exist. And therefore, to understand Rhetorical repertoire (repertoire from before the Romantic Revolution)—as far as we can grasp it from this distance—entails an attempt to perceive music with*out* the Canon in the background. "If we are to understand the canon historically, we must become sceptical of it, and free ourselves from its authority, its ideology, and the whole manner of speech that surrounds it."[46]

Originality and the Cult of Genius

Craftsmen take pride in their ability to make the same thing many times (or something very close), which shows a command of technique and materials. They tend to see originality as a euphemism for lack of control or technique. A modern-day potter or instrument maker, for instance, tends to discount the skill of colleagues who can only make one-off pieces, which he regards as products of chance. The artiste, however, sees things differently. For him, the discovery of a new and original object (by preference non-functional) is a sign of *genius*.

Genius, according to Carl Dahlhaus, consists of "radical originality," which means two things: first, that the composer is using his piece to express himself (composing "from within," in the sense of a personal autobiography, with a focus on the artist's passions and inner struggles), and second, that "if a composer wishes his music to be heard in those circles whose opinion matters he has to say something new"[47] (a view no doubt inspired by the nineteenth-century belief in progress).

In his *Critique of Judgement*, Kant spoke of genius as "breaking the mold," producing new rules of form in art and of rising above antique forms.

Why, one wonders, is genius so often associated with Romantic music but seems beside the mark when applied to Machaut or Dowland?[48]

Musicians in the Rhetorical era composed and performed using rules of thumb and craftsmanlike formulas. Where a Romantic composer would show their genius by transcending or reinterpreting mere rules, a Baroque musician would prove their ingenuity not by breaking but by fulfilling the rules.[49] Composition "was an art in the 18th-century sense of the word— a skill in the performance of actions using accepted, proven techniques and precepts."[50] Sounds like a craftsman talking. As Roger North put it, "In musick nothing is left to accident; all must be done either with designe or by inveterate habit, in a course duely establisht; and the cheif industry lyes in procuring variety."[51] To a Romantic, this would not have done at all.

Attribution and Designer Labels

The true Canonic musical experience requires knowing who wrote the piece one is hearing, knowing when they lived, and knowing where they fit in the hierarchy of the Pantheon. For his dissertation, John Spitzer traced the histories of works attributed to great composers that were later proved spurious; they disappeared from the repertoire when they lost their pedigrees. Spitzer observed how, when in 1964 they were re-ascribed to Hofstetter, Haydn's Opus 3 string quartets began to disappear from the repertoire.[52] The same phenomenon occurs in painting and literature.

The label, it seems, is more important than the product. This is disgraceful, but I have to say that for myself, and I believe most musicians, a true appreciation of a piece is not possible until its composer is known. Spitzer writes of how this influences our perception of the work's identity and qualities. As he says, "changing the name amounts to altering the work itself."[53] Think of the discomfort we experience in turning on the radio in the middle of a piece and impatiently waiting for the end, to identify the composer and performers! Spitzer talks about being in this situation and realizing the piece is, say, Beethoven's Fourth:

> When the listener suddenly exclaims to himself "Beethoven," he does more than just hang a label on the music. With one word he calls up an entire context of Beethoven's biography, Beethoven's other works, Beethoven's patrons, early 19th-century Vienna, what critics have said about Beethoven, and so on. The listener hears the remainder of the Fourth Symphony in a different frame of mind, because knowing its authorship has greatly enriched the context in which the work is perceived and appreciated.

As Spitzer observes, knowing its authorship satisfies our need to put art into its historical context (since it is no longer in one). It also contributes to our sense of a piece's identity, since each performance is a little different (and in some cases so different as to render the music unrecognizable).

Musicology was invented in the Romantic period, and its first activity was the production of countless biographies and collected works of artist-composers. This was natural, since the dominant paradigm in Romantic music was the hero/composer and the "masterpiece." But it gave the Romantics an unholy obsession with attributing works, and who influenced whom.

One obvious result of this fixation on who wrote the music and its catalogue number is our modern need for documentation at concerts. "The audience was provided with printed or typed programmes in which the names and composers of the works to be performed were always included, sometimes supplemented by written 'programme notes' summarising the main features of each work which could be followed by the listeners during the performance."[54] Written programs are even supplied by kids doing plays for their parents, and in fact serve as an important attribute of formal performance. Since music at concerts is normally from the past, programs serve the function of announcing their historical credentials, especially for those who might not recognize an otherwise unintelligible sound mass as a rendition of Purcell or Beethoven. Giving it a label endows it with some kind of intention, and at the same time encourages a tolerant attitude.

As might be expected, in the days before genius-personality became a dominant issue, attribution was of less concern. Spitzer observes that for roughly the first four centuries that music was notated in Europe, it wasn't ascribed to "composers" at all. And even after that, attributions of songs often seem not to have been for the music but for the texts.[55] Manuscripts start regularly giving composers' names toward the end of the fourteenth century, but attributions were sporadic as late as the sixteenth century.

Even today, attribution is not an important issue except in Canonic music. The status of a piece of music as high art is probably directly related to the accuracy of its attribution. One can observe a spectrum from the extreme precision of a concert program with register and opus numbers and composers' full names and dates, to the casual (and usually unread) credits at the end of movies, to the chance mention of composers of popular songs, to the absolute anonymity of TV jingles. By contrast, the names of the most trivial opera arias are scrupulously identified (even to their act), Mozart's pieces are almost never mentioned without their Köchel catalogue numbers, concerts are unthinkable these days without a program, and even the names of encores are announced by the players. Identity and attribution are the life-blood of the Pantheon mentality.

The snobbism implied by the Haydn/Hofstetter example above is confirmed by Spitzer's observation that people also rate pieces lower if they are unascribed (that is, anonymous). His evidence indicates that "people's intolerance for anonymous art seems to be a comparatively recent phenomenon"[56] unshared by musicians and audiences during the Renaissance.

> In the Renaissance an attribution seems to have been a contingent feature of a painting or a musical work: people could take it or leave it, they could transmit it or neglect it. Today attribution seems to be essential. If an art work is not attributed, a whole scholarly industry tries to give it an author. Rational and scientific methods have been developed for attributing anonymous music, literature and painting and for testing and verifying attributions already made.[57]

The identity of the artist-composers is important to Canonists because works by hero/genius composers are by definition imbued with "greatness" (regardless of their perceived musical qualities, or lack of them). And, like the star phenomenon in modern culture, a work takes on interest when it is associated with a big name, and becomes worthy of reconsideration, no matter how mediocre it may seem at first glance.

> The discovery that a work of art is spurious points up in a concrete way just how precarious a construction the author really is. . . . If people could continue to listen to the Opus 3 quartets [of Haydn]—now as Hofstetter—and to derive just as much satisfaction from them as when they were Haydn, this

might suggest that there was never anything so special about Haydn's authorship in the first place.[58]

This in turn threatens the whole Canonic house of cards, as maybe there never was anything so special about hero/god composers except their music itself. "The very possibility of any intelligent standards of appreciation and taste seems to totter at the edge of the abyss."[59]

No wonder, then, that art forgers are sometimes thrown into the slammer: their work tends to confuse identities, which has the effect of watering down the greatness of individual artists and artistic works, requiring them to be judged on their merits alone. In the end, art forgery is an issue of attribution: whose name goes on the work. One would think, therefore, that it would be a minor matter. But the Romantic cult of personality is very deep-seated in our culture. Kurz, writing in 1948, goes as far as to call all art forgeries "potentially dangerous. . . . A great artist, whether a Shakespeare, Michelangelo, or Corot, is entitled to have his *oeuvre* purged of unwelcome additions."[60] "Dangerous" seems an odd word to use in this context. Kurz uses three of the symbolic attributes of Canonism here: the "great artist," the "*oeuvre*" or "works," and the purity of Art.

We could in fact take this a step further and suggest that the idea of art forgeries can only exist in a climate of "great works," a Canonized, Classical art. The idea of fakes is non-existent in Chinese painting, for instance, where copying early masters of past centuries is a common practice.

In an intriguing fictional story written in 1939, "Pierre Menard, author of Don Quixote," Jorge Luis Borges tells of a most refined French writer who was inspired to attempt to write several chapters of *Don Quixote*. (Not "another *Don Quixote*—which would be easy—but *the Don Quixote*. . . . he did not propose to copy it. His admirable ambition was to produce pages which would coincide—word for word and line for line—with those of Miguel de Cervantes.") In the same vein, Le Cerf de la Viéville writes of the musicians of his own day (a generation after Lully's death) writing pieces that resembled Lully's "without their having thought of him. Just so, it happens every day in poetry that one has the same ideas and says the same things as an author one has not intended to imitate. For instance, M. le Marquis de Racan wrote four lines similar word for word to a quatrain from the *Tablettes* of Mathieu which he had never read."[61]

Borges has his character Menard saying, "To compose *Don Quixote* at the beginning of the 17th century was a reasonable, necessary and perhaps inevitable undertaking; at the beginning of the 20th century it is almost impossible. It is not in vain that three hundred years have passed, charged with the most complex happenings—among them, to mention only one, that same *Don Quixote*." "The text of Cervantes and that of Menard are verbally identical," says the narrator, "but the second is almost infinitely richer." He cites passages from both authors, quite indistinguish-able, and marvels at how unlikely Menard's text is, considering when it was written. He also comments that "the archaic style of Menard—in the last analysis, a foreigner—suffers from a certain affectation. Not so that of his precursor, who handles easily the ordinary Spanish of his time." Borges seems to have been playing with the idea of how ascription alters the identity of a work (suggesting, for instance, that *The Lord of the Rings* would be seen very differently if ascribed to James Joyce). But it provokes speculation. What can we discover now in the performing protocols of earlier times that were invisible to the people of those times? And on the reverse side, what can we discover about ourselves in those Rhetorical pieces by totally identifying with the style of the period (which was one of Menard's inspirations)?

Repeatability and Ritualized Performance

If a work could enter the Pantheon and acquire Canonic status, it would be heard more than once. This is *repeatability,* which became common in the nineteenth century and is habitual and standard today. One of Dahlhaus's most appealing ideas is that with repeatability, works could be incomprehensible, or only partly intelligible, on first hearing.[62] This is probably what Liszt was thinking when he said his ambition was "to fling a spear into the limitless distances of the future."[63] Of course, one has also to be interested in listening more than once. "One can't judge Wagner's opera *Lohengrin* after a first hearing," Rossini is said to have commented, "and I certainly don't intend hearing it a second time."

If pieces were destined to stand for eternity, there was a built-in brake on changing style. If style moved too far away from Beethoven, for in-stance, there was a chance that his music would begin to sound out of date and irrelevant. This contrasts with the sense of constant change right through the eighteenth century. The comment of one good composer to another in 1778 about a third composer he had heard the night before was that his music "ein wenig in den ältern Styl fällt"[64] (smacks a little of the older style). This is Leopold Mozart in a letter to his son on the music of Carlo Besozzi, who was nineteen years Mozart's junior.

As Derek Bailey observes, "nothing reflects change more speedily than popular music,"[65] and that is of course because it involves so much improvisation; it isn't slowed down by being written and fixed. That would explain why musical style (and indeed, performing style and in-strument-making style as well) was changing so quickly in the Baroque period. This was not only because it was only partly written down but be-cause, like popular music, it was not intended to last—to become timeless and Classical. Musicking in the seventeenth and eighteenth centuries—whether playing, making instruments, or composing—rarely survived the generation in which it was first developed. If a performer, composer, or

maker ever got a reputation for being old-fashioned or *passé,* it was disastrous for their career. Familiarity was a negative quality; perhaps earlier musicians wished to avoid the ultimate effect of it, which is to turn
brilliance into empty ceremony:

> Familiarity softens discomfort: how many times can *The Rite of Spring*
> shock? Time and history accommodate discomfort: the Wagnerian revolution
> may have consigned Rossini's musical practices to history, but now Wagner
> sits beside Rossini in history and in the repertory. Classical status itself trans-
> forms discomfort: Monteverdi's or Schönberg's boldest progressions have be-
> come like inscriptions on a monument, stirring but no longer inflammatory.[66]

I mentioned before the analogy to film today. Imagine if films were
Canonized in the same way nineteenth-century music is! That audiences
would only watch the same two hundred films over and over again, ignoring the existence of others, and watch them in a kind of religious awe.
Not only that, but a discipline known as "cinematology" would grow up
that used sophisticated vocabulary to argue essentially for the mainte-
nance of this film Canon.

The fact that seventeenth- and eighteenth-century music was not
meant to be heard repeatedly tended to make it easy to understand and
conventional in form. Because there were rarely second chances to hear
new pieces, a piece that could not be directly grasped (by an intelligent
and educated ear) risked failure. This idea leads to two corollaries:

- It reflects rather poorly on our level of musical sophistication that
  we are willing to listen to these non-Canonic pieces over and over
  again, and
- It would not have been prudent for a composer to present too
  many experiments. In the Baroque period, as Laurence Dreyfus
  says, "the very idea of an idiosyncratic or adversarial music is unthinkable."[67]

One problem with repeatability is that surprise disappears. "A deceptive cadence that one already knows no longer deceives. . . . The essential difference between the listening habits of earlier times and those
of today lies in the fact that we desire to listen often to a work that we
love, whereas people of earlier times did not."[68]

Christopher Small points out that Beethoven's symphonies are a good
example of music that we have heard repeated so often that they provide
comfort, while for Beethoven's contemporaries they struck "like a fist in
the face."[69] Early audiences did not have the benefit of hindsight, as we do.
Hindsight in history can seriously distort the past. "To the men of 1807,"
for instance, "the year 1808 was a mystery and an unexplored tract; . . .
to study the year 1807 remembering all the time what happened in 1808
. . . is to miss the adventure and the great uncertainties and the element
of gamble in their lives; where we cannot help seeing the certainty of a desired issue, the men of the time were all suspense."[70]

I think the most serious effect of repeatability is that, knowing we can hear a piece again, we do not feel the imperative to listen carefully. It can also turn listening to a piece we know well, like a Beethoven symphony, into an empty routine. Instead of hearing the composition itself, one's attention is focused on how performances of the piece differ. "There was vastly more interest in the work itself [in the eighteenth century] than in its rendition; critics reserved most of their comments for the piece, devoting only casual attention to its performance—whereas today usually only the details of performance are discussed and compared."[71] We have even developed, then, a Canonic way of performing each of these Canonic pieces. Back in the 1940s and 1950s, comparing different Toscanini recordings of the same Beethoven symphony was already a cult ritual.[72] Music of this type thus risks becoming liturgy, unthinking and unprovocative; liturgy, in other words, ritual. Ritual actions are those that, because they are often repeated, lose the meaning they once possessed, and become automatic. Nicholas Cook, in pointing out that CD sales are often motivated by individual performers who are marketed as much as the pieces they play, suggests that "perhaps the Canon might be defined as a set of works so familiar that they function more as medium than message."[73]

Several writers have suggested that there are reasons to think of the ritual intoning of a symphony concert as a bedtime story for adults.[74] Among the similarities is that the stories are so familiar that they have lost any power they might once have had to disturb. Burnham writes how he loves repeated hearings of Beethoven: "it always brings us to the same place, always invokes the same uncanny presence. . . . we like being there."[75] Performing Canonic works is reassuring, it gives comfort. "Each work has been validated over and over again by the admiration of generations and is being performed in these sumptuous surroundings [i.e., a concert hall] backed by the full weight of social approval of the whole symphony concert ceremony."

Another similarity is the obsession with letter-perfect repetition. Motivated "by the same desire for reassurance that makes the five-year-old correct his father's momentary stumble in the reading of a familiar bedtime story," our literacy extends to insisting not only on note-perfect accuracy; we demand that every detail be rendered exactly as in the composer's manuscript, every grace and slur. Sometimes we go back even further, to the composer's sketches.[76]

This note-perfect accuracy extends at moments of weakness even to so-called "historical" performances, so that no graces can be either added or taken away.[77]

Repeatability is implicit in literate music; writing down a piece is for the purpose of repeating it. But the number of repetitions is important. When a listener understands a sufficient amount, their experience of listening mutates into ritual. As North says, "It is remarkable that melody is never so good the first, as at the second time of hearing, and few [melodies] will hold much longer."[78]

5

The Transparent Performer

"Executio Anima Compositionis"
(Performance is the vital principle in composing)

(Motto in the scroll of G. F. Schmidt's engraving
that closes Quantz's book)

*It is in fact wickedly presumptuous for a player to alter a work of
art according to his mood, since in doing that he suggests that he
understands the work better than the composer who invented it.*

(A. L. Crelle, *Einiges über musicalischen Ausdruck und Vortrag*, 1823)

*[The performer should play] so that one believes that the music
was composed by the person who is playing it.*

(Wolfgang Mozart, in a letter of 1778)

Composer-Intention ("Fidelity to the Composer")

Mark Twain is said to have quipped, "Wagner's music is better than it
sounds." This sense of obligation is worrying. Who are we trying to
please nowadays with our Canon? Are we really required to admire Wagner's music, whether we like it or not? If so, who's doing the requiring?
Wagner himself hasn't been around for some time.

I find it difficult to imagine that whatever we do to their music, the
original composers will be affected. Let's admit it, what we're really doing
is plundering and pillaging the past, looking for what profit we can extract. Original repertoire is all in the public domain now. "These [old
composers] are dead. They no longer exist. They need nothing from us.
Their surviving remains—those documents and artefacts that have not
been destroyed over time—are all that there is. Heartless as it may sound,
those remains are ours now and for us to use as we think best."[1] I suggest
that far from being "faithful" to a composer's intentions, we are in fact

merely stealing ideas from them, and doing it selectively. But obviously, to get the most value out of our theft, it is in our own best interest to be conscious of the composer's wishes. This will give the music the best chance of being understandable. Our own wishes, in this case, coincide with the composers'. As Godlovitch put it, "Nor is attending to scoring, etc., merely to honour the last will and testament of the composer. It is a respect for craftsmanship and not for the wishes of the dead."[2]

Charles Rosen raises a related point. He complains that HIP

> does not ask what the composer wanted, but only what he got. Intentions are irrelevant. . . . We no longer try to infer what Bach would have liked; instead, we ascertain how he was played during his lifetime, in what style, with which instruments, and how many of them there were in his orchestra. This substitutes genuine research for sympathy, and it makes a study of the conditions of old performance more urgent than a study of the text.[3]

Rosen seems to think Bach didn't get what he wanted. Bruno Walter had thought that, as well. In Rosen's case, it may be because he is a pianist, and he thinks that what Bach really wanted was the piano—the modern one, like his. The presence of Absolute Music is palpable in these words as well: that Bach thought in "pure music" rather than the music produced by the real world he lived in. Gould thought this way too. Maybe everybody used to think Bach was an unhappy genius born ahead of his time.

But it seems more plausible to me that composers like Bach didn't have time for speculative inspirations and Romantic fantasies; they had to write music that worked immediately. Thinking like them means thinking of the conditions of the time, not of some imaginary future where one's music would be transcribed onto Romantic grand piano or performed by a symphony orchestra in some nineteenth-century style. Rosen can do that if he wants, but he can't convince me that Bach wanted to do it. What Bach wanted was inextricably bound up with what he expected to get. And so we come to composer-intention.

Composer-intention, or author-intention, is a concept shared with other arts, where it is often called the "intentional imperative."[4] For many people, composer-intention is identical to authenticity. But in some ways, it is difficult to take musicians seriously on this issue when so many of them ignore the intentions of composers. They perform certain pieces into the ground, like the Brandenburg concertos or the Four Seasons— much more frequently than they were ever performed, or intended to be, effectively Canonizing them. And the fact that I see many concerts in which Period performers make little attempt to reach out to move their audiences in the Rhetorical sense, or to bring to life some of the stylistic attributes that are inherent in the written parts, makes me wonder how seriously they consider the intentions of any Baroque composer. Observing one of these commercially successful orchestras do a series of Christmas *Messiah*s with half of the musicians Modern-style pickups, when the original objectives of the music are abused in such fundamental ways, it is difficult to take seriously any talk about "fidelity to the composer."

What Is a Piece of Music?

Talking of modifying a piece brings up the perilous (and modern) question of what a piece is. A number of recent writers have been trying to find a satisfactory definition of a musical "work." Even philosophers are involved, using the subject as an example of metaphysics.[5] Although I'm incapable of understanding it all, I've read enough to see that much of this literature starts with premises that are irrelevant or out of date; the discourse is heavily Romanticist and the orientation is that of the theorist and the composer. I have little interest in attempts to define music that separate composition and performance or ignore the Rhetorical approach. The published discussion recalls many acoustical studies that treat music in terms that omit or ignore elements that are important to musicians.

A score might also be seen as a gene map of a series of potential performances, each differing by individual traits. A gene map is not in itself any single living creature; it is merely an abstraction of what is common between groups of living things. In the same way, a piece of music can be defined as the musical content that is shared in all its performances. It's when you hear a piece performed by someone else that you begin to understand the real piece, that is, what the performances have, and don't have, in common. The real piece, the irreducible, unchangeable heart of a piece, is the aspect that doesn't change from performance to performance. That doesn't mean you have to know every performance in order to have a powerful impression of what a piece is. One good one is all you need. But what you are hearing is one particular "take" on the piece.

Some parts of a piece are automatically altered every time it is played. Two consecutive performances of a piece by the same player that use the same instruments and notes (i.e., sequence of pitches and rhythms) "vary in virtually every other respect."[6] So the only parts we could change that would affect its identity would be the instrumentation and the tunes. If we change phrasing, for instance, no one considers it changing the piece.

A sense of what constitutes the essential qualities of a piece and what can be changed without affecting its identity is constantly shifting, however. Presently, we don't countenance changing the pitches in the score, but, as José A. Bowen wonders, what about "tempo, dynamics, timbre, instrumentation, orchestration, phrasing, or portamento? . . . Is it possible . . . that a future generation will find Haitink and Harnoncourt as corrupt as Toscanini found Nikisch, and we now find Toscanini?"[7]

Bowen talks of Toscanini's and Furtwängler's alterations of Beethoven symphonies.[8] In his day Furtwängler, like Wagner before him, was regarded a great defender of the composer's intention. Yet his free interpretations of Beethoven's "inviolable" texts contained countless unnotated nuances, varying tempos, and frequent changes of notes.

E. T. A. Hoffmann, as spokesman for the new artistic aims at the beginning of the nineteenth century, wrote of the hero/genius composer sealing their work, presumably hermetically, so messing with it might cancel its "magic." But as we have seen, notation is always ambiguous to some degree, and this is especially true of music from before the Romantic Revolution.

For those familiar with a given piece, it can be called to mind by quotation in another piece, sometimes with as little as two notes. If reminding listeners of a work with only the vaguest and most fleeting of means is enough to summon its presence, altering parts of it should not be a threat to its identity.

When musicians perform a well-known tune in jazz, R&B, Funk, Soul, Pop, and so on, they start varying it even before the first version is completed. Two options that are common in Classical music are unacceptable here:

- playing a melody completely straight,
- or exactly imitating somebody else's riffs.

In other words, what amounts to passaggi—improvising—is not only encouraged, it's obligatory. Here's an example, Stevie Wonder and Take 6 doing a well-known piece of Handel.

AUDIO SAMPLE: 38. Stevie Wonder and Take 6, 1992. "O thou that tellest good tidings to Zion," *Handel's Messiah: A Soulful Celebration*

And it seems it was very much the same with music until the end of the eighteenth century. Bacilly considered the simple, ungraced melody as a framework, having no beauty of its own, merely the potential for beauty through well-judged embellishments applied by the performer.[9]

As Bowen observes of jazz, Italian opera, and eighteenth-century Adagios, "We need to hear enough pitches to be convinced of the identity of the work, but if we hear *only* the traditional pitches, the performance will be labeled 'derivative.'"[10] It's interesting that this word isn't used for the rest of the Classical literature, where "derivative" is respected as "*Werktreue.*"

Werktreue *(Work-Fidelity): The Musical Analogue of Religious Fundamentalism*

The respect for the composer as a great artist extends to their work, and is known in the trade as *Werktreue* (work-fidelity). And around *Werktreue* a

number of familiar dogmas about Classical music orbit, such as untouchability, the Urtext Imperative ("If it's not commanded, it's forbidden"), and
text fetishism. Ideas like this lead to an image of the "transparent" musician as a selfless vehicle, a concept very far from the performer's role in the
Rhetorical period.

Nicholas Cook suggests that *Werktreue* resembles religious fundamentalism, which is, at base, a linguistic error. "Fundamentalism arises
from the false belief that language can circumscribe and contain reality,
from which it follows that what cannot be said does not exist."[11] In the
same way, *Werktreue* arises from the belief that a musical text can circumscribe and contain a performance—all of it. Since that is impractical,
just as fundamentalism usually has the effect of limiting actions and
choices in a society, *Werktreue* acts as a constraint on musical performers,
leading them to try to play only the notated parameters and suppress the
others.

Derek Bailey writes from the perspective of a modern improviser:

> Music for the instrumentalist is a set of written symbols which he inter-
> prets as best he can. They, the symbols, are the music, and the man who
> wrote them, the composer, is the music-maker. The instrument is the medium
> through which the composer finally transmits his ideas. The instrumentalist
> is not required to make music. He can assist with his 'interpretation' perhaps,
> but, judging from most reported remarks on the subject, composers prefer
> the instrumentalist to limit his contribution to providing the instrument,
> keeping it in tune and being able to use it to carry out, as accurately as pos-
> sible, any instructions which might be given to him. The improvisor's view of
> the instrument is totally different.[12]

Linguists say that languages change more slowly when the people who
speak them become generally literate. Spelling, for instance, becomes stan-
dardized. Literacy has become a factor in music in the last 500 years, and,
over the last two centuries the fixed Canonic repertoire has become so influential that the notated script is sometimes confused with the music it is
supposed to represent. As if these pages with black dots were something
more than mere reminders of a myriad of indications too subtle to notate.

The Urtext Imperative and Text Fetishism

Reflecting on the score lying open on its stand on the podium before a
symphony concert begins, Christopher Small observes, "The authority of
the conductor, supreme as it appears, is contingent on his obeying, like
everyone else on the platform, the coded instructions that the score contains."[13] Failure to execute a Romantic piece just as it is written is seen
by some people nowadays as a violation, as mutilation or disfigurement
of the work.[14] Manipulating or juxtaposing pieces is not acceptable in
anything but joke performances like the *Hoffnung Festival*. To take
Harnoncourt's example, if someone tried to mount a production of Wag-

ner's *Meistersinger* in all sincerity with an orchestra of pianos, harps, guitars, saxophones, and vibraphone, it would probably be seen as an attack on a work of art, an unjustifiable misrepresentation of the artist-composer's idea.

Two generations ago, Landowska had also noted the same numbing tendency:

> The fear of adding a note which cries out to be inserted . . . is a misconception of the spirit of the music of the past. This sobriety has for its aim the objective presentation of the text without any personal involvement. . . . the average person is suspicious when a phrase of Bach is played freely. For this reason style is rectitude. He considers any deviation from the printed text an act of dishonesty.[15]

And Landowska was lined up against Romantic style, a much more spontaneous and expressive æsthetic than Modern style.

Old habits die hard, and texts still form the principal subject matter of the history and analysis of music. Arthur Mendel, for instance, in distinguishing the history of arts from other kinds of history, wrote that "what we have before us in an old manuscript or print—or in its modern reprint, for that matter—is much more than a trace of the doer [of a deed]: it is his deed itself."[16] This statement breathes the assumption that a musical deed—all of it—can be captured on paper. But an antique manuscript or print is hardly all of a composer's deed; at best it is only a record of certain aspects of it. Not only is music invariably under-notated, but those signs—the ones that are there—can mean many different things.

This is one of countless examples of what Taruskin calls "text-fetishism, the exaltation of scores over those who read or write them."[17] Text fetishism is strong in every branch of concert music—literate music—but seems stronger in Modern style, maybe because there is less skepticism regarding editorial intervention than in HIP. Henry Kingsbury, in his ethnomusicological study of a conservatory, describes a violin master class where the teaching, as mainstream as it is possible to be, emphasized that

> the score was of paramount importance . . . [but its] authority is frequently impeached with reference to another edition of the composition, a version of the score that is held to be more authentic. . . . Goldmann's invoking of the score as the paramount authority can itself be seen as part of a particular aural tradition; rigorous adherence to the score is unquestionably a hallmark of the Schnabel legacy that Goldmann inherits.[18]

This, at least, is the tradition. In actual fact, as Kingsbury observes, the score is used as a symbolic standard, but the final authority (apparently never openly acknowledged) rests with the teacher, who bends the text as necessary to get out of it what they want to play and hear. Thank goodness.

At times the curious fixation on the written score that seems to afflict certain musicians slips into pedantry. Gunther Schuller's book on conducting (1997), which surveys many recordings, likewise ignores the variety of Period styles they document, since for Schuller "authenticity and the composer's intention reside solely in—and are recoverable solely from—the printed score."[19] Schuller discredits any conductor's interpretation that does not correspond to the score (in this case Brahms's First Symphony). Despite considerable supplementary information on Brahms's intentions, he accuses these conductors of "arrogant willfulness." Frisch comments that

> it is not these conductors, but Schuller himself, who shows "arrogant willfulness" in failing to recognize the validity—the real "authenticity"—of the practices represented in these recordings. Schuller reductively equates the score with the composer's intention, and does not acknowledge that the score is only a notational intermediary, and a wonderfully imperfect one at that, between the composer and his realization of his music in performance.[20]

Looked at with a little perspective, this obsession with correct texts seems directly connected to the Romantic cult of genius-personality that confers absolute authority on the artist-composer's text as a document and requires, as Christopher Small writes, an "enormous effort to be expended in ascertaining exactly what the man who set it down really wrote, or intended to write, since a corrupt text will surely corrupt the ritual of performance."[21] Small is irresistibly reminded of koranic, talmudic, and biblical scholars "with their obsession for documentation, their reverence for any written text and their often centuries-long arguments over the meaning of a single phrase."[22] Taruskin comments:

> Central to this concept is an idealized notion of what a musical work is: something wholly realized by its creator, fixed in writing, and thus capable of being preserved. Fidelity is that which enables preservation: scrupulous execution according to the creator's intentions, divined either directly from explicit notation or indirectly through study of contemporary conventions and circumstances. At the center, then, stands the text, and the werktreu performer (and scholar, and editor, and critic) is there to serve it.[23]

It must have been a score-oriented mind that produced 78 rpm records in which the da capo section was not included and the listener was instructed to play the first side again.[24] This satisfied the need for a da capo, technically, but cancelled out the illusion of hearing a musical performance. The score-oriented mind is also the reason recordings with splices often sound so strange to the performers who have made them. The musician is actually playing several different "pieces," spliced together in arbitrary ways. What all these varied takes have in common is that they follow the same text. If the score, the text, is seen as paramount, rather than the performance of the music the score tries to encompass, then edited recordings are speciously perceived as musically cohesive.

Kingsbury noted the comments of the teacher in a master class. In disagreement with the written indications in a passage in the Brahms violin sonata, he commented, "I know I'm wrong, but I just cannot feel it that way." Kingsbury observed, "His 'I know I'm wrong' was an unambiguous gesture of deference to the supposedly ultimate authority of the score. At the same time, he was demonstrating that when the values of performance are perceived as conflicting with those of fidelity to the score, then good performance takes primacy over adherence to the score."[25]

Untouchability

The concept called by Goehr "untouchability," an obligation to transmit—literally—the intentions of a composer without changing even the smallest detail, is another curious expression of the Canonic mind. What if you would like the phrase to "go up" the second time, for instance? There is no allowance for that option; even as a performer you are obliged to play what is written.

Untouchability seems not to have been a strong imperative in Baroque times. There are striking examples of seventeenth- and eighteenth-century musicians changing a piece in the presence of its composer and obviously pleasing him or her. Bénigne de Bacilly, for example, described in 1679 how his mentor, Pierre de Niert, sang some of Luigi Rossi's songs to him. Niert brought the Italian composer to tears of joy: "Especially Signor Luiggi had to admire him, weeping for joy to hear [Niert] execute his airs. Did I say "execute"? He ornamented them and even changed notes here and there to better frame the Italian words."[26] Boorman lists some other examples of serious reworkings of pieces:

> Later composers or scribes could add voices to, or recompose sections of, early Renaissance chansons; composers and performers could substitute arias and larger sections in operas; performers could rearrange the order of movements or embellish to the point where the original was completely lost to view. Yet the same composer's name was retained throughout the process. Soriano could add a second four-voiced choir to a mass by Palestrina, while the original composer's name was retained; and Chopin's First Piano Concerto could be radically rewritten by Tausig, among others, and still be ascribed to Chopin.[27]

As late as the 1780s (when Mozart was in his twenties), "touchability" was still in vogue. A source written then declares that "either an air, or recitative, sung exactly as it is commonly noted, would be a very inexpressive, nay, a very uncouth performance."[28]

The *"Transparent" Performer and "Perfect Compliance"*

"With the establishment [in 1843] of Mendelssohn's conservatory in Leipzig," Bowen believes, "the doctrine of the transparent performer spread throughout Europe."[29] Mendelssohn was known for "his absolute and unqualified devotion to the master whose work he was executing," adding "nothing of himself."[30] Berlioz, too, thought of performers as transparent intermediaries of fixed musical works. For him, expression did not involve creating, but "'reproducing' the composer's feelings or intentions. This attitude was accompanied by an extreme regard for the score, which was an especially radical proposition for 19th-century Paris."[31]

The latest edition of the *New Grove* enunciates that same *Werktreue* principle: "There is no single 'correct' interpretation," it says, "but there may be incorrect ones—those that 'manifestly defy the composer's instructions'"!

Taruskin draws attention to the appalling definition of "performing practice" in the same encyclopedia (the latest version, 2002, has not changed).[32] It is presented with the modern assumption of a clear separation between composer and performer; even more, an opposition, casting the composer as "permitting" certain liberties to the "transparent performer." It begins with an observation that could have come from Stravinsky himself: "Musical notation can be understood as a set of instructions indicating to the performer how the composer wished the music to sound." This is like a cake recipe (actually, more like a pre-made cake mix). Relations of this kind between the performing musician and composer no doubt existed in some cases before the nineteenth century, but in general the connection must have been more supple and more empathetic; and of course often the performer was playing their own music, or that of a colleague they worked with regularly.

This is the dominant attitude today, a direct continuation of the Romantic mentality. It seems to be sustained by everyone concerned. But no one can convincingly explain why we should show such exaggerated respect for dead musicians.

Live composers certainly weren't so privileged in the eighteenth century, when "singers simply assumed they could dictate to the composer how they wanted their arias to be composed! If the composer did not comply with the wishes of his singers, he was criticized, indeed, he would have been thought unsuitable as a composer." This is Harnoncourt, speaking about Mozart (in this case, Mozart the composer).[33] As late as the 1830s, Berlioz complained of "all those abuses which have made of melody, harmony, tempo, rhythm, . . . poetry, the poet, and the composer the abject slaves and playthings of the singer."[34]

Clive Brown describes the growing separation between musicians and composers during the nineteenth century, the new hero/genius composer, the tendency to look on manuscripts as scripture to be read hyperliterally, and how composers played into this game by writing with greater precision and more specific demands or instructions.

The change was gradual. Schulz, in 1771, still speaks in generalities, describing a "cake" rather than prescribing how to cook (or "execute") one. But he also turns Mozart's inspiring advice on its head. Mozart had said that the performer should play "so that one believes that the music was composed by the person who is playing it."[35] Performers like this idea. But Schulz goes much further, already bestowing dominance on the composer and thereby driving a wedge between the two roles of performing and composing. He would like to see the performer play "as if from the soul of the composer."[36] This is the direction of future thinking in the nineteenth century.

The transparent performer was described with approval by E. T. A. Hoffmann in 1810:

> The true artist lives only in that work which he has comprehended and now performs as the master intended it to be performed. He is above putting his own personality forward in any way, and all his endeavours are directed towards a single end, to call to life all the enchanting pictures and shapes the composer has sealed into his work with magic power.[37]

Here, expressed in one short paragraph, are the new concepts of text fetishism, "perfect compliance," the transparent performer, and the division of roles between composer and performer.

The transparent performer appears in the changed meaning of *Vortrag* between the mid-eighteenth century and the later nineteenth. As I will discuss later, *Vortrag* for Quantz and Emanuel Bach meant "eloquence" or good "delivery"; being effective, in other words, at touching an audience and moving their hearts. By 1882, however, *Vortrag* in Hermann Mendel's *Lexikon* was a very different thing (as it is today). Mendel reckoned *Vortrag* required two things of a performer:

- a complete understanding of the notational signs employed by the creative artist.

This latter is the composer; the wording makes clear that the performer is not considered a creative artist.

- the technical skill to "execute" what they indicate.[38]

The poor "uncreative" performer's job was to practice scales and be an expert at deciphering bad handwriting.

The idea of the transparent performer was developed still further by the Modernists. The well-known organist and composer Marcel Dupré (active from 1898 to the 1950s and renowned for his improvisations) is quoted as saying, "The interpreter must never allow his own personality to appear. As soon as it penetrates, the work has been betrayed. By concealing himself sincerely before the character of the work in order to illuminate it, even more so before the personality of the composer, he serves the latter and confirms the authority of the work."[39] Dupré's attitude is the norm in Modern style.

A virulent strain of transparency can be seen in a recent talk by Jay Nordlinger, a music critic, who said that he considered it part of his job "to hold musicians to account. If the critic has any role at all, it is that of defender of music." What he means by "critic" and "music" is clarified in the following: "Here is something that drives me a bit crazy: when a performer says, 'Oh, I'm doing this in order to be creative. This allows me to express myself.' We all know singers, violinists, and others who talk this way." (To be honest, I've never heard a performer talk this way. But that's beside the point.)

> I always want to pipe up, Oh yeah? You want to be creative? You want to express yourself? Fine: Get yourself some manuscript paper and compose something. Then you'll really be expressing yourself. But you aren't the creator here, you're the servant of the creator, the composer of the music. Mr. Handel has expressed himself already, or Mr. Schumann, or Mr. Prokofiev, or whoever. Your job is to bring it out, to be faithful to him.[40]

Notice the subliminal Romantic messages. Although it's not likely Handel would have put it quite this way, for Nordlinger composing means "being creative" and "expressing yourself"; Schumann might have agreed. Also, Nordlinger associates composing with manuscript paper; improvising is not part of his picture. Finally, the vehemence and length of the "servant of the creator" argument suggest that he feels this point is not obvious or shared by everyone.

The Romantic Invention of the Interpretive Conductor

> *When you see a guy in a white tie and tails actually conducting an aria, you wonder: what is this?*

> (Susie Napper, nonstrait HIP cellist)

In Rhetorical times, being dead was a definite disadvantage to a composer. After 1800, however, it was almost required in order to achieve greatness. The new Canon included more and more music by dead composers, and as a consequence the "conductor" appeared. Conductors acted as the dead composer's surrogate.

Through most of the nineteenth century the conductor limited their word to generally "implicit" rather than "explicit" tasks; they were not, in other words, playing the group as if it was their instrument (like most modern conductors), but rather coordinating and facilitating a performance still driven by style rather than individual and arbitrary "interpretation." In 1836 an anonymous writer (probably Schumann) was suggesting that a conductor should only beat time at the beginning of a movement or at tempo changes, and perhaps for very slow tempos. According to Brown, this may have been the way Mendelssohn conducted.[41]

"Maestro" is a word that has been used to designate conductors only since about the middle of the twentieth century. Christopher Small compares the "maestro" to a magus, or shaman, who summons the spirit of the dead composer.[42] He also likens them to the priest in the service of the composer/prophet, with the score as the sacred text. Conductors, like priests, claim the right to interpret the holy word and to impose their interpretations on others.[43] The conductor even does a shaman-dance up there on their little podium.

Davies wonders whether composer-intention is a kind of instruction that must be obeyed by the performer, or more of a recommendation that might be ignored.[44] We will never know, but I can tell you what would happen to a member of the orchestra, say, the first flute if he decided to ignore a composer's "intention" (as construed by the conductor, of course).

First of all, the dynamics of power in an orchestra are very simple. As Elias Canetti wrote, "There is no more obvious expression of power than the performance of a conductor."[45] The conductor can fire any musician pretty much at will.

Bowen is probably right that interpretive conductors appeared at about the same time as the transparent performer. The two phenomena actually need each other; a musician who has lost confidence in a stylistic interpretation needs someone to tell them what to do. And the "maestro's" authority is underscored by the idea that musicians should be transparent. Nicholas Avery calls this a "pernicious symbiosis."[46]

Conductors are commonly found in large groups of upwards of a hundred or more performers, where a central figure is often essential to coordinate the activity. They act as alpha-dominant figures, much like an alpha gorilla provides the center pillar around which the rest of the troop moves. The modern interpretive conductor has done quite well for himself. In the hall where they produce their work, the seats are all oriented concentrically toward them, so they are automatically the point of attention of the entire hall.[47] Considering that the "maestro" did not write the music, does not play it, makes in fact no sound, has only to tell the musicians what to do and take the credit for what they have done, one wonders how they have created this niche out of nothing but their personal charm and strong opinions about how the music should sound. In many respects, the conductor meets the biological definition of a parasite, certainly in their ability to take charge of most of the money otherwise destined for the musicians.

An example from the heyday of conductor intervention is the performance by Glenn Gould of the Brahms D-minor concerto, and the conservative, even Romantic position taken by the conductor Leonard Bernstein, who gave a famous speech of disclaimer before the performance. Bernstein called Gould's ideas "unorthodox," thereby immediately evoking the orthodox. The implication was that there was a standard, Classical way to perform standard, Classical pieces, and that conductors had a natural right, even a responsibility, to guard that tradition. Bernstein said further that he disagreed with Gould's changes in the dynamics as marked by Brahms, thus reinforcing the iron hoops of Romantic text fetishism and untouchability. Bernstein also asked "who's boss" in a concerto, the one who plays or the one who conducts, calling it an "age-old" question. (In fact, it would rarely have been an issue before 1800; why is it not surprising that Bernstein, personifying the mainstream in 1962, did not know that?) "Only once before in my life have I had to submit to the will of a soloist," says Bernstein, "and that was the last time I accompanied Mr Gould." It is to his credit that he went ahead, no doubt under threat of a pullout from Mr. Gould.

Now, a first flutist with the clout that Glenn Gould wielded does not exist. It is therefore clear to us all, and especially to the first flutist, what would happen to them if they decided to ignore a conductor's—whoops, I mean a composer's—intention.

In modern symphony orchestras the frustration of players is palpable, brought on by the performer's general loss of status and sense of responsibility, assumed—indeed, usurped—by the conductor. The composer Grétry (clearly a sensitive person despite writing truly banal music) had already noticed this in 1797: "Orchestra musicians become cold and indifferent when they do not follow the singer directly. The stick that directs them humiliates them."[48] I have observed this situation in Period groups as well.

The commercial/promotional side of baton-conducting in the modern sense began with Toscanini, whose cult fame was deliberately created by NBC just after World War II.[49]

Thus the modern idea of the interventionist-conductor who interprets the composer's "intentions" is yet another albatross we have inherited from Romanticism. You'd never guess it. I recently ran across one of Gardiner's recordings with his picture on the front: he is dressed in symbolic white tie and tails, and holds a baton of the type developed in the twentieth century. The picture is autographed. The striking thing is that amidst this panoply of Romantic attributes, the recording is of Monteverdi.

Horowitz describes the booklets that come with the complete Beethoven CDs conducted by Herbert von Karajan: "Karajan . . . is photographed alone. He is not conducting, but immersed in thought, eyes closed. He grips his baton at either end with his fists."[50] "The 19th century," Peter Gay writes in the first sentence of his book on Romanticism, "was intensely preoccupied with the self, to the point of neurosis." Karajan's "tousled silver hair and stern brow are brilliantly lit from the side. . . . Karajan's Rembrandt-like portrayal of the Romantic genius connotes Karajan focused on himself."[51]

George Houle commented:

> The rise of the virtuoso conductor in the 19th century brought with it a technique far removed from the apparently simple down-and-up gesture of the *tactus* beater [of Rhetorical times]. The modern conductor has a powerful and efficient technique, commanding meter, rhythm, dynamics, accentuation, tempo, and nuances of performance that were formerly controlled only by individual performers.[52]

This may be true, but any parameters that can be communicated by a stick were once the purview of the musicians making the music; each of them represents an appropriation on the conductor's part. Even strong personalities like Handel and Bach, who probably intimidated their players, would not have controlled meter, rhythm, dynamics, accentuation, tempo, and nuances of performance with a stick technique.

The Maestro-Rehearsal

What happens on stage as the conductor raises their baton for the first note of the concert? Everyone, including the conductor, is aware that the conductor is suddenly powerless; if things don't go as they demanded in rehearsal, they can't stop the concert and confront the individual musicians. Things could easily go very differently than the conductor had wanted.

That is, in fact, the challenge for a guest conductor: to get the orchestra to pay attention to their particular ideas, to get them to play differently from how they usually do. Their only chance is their rehearsals because both they and the orchestra know they could play the piece without a conductor.

With his Original Shakespeare Company (founded to experiment with historical performing practices), Patrick Tucker has discovered that good actors seem to function fine—better, in fact—without rehearsals and directors.

That is also the experience of many orchestral musicians, including myself. With Rhetorical repertoire, orchestras are often able to function better without conductors, since responsibility devolves on each member of the group to act together. Group attentiveness and competence is measurably lower when individuals are required to do what they would otherwise have done voluntarily.

Robert Levin commented on this question:

> As soon as you have a conductor you surrender the responsibility for the performance into the hands of that conductor. When you play without a conductor and you have a concertmaster and a fortepiano (or Steinway) player, and they're seated in an intimate circle around one another, they all listen because they have to make that ensemble by themselves. The result is a performance that is likely to be much tighter, much more active, and much more engaged than one with a conductor, because there's collective responsibility.[53]

No director = no rehearsal, as the Original Shakespeare Company has found. Thus logically, we can venture to propose that rehearsals exist, in fact, for the sake of the conductor. If we had no conductor, we would not need rehearsals. Tucker writes,

> Many people feel that because they themselves need rehearsals before they perform, this is what all performers need. But the modern world of film and television has so developed that rehearsal is very much the exception. Most

professional actors going to work in front of a camera bring to the screen
what they themselves have privately prepared, and their work is not guided,
but reacted to—just like the Elizabethans.[54]

The custom of rehearsing in the modern sense seems to have begun
towards the end of the eighteenth century, when composer-intention took
hold as an ideology. This kind of rehearsal, in which the main thing that
happens is that the conductor tells the musicians how to play his interpretation of the music, I'll call the *Maestro-Rehearsal*. One of the first
times the existence of rehearsals is mentioned is in Petri (1782); he writes
that a rehearsal is "where the music director makes the players aware of
'the hidden intentions of the composers.'"[55] It was probably at this point
in time that actors also found themselves being informed of Shakespeare's
intentions by the new stage directors.

If original rehearsals were basic, dealing with essentials (since there
was apparently no need of interpretive discussion), rehearsals would indeed have been minimal, as they are described (or rather *not* described)
in historical documentation. Because performers were good (often practicing the family trade, specializing early and wasting no time on modern
"nonsense" like learning to read books and write letters), this system
could work.

In music, bare-bones rehearsals are certainly needed for other reasons, like agreeing on tempos, how pieces begin and end, when to tune,
whether to repeat, and so on. It is for these practical reasons that musicians think rehearsals are necessary, although all of this could easily be
done by one of the leaders of larger ensembles. None of it needs an interpretive conductor.

Thus the work of Tucker and the Original Shakespeare Company
rings a sympathetic bell with many musicians.

Tucker adds another element. Without rehearsals, he notes, there is
"no way the author [i.e., Shakespeare] could inform the actors how to
perform except through the text itself."[56] Experience indicated to him
and his company that they needed what they call "verse-nursing" sessions
to help the cast notice the many hints and clues found in the scripts.

> A verse nurse session has become the time when the actor is confronted with
> the clues [contained in his lines] . . . and asked to wonder why, at this par-
> ticular time, his character changes from poetry to prose, or from complex to
> simple language, and, the glory of it all, why they are changing from *you* to
> *thee*. It is in these sessions that the actors find their characters take hold, and
> get the framework their acting will fit into . . . At these meetings, the actors
> are never told how to perform, or indeed whether the decisions they have
> made are valid or not. They are simply reminded of the clues, with the in-
> junction that if they have a clue, they must do something about it.[57]

With music, the parallel to learning to recognize the implications in original parts, such as the ones discussed above, like delivering the Affection

of a piece, stress differences, bringing out and inflecting figures and gestures, dynamic changes, changes in tempo, the use of rubato, dynamic inflection and note shaping, agogics of various kinds, contrasting articulations, pauses, and bowings based on note importance. An individual who could lead sessions like this for musicians would be highly revered. He or she would have to be experienced and knowledgeable, a genuine "maestro" whose wisdom and insight were recognized by the players.

Performing concerts without Maestro-Rehearsals doesn't mean performance need be less individualized. Even sight-reading sessions can be full of personality; it depends on the quality of the players as well as whether they are used to working in this way. Changes of tempo, bringing out accents, using contrasting articulations, inflection, and agogics are all possible to coordinate subtly if the members have worked regularly together. Of course, they have to know how to read their parts; this is what I will discuss in the next chapter.

6

Changing Meanings,
Permanent Symbols

*Just as there is a great distance between grammar and Eloquence,
there is the same infinity between notated music and music played
well.*

(François Couperin, *L'Art de toucher le clavecin*, 1717)

Most music in the world is communicated orally from musician to musician (that is, by ear). Western concert music is exceptional in depending on writing for transmission. If most Classical musicians cannot play by ear and need a written page in front of them, the page itself takes on importance. Thus the way music is written down and the way we understand the writing have an important effect on the music that results. The issues of what was intended by the writing and what should be read back out of it become central to our musicking.

Over time, however, the meaning of written musical symbols has gradually shifted. The writing and reading of music has changed in fundamental ways, especially around 1800. That is the subject of this chapter.

Changing Meanings, Permanent Symbols

"Is it not astonishing," writes Harnoncourt, "that musical works which are completely different in essence and style, such as an opera by Monteverdi and a symphony by Gustav Mahler, can be written down using the same notational symbols?"[1] The kind of change—both in sound and in meaning—that Harnoncourt is talking about is not well understood by most musicians, but it has been studied in languages for a long time; we have all heard examples of readings of Chaucer or Shakespeare.

Preserving style, including styles of speaking, is like trying to hold water in your hand. One of the primary purposes of opera coaches and teachers, for instance, is to serve as guardians of tradition, maintaining "correct" and often fixed interpretations of roles—preserving idiom. They can slow down the process of change, but they cannot arrest it, as a comparison of recordings by Caruso (b. 1873) and Pavarotti (b. 1935) shows.

The connotations of words change during our lifetimes. I think of "leading-edge," "bottom-line," or "icon." If language can evolve so quickly even in a highly literate society (where literacy usually acts as a brake on evolution), surely musical meanings are also on the move. But, while this is happening, nothing changes on paper; the old manuscripts abide, speaking a language that was leading-edge in 1750, or 1650; many lifetimes ago.

Thus, with musical documents three to four centuries old, there is every prospect that, without special knowledge, we will mistake the meanings of their symbols. It is convenient to ignore this, and Modern style musicians often read Rhetorical music with results that are not very satisfactory. An example is the distinction between *descriptive* and *prescriptive* notation. This is a distinction a musician needs to be able to make.

Descriptive and Prescriptive Notation

There is a long-standing debate among grammarians about whether they should be discovering structures in language or dictating them; whether, in other words, grammar tells you what you do, or tells you what to do. This is similar to the distinction in music between the descriptive and prescriptive ways of writing,[2] which in a general way distinguish Rhetorical music from Romantic.[3]

In *descriptive* writing, "the composition itself is notated," as Harnoncourt puts it, "but the details of its interpretation cannot be deduced from the notation." The musician is presented, then, with the composer's inspiration, which they have to realize as best they can. It is the performer who is responsible for the practical details of the performance, choosing the instruments to be used, for instance, the movements to be included or omitted, and so on.

By contrast, *prescriptive* writing consists of reasonably detailed directions for performing the music: in this mode, the form and structure of the piece itself are what is not clear; they emerge "automatically, as it were, during performance," as a result of following the instructions.[4]

Descriptive writing is halfway to being as "thin" as a lead-sheet in jazz. It is typical of Baroque music in general. Extreme examples are the unmeasured preludes by seventeenth-century French composers like Louis Couperin and Jean de Sainte-Colombe. Bach's solo violin pieces written with four-part chords are an example of another kind of descriptive writing: passages that are impossible to play as written, but nevertheless help

the player to visualize the effect. Because the low G-string stops sounding when the bow touches the top E-string, it is impossible to keep the
G-string sounding, and yet writing the music in this way (playing "as if"
sounding four notes, a kind of musical metaphor) helps the player visualize Bach's "description" of the piece. Prescriptive readers don't get it.
They invented a "Bach-bow" to play all four strings—a bow Bach and his
contemporaries had never seen.

Descriptive notation offers a picture or vision of a piece, an ideal toward which to strive. But it does not necessarily provide the technical
means to realize it. These are left in the performer's domain. The goal of
prescriptive notation, on the other hand, is just the opposite: to direct the
player in a particular series of acts that produce a piece of music. It is like
drawing by connecting the dots—the picture does not emerge until the
dots are joined in the correct sequence. As Nelson Goodman puts it, reading prescriptive scores is like being able "to recognize, so to speak, correct
pronunciation though without necessarily understanding what is pro-
nounced."[5] Unlike descriptive writing, where the performer is in on the
plan from the beginning, in prescriptive writing one tends to realize rather
late in the process what one is saying—sometimes, like newscasters, only
at the moment of saying it.[6]

Lydia Goehr makes a useful distinction between "composing through
performance and composing prior to performance."[7] By "composing
through performance," she means the dominant mode of seventeenth-
and eighteenth-century music, improvisatory and informal. The opposite,
"composing prior to performance," implies the existence of an artist-
composer separate from the performers, who creates a fixed conception
that the performers are not expected to change through their execution;
a Romantic prescriptive piece, in other words, with explicit instructions
(what Goehr curiously calls a "sufficiently well specified" score).

The prescriptive approach was the norm during the twentieth century.
An example is Anton Webern's music. Because only a single note or a few
notes within a line are given to each separate part, the full piece is invisible
to each individual player.

The model of the prescriptive mode is like a recipe for baking a cake;
recipes are sets of instructions from a chef/composer to a cook/performer.
Accurately follow the instructions, and a cake will be the result. So what
about a *descriptive* score? How could a recipe be presented in that mode?
What would have to change? What if, instead of a recipe, one described
a cake in terms of its taste, moistness, size, color, consistency, and general
ingredients, rather like two cooks in conversation? In fact good, creative
cooks do often work this way, eating something in a restaurant, for instance, and then going home to try to make it themselves (better, they
hope). In Stravinsky's terms, they would be called "interpretive" cooks
rather than "executants."

The Incomplete Musical Score

Anyone who has ever tried to convey a musical idea by means of notation knows how approximate it is. No matter how clever one is at accurately writing the idea, no matter how much detail is included, it always seems a small miracle if someone else can seize the meaning by eye without having first heard it.

The gamba virtuoso André Maugars heard Frescobaldi play in 1639 and commented, "Although his printed works give sufficient witness to his ability, one has to hear him in person improvising toccatas full of contrapuntal devices and admirable inventions in order to fully appreciate his profound knowledge."[8]

Musical notation is always under-determined; imprecise and incomplete in one way or another, "concealing" (as Boorman puts it) "many well-understood elements"[9] that are in effect the performance practice of the period. Boorman writes, "No practical notation has been (or has been devised to be) comprehensive or precise. Each notation, and each source using it, assumes a series of understandings on the part of the reader."[10] Randel notes the general imprecision of modern Western musical notation: "For all of its weakness at dealing with pitch, it is downright crude with respect to duration and worse yet with respect to timbre."[11]

There are always important performance variables missing from the page: vibrato, for instance, frequency of dynamic changes, dynamic nuance, balance, rubato, exact tempo, and beat hierarchy.[12] No matter how literal the performer wishes to be, they are obliged to make some decisions: on timbre, for instance, or the tuning system and (if given as a word) the tempo.

In his influential book *Languages of Art*, Nelson Goodman proposes his notorious definition of a musical work that requires it to be note-perfect: "full compliance with the specifications given [in the score] is categorically required."[13] This definition can only be taken seriously if one believes that musical notation really was intended to define exactly the identity of a piece, and was capable of doing so. Goodman's language analogy also leads him into the concept of "compliance" with its sado-masochistic overtones; other philosophers have taken up this dubious concept.

Written Music's Oral Element

The reason musical writing succeeds is because, alongside the notation system, there is a parallel oral tradition. The oral element is necessary to decipher the musical symbols, and everybody who reads music has learned it. Reading music successfully depends on agreements on what the signs mean, on what kinds of things may be added or substituted, and what to do for the unwritten elements. These conventions are passed on from one generation to the next. According to Bowen, "many of the 'rules' which we take for granted—like 'Don't speed up when you get louder', or even 'A minim is twice as long as crotchet'—are simply conventions which were drilled into us at an early age. (These conventions . . . are invisible, like the rules of grammar, to the native speaker.)"[14]

Harnoncourt gives the example of the Viennese waltz. As he says, "It is not possible to write down such dance music precisely as it should be played," and if musicians were to play it literally (at least, what *we* think of as "literal"), it would be very far from the real waltz style. Harnoncourt wrote this before music software like *Finale* and *Sibelius* was developed that transcribes exactly the rhythms one plays into it. Played in traditional style, Strauss waltzes look very complicated in a music notation program. This software is the perfect reflection of the literal approach to notation that has been gaining ground since the nineteenth century; computers have trouble with ambiguity, a great deal of which was purposely written into seventeenth- and eighteenth-century scores. Because ambiguity is impossible in these programs, they transcribe simple human rhythms into complex figures that are difficult to read.

"If the correct understanding of notes is this problematical for the music of Johann Strauss, despite its unbroken tradition—how much more problematical it must be in the case of music whose playing tradition has completely vanished."[15] Imagine, he suggests, how Strauss waltzes would be played if they were to fall into disuse for a hundred years and were then rediscovered!

Music historians often speak as if a complete musical "work" could be communicated solely through paper and ink. They forget this oral element, the decoding device, without which music on paper is a locked document.

Writing Only the Essential in Rhetorical Music

A common characteristic of Rhetorical scores is that they are thin, containing very little more than the essential—a notation for professionals. No one bothered to write what would already have been understood. The convention was that the composer marked only the unexpected: that which deviated from the norms of the ambient style. This basic principle is evident everywhere.

When nothing, or at least very little, was written needlessly, a corollary is that nothing or very little on the page was without significance or implications. The signs that found their way onto the page often represented the exceptional or unusual. When there is a "forte" marked, it means a musician would normally have played "piano" there. Every sign is thus potentially describing performance practice, but in reverse.

Because they were exceptional, markings would have attracted the attention of the eighteenth-century player. When presented with an unexpected articulation, for instance, they would not only have emphasized it (since it was unusual), but, because it was part of the special character of the piece, would have articulated analogous passages in the same way. (The copyist, knowing this, would not have bothered to mark it after the first occurrence.[16])

Let's take the slur as an example. A slur is nowadays rarely thought of as a grace; it is an instruction for articulation (or rather, the lack of it). But in the eighteenth century, a slur of up to three or four notes was only incidentally an indication of legato playing; it normally implied an emphasis with a diminuendo.[17] A bar of six 8ths tied 2-2-2 would describe something like three sighs with an emphasis on the first of each pair and a decrescendo over each pair. Brahms, in several of his chamber works, depended on such a nuanced performance of slurred pairs. By that time it was unusual. In 1845, Mendelssohn had to point out to the players, since they did not read it automatically, that for Bach these figures would have been given an accent-diminuendo treatment.[18]

A performer in Modern style would see this passage differently. Not thinking of slurs as anything exceptional, they would read them as mere technical instructions for legato, for which the performer as "executant" takes neither responsibility nor credit.[19] Having thus missed their original significance, the modern player would omit the slurs in later analogous passages.

Here is an example of the same piece played with slurs as graces (= accent-diminuendo) and as articulations (merely legato):

◀🔊 AUDIO SAMPLE: 39. Bach: Leonhardt Consort, Equiluz, Leonhardt, 1987. "Jesu, meines Todes Tod" in BWV 165

◀🔊 AUDIO SAMPLE: 40. Bach Collegium, Japan, Sakurada, Suzuki, 1996. Bach: "Jesu, meines Todes Tod" in BWV 165

The literal approach, where initiative is discouraged ("the highest quality in an executant is submission"), makes it easy to fall into this trap. After all, slurs looked then like they look now. Let's try this idea as a rehearsal sketch:

> "You want an 'expressive event,'" says the hard-boiled Modern-style musician, "you write 'Espressivo' over it." More than once in their career they have been reprimanded for "adding" things to their part.
>
> "Vat are you talkink about, didn' you see dose slures I put in duh first time?" replies Handel's ghost.
>
> "You want slurs the second time, too? Why didn' you write 'em?" This guy is almost as bad as Corelli and his French hangup. (They're wondering, meanwhile, what the fat German is talking about, that a slur somehow means "Espressivo"?)

Taruskin writes of players who tend to see their performance as "texts rather than acts," that is, they play like textual editors edit: removing later

editorial additions or changes. In itself, this is indeed a necessary procedure if one has to deal with editions. Although—as he says—it is the point
where the editor stops, the performer should be just beginning. All too
often, Strait performers produce "the aural equivalent of an Urtext score."
"This seems to be most characteristic—dare I say it?—of English performances."[20] Taruskin wrote this in 1984, but it is even truer today (and Strait
style these days is by no means limited to Britain or the Anglo-Saxons).

Implicit Notation

The *Harvard Dictionary of Music* calls performance practice "the gap between what was notated and what was thought necessary for a performance."[21] Put another way, the thin notation of Rhetorical music is normally
in *implicit* mode because a large proportion of what it communicates is
not explicitly written but is implied through performance practice.

This idea is developed further by Peter Jeffery:

> From some perspectives the difference [between oral transmission and per-
> formance practice] may be primarily terminological, for "performance prac-
> tice," can be seen as merely a customary term for the oral component of all
> Western art music, the unwritten conventions performers use to interpret the
> written sources. . . . In this sense, performance practice is at its base really a
> matter of musical "literacy."[22]

A similar idea was expressed by Peter Walls: "One way of looking at the
whole enterprise of performance practice is to see it as a matter of literacy. How do we read this score (the composer's way of communicating
intentions)? On one level, this amounts to no more or less than a thor-
ough understanding of the implications of the notation, an ability to read
it with a proper sense of the idiom."[23]

If you are used to explicit parts, the idea that the information on the
page is supplemented by a well-defined style (mainstream in the Baroque
period, learned now as performance practice) would not be immediately
obvious. Baroque notation implies many things that are not obvious on
the page. Besides stylistic conventions, thin notation implies the higher
status of a performing musician at the time, not yet "transparent" or "com-
pliant." Their part leaves ambiguity, which allows considerable individual freedom, and gives them some of the discretion now allotted to the
composer. I'll evoke once more the jazz musician as an ideal, playing
somebody's tune, but nobody else's composition. The Baroque musician
is halfway there, playing a very elaborate "tune" but adding to it enough
material to make it uniquely their own, and playing in a way that will
probably be heard only once.

As I mentioned above, since the markings represented the exceptional
or unusual, some performance practice was also indicated in negative

image every time a performance sign appeared. Markings indicated, in other words, what one would not normally be expected to do; a "piano" marking would normally have been played "forte," and so on.

To play literally "as written" from the page, Urtext style, would thus—paradoxically—be to play *not* as written, as it would overlook the shorthand messages embedded in the notation and assumed to be understandable. Many expressive gestures built into the notation can be recognized by the trained eye. Together with an understanding of musical grammar, which was assumed of any competent professional musician, musicians routinely read or recognized:

- figures and gestures and their functions within phrases,
- many dynamic changes,
- changing tempo, both long-term and short,
- inflection and note shaping,
- rhythmic freedoms used to distinguish the relative melodic importance of notes (agogics),
- prolonging the first of a group of notes in faster passages and making it stronger, in order to clarify metric groups and delineate figuration (the agogic accent),
- contrasting articulations,
- pauses,
- bowings based on note importance.

These and other expressive elements were integral and implicit in the notation. Beat hierarchy was also unmarked; George Houle commented, for instance, that

> The perception of *quantitas intrinseca,* or "good" and "bad" notes, gave essential information to performers about articulation patterns. Instead of relying on markings for slurs, staccato marks, sforzandos, and accents, 17th- and 18th-century performers interpreted their unmarked scores through habits and formulas learned as part of their elementary instruction.[24]

We have not yet come to the more elaborate Baroque freedoms, like the essential graces, passaggi, cadenzas, and preludes. Nor have I mentioned the orator's special style of declamation in delivering the Affection of a piece (usually implied in a movement's title, like Adagio, Dolce, Mesto, or Pesante). All these attributes are implied or intimated on a Baroque page of music.

After 1800, apparently in response to the widening gulf between musicians and composers, there was a gradual shift from implicit to explicit writing, so that a language that was once descriptive was converted into a set of technical instructions telling the player what to do or how to do it. This is the kind of notation modern musicians are used to, and they tend to be pretty literal in playing what's on the page, applying mathematical precision (a note with five flags is a 1/128th note, not just—as in the Baroque period—a "very short note"). This can be called "thick reading."

When it is assumed that the performer reads literally what is written on the page, the writing has to be very precise. But if the performer is expected to embellish what they see on the page, a sketch is enough.

The switch to explicit writing was not sudden and complete; the difference between the eighteenth and nineteenth centuries was a question of degree.[25] "During the 19th century there was a proliferation of markings, designed to show finer grades or types of accents and dynamic effects, and performance instructions of all kinds were used ever more freely."[26] Essential graces, as we have seen in the case of the slur, were originally understood to indicate expressive events, fairly specific but subject to slight changes in detail.

Graces declined after the Romantic Revolution, along with performer status. By the late twentieth century, gracing was so little understood that a well-known writer on music could suggest writing out Tartini's trills "in full,"[27] which is an oxymoron, a conceptual contradiction. Trills are by definition indeterminate and ambiguous (played longer or shorter, for instance, depending on tempo, amount of rosin on the bow, how old the string is, one's mood, etc.). That is why they were notated in imprecise symbols rather than "plaine notes." If they were to be written in explicit mode, their creative character would be dampened or removed, and they would atrophy into mechanical formulas.

Strait Style and the Neutral "Run-Through"

Joshua Rifkin has suggested that an eighteenth-century concert was "an interpretation that does not differ superficially from many a run-through— in other words, does not engage in very noticeable modifications of tempo, does not go to extremes of accent or inflection, and so forth."[28]

A modern "run-through" tends to be a literal reading similar to Rifkin's description. The musicians keep strictly to the explicit directions printed black on white, and they tend not to become musically engaged with the material; a run-through is a "generic" reading. Rifkin compares the "run-through" approach to a "jingle session" in which musicians come into a performing space of some sort, are handed a newly written piece of music, read it once or twice through, play it more or less flawlessly, with a sense of its basic stylistic assumptions, and then go home.[29]

Because Rifkin's recordings of Bach represent the Strait style very well, his vision of eighteenth-century performance as similar to a run-through offers an understanding of the background reasoning that has created this image of Rhetorical music so different from my own. A sample of his approach can be heard in the "Alleluja" from Cantata 51, *Jauchzet Gott,* which, when compared with the version by Leonhardt, seems extremely laid-back and detached.

🔊 AUDIO SAMPLE: 41. Leonhardt Consort, Kweksilber, Smithers, Leonhardt, 1976. Bach: BWV 51/5

🔊 AUDIO SAMPLE: 42. Bach Ensemble, Baird, Holmgren, Rifkin, 1986. Bach: BWV 51/5

In the recordings conducted by Rifkin that I've heard, my ears do not pick up signals that indicate that the performance is intended to move and touch me—"si vis me flere, dolendum est primum ipsi tibi [if you would have me weep, you must first show grief yourself]."[30] Among these signs would be hesitations or other disturbances of the regular tempo, dramatic contrasts in dynamics such as a sudden pianissimo or messa di voce (this latter is attempted occasionally, but is usually curtailed before it develops). Nor is there a sense of unpredictability or spontaneity; the performers know exactly what is coming next. Here is an example:

🔊 AUDIO SAMPLE: 43. Bach Ensemble, Schopper, Rifkin, 1995–96. Bach: "Starkes Lieben," BWV 182/4

Here is another approach to the piece, where the instruments especially manage to reach the listener.

🔊 AUDIO SAMPLE: 44. Amsterdam Baroque Orchestra, Mertens, Koopman, 1995. Bach: "Starkes Lieben," BWV 182/4

Strait performances usually sound as if the musicians think that the mere act of performing the music is enough to justify making an audience listen. The effort to evoke and arouse emotions in listeners is missing, the sense of Mattheson's expression *"Klang-Rede,"* musical declamation.

"Early music" as a manifestation of Rhetoric does not engage Rifkin. In an interview several years ago he offered the idea that "rhetoric is simply effective speech—good public speaking, if you will."[31] It can't be denied that that is Rhetoric's status today. Rifkin questions the historical basis of the connection between music and Rhetoric, characterizing attempts to apply it as "milking every little gesture for all it's worth." This view, by a thoughtful Strait style musician, corresponds with the reserved character of the performances he has directed.

Style versus Interpretation

The idea that there is implied or built-in performance information that is not explicitly written in the score is a very different one from the modern idea of "interpretation." At least, from the kind of interpretation that amounts to arbitrary intervention; adding personal ideas to the music, or even (God forbid) improvisation. It is known that Beethoven made disagreeable scenes when a musician dared to add a few trills.[32]

Rifkin's conception of interpretation is clarified by a question he poses elsewhere. He asks, "How far does interpretation take us from the original, how much of that is legitimate?" The opposition of "interpretation" to "the original" is a not-uncommon twentieth-century view of things, and my guess is that it is shared by most or all Strait style performers. What, one wonders, is "the original" of a piece of music? Presumably, it has to do with the intention of the composer. In that case, any personal input by performers leads away from the composer's conception. This separates "interpretation" from the "music," the way mustard is separate from a hot dog; some people don't take mustard, and some people prefer their music "plain," without interpretation.

The attitude behind "interpretation as mustard" was famously articulated in 1810 by E. T. A. Hoffmann in a passage I quoted at the beginning of this chapter: "The genuine artist . . . does not make his personality count in any way. All his thoughts and actions are directed towards bringing into being . . . the pictures and impressions the composer sealed in his work."[33]

Seeing the interests of the composer and performer as different is a view of historical performance born of an assumption that the music is a separate thing from what the performer does—that the performer can somehow damage the object called "the music"—rather than that the music achieves its identity in being performed (as a cake recipe achieves its identity when the cake comes out of the oven).

The word "interpret" defined as "to bring out the meaning of a musical composition by performance" is, according to the *OED*, "in recent use"; its first example dates from 1888. "Interpretation" can mean "taking liberties" or making assumptions not based on explicit indications; or the arbitrary addition in performance of personal mannerisms not necessarily designed to bring out the piece's invention and essential identity. This is definitely something added to the music, like mustard. It seems possible that "interpretation" in this sense of arbitrary addition has only existed since Romantic times? Is it possible that before that time there was only what we saw above, stylistic reading based on performance practice, a performing style attached to the music, like the Viennese waltz?

Brown points out that in the course of the nineteenth century the performer stopped depending on style and began looking for intention.

> The change of attitude implied by these differences is profound. The onus
> for the performer had decisively shifted from one of determining in which

of a number of different ways to realise the notation, on the basis of general conventions of appropriate style, to one in which it was primarily necessary to know the precise meaning and intention behind the composer's symbols and instructions.[34]

It is ironic that figures, graces, and other expressive devices often came to be regarded in the nineteenth century as extraneous impertinence, whereas in the eighteenth century and before they were not seen as personal interpolations but rather as enhancements that were part of a common language, expected and welcomed by composer and listener alike.

I don't mean to suggest that musicians in the Rhetorical period played like automatons, putting nothing of themselves into their performances. Quite the contrary: when parameters like dynamic nuance, individual note-shaping, rubato, agogics and note placing, pauses, beat hierarchy, and emphasis are regularly present in one's performance, they act like windows into the soul. It's pretty difficult to do all these things while maintaining a distant, mechanical persona. But what I do mean to suggest is that the kind of neutral "run-through" (with windows closed and nobody home) personified in modern Strait style would have been almost impossible for the musician of Rhetorical mentality.

I wonder, in other words, whether much of what Rifkin and other Strait historical musicians see as unwarranted personal license (that is, arbitrary interpretation) is thought of by musicians like myself as performance practice, the common attributes of Period style.

"Saying Bach, Meaning Telemann": Composer-Intention before the Romantic Period

Composer-intention derives a lot of its force from the role of the composer in the Romantic period and the rise of the cult of genius.[35] That attitude is still with us, to the point that Josef Mertin, in a book on Period musicking full of wisdom, compares "fidelity to the composer" for musicians to the Hippocratic Oath for physicians.[36] Surely this is an exaggeration.

To be sure, the idea of artist-intention already existed in the eighteenth century. Charles Avison wrote in 1753 in his *Essay on Musical Expression:* "For, as Musicall Expression in the Composer, is succeeding in the Attempt to express some particular Passion; so in the Performer, it is to do a Composition Justice, by playing it in a Taste and Stile so exactly corresponding with the Intention of the Composer, as to preserve and illustrate all the Beauties of his Work."[37]

Quantz also talks of satisfying "the aims of the composer and the ideas they had when writing the piece."[38] Walls gives other examples.[39]

It might be more enlightening, however, to try to imagine what would have been the reasonable expectations of a seventeenth- or eighteenth-century musician writing down a composition. How much "compliance" (so-called) would they have expected? Indeed, to what would they have expected compliance? Mattheson wrote in 1739, "Those who have never discovered how the composer himself wished to have the work performed will hardly be able to play it well. Indeed, they will often rob the thing of its true vigour and grace, so much so, in fact, that the composer should they themselves be among the listeners, would find it difficult to recognize their own work."[40]

Performers "who have never discovered how the composer himself wished to have the work performed" would have had to fall back on a common sense of performing style. Then as now, style in this sense is a social category, like language, and performance practice. It is not a private, individual taste; it is shared by a group of people. Style is a broad category, of course, and while it is bigger than individuals, it accommodates many individual approaches.

Jeanne Bovet writes of old treatises on declamation:

> Although they may not give us the ability to hear the actual voices of actors, they do allow us to "understand" ["entendre"] in the old sense of the period; that is, to comprehend in the way contemporaries did. . . . What is communicated in the 17th-and 18th-century treatises is a state of mind, a cultural perception. . . . To adequately grasp the basic principles of classical declamation, it is less relevant to try to reconstitute one or several particular instances than to recognize the vocal poetics of which they are all a part.[41]

Trying to reproduce the *individual* composer's personal intentions is a Romantic idea. Baroque composers did not expect anyone to do that, even in their own time. Bach's purpose in writing down his music, for instance, was to communicate it to others. He already knew how the music went and did not need to read his own score. Think of Gesner's description of Bach's conducting:

> If you could see him, I say, . . . singing with one voice and playing his own parts, but watching over everything and bringing back to the rhythm and the beat, out of thirty or even forty musicians, the one with a nod, another by tapping with his foot, the third with a warning finger, giving the right note to one with the top of his voice, to another from the bottom, and to a third from the middle of it—all alone, in the midst of the greatest din made by all the participants, and, although he is executing the most difficult parts himself, noticing at once whenever and wherever a mistake occurs, holding everyone together.[42]

Bach's main motive in writing was no doubt to convey the piece as it existed in his mind to his immediate colleagues in a sufficiently detailed manner to allow them to reproduce it in a recognizable form. His "intention," then, was satisfied when a musician could perform his music in a way he would recognize as that of competent performance practice.

That phrase, "competent performance practice" is, I believe, a key. It could even serve as a tentative definition of Authenticity.

The Romantic veil obscures a subtle but important distinction here. When Adorno fulminated against HIP ("They say Bach, mean Telemann"[43]), he was thinking of the Bach and Telemann of the mid-twentieth century. Bach in those days was still an honorary (if premature) member of the circle of immortals, a genius in the Romantic sense, compared with whom Telemann was useful only as a symbol of the mediocre.

In Bach's time, we now know, musicians saw these things differently: Telemann's position was reversed; he was generally regarded as Germany's greatest musician. Bach's post at Leipzig had first been offered to Telemann. By the criteria of Bach's time, to play Bach as Telemann might have played him would hardly "reduce" him to the norms of his historical environment, as John Butt puts it;[44] Bach himself would surely have been delighted with—or at the very least interested in—Telemann's interpretation.[45] In fact, Adorno's criticism is very astute (and thoroughly Romantic); HIP—doing its best to apply the criteria of Bach's time—*does* want to hear how Bach's music would sound if it were "Telemann." It is what these composers shared—a common style—that most interests the movement, not the differences between them as individuals (as Romantic "artistes," in other words). What HIP offers is a way to get pleasure from both Telemann and Bach. We could say that Period musicians are "transparent" to the ambient style rather than any particular composer's style.

It is not that the thinking and goals of individual Baroque composers are unimportant to HIP. Knowing the ambient performing protocol in Bach's time and place does not exclude knowing what he himself wished for his pieces.[46] It's the emphasis that's different. Not many musicians today prefer Telemann to Bach, no matter what their stylistic stance. But Bach's originality is easier to see, in fact, by comparing him with his contemporaries, not in removing him from the context in which he worked.

So it is not the particular composer who is at the center of the movement's concerns.[47] Details of the notation of an individual that may be difficult to understand, for instance, are sometimes clarified by knowing what other musicians at the same time and place took for granted. Composer-intention thus shifts from being a personal affair of the individual composer into a question of performing style.

III

ANACHRONISM
AND AUTHENTICITY

7

Original Ears

Vintage Compared with Style

It has always puzzled me why, if we put old buildings on lists to protect them (I'm talking about pre-twentieth-century buildings), and pay large sums to own and live in them, we do not build new ones in that style. A new house, built using, say, seventeenth-century principles, would inspire enormous interest. People would drive miles to see it. Of course it would be expensive to build, which is the usual explanation for not doing it. But its value would correspond to its cost. And it would be a pleasure to see and to use. Why don't we do it?

The same with furniture: people pay huge amounts for old antiques—far more than they are worth—simply because of their style; but very few furniture stores sell new furniture in authentic antique styles.

Could it be that most people don't actually appreciate the beautiful qualities of old things? That it is the age of the object, rather than the style of its design and construction that gives it its monetary value? All the more reason, I would think, to encourage people to make copies of objects made in older styles. Then they don't have to pay for age.

"Old" evidently has more value than "new." No dealer would sell a Rembrandt as a Picasso. Pico complained in 1512, "Any sculpture which is reported to be of recent make, even if it excels those made in ancient times, is considered inferior."[1] Dürer was actually told in Venice in 1506 that the piece he was trying to sell was "not in the ancient manner and therefore no good."[2] It was not, as dealers say, "antique enough." Imagine a composer, or graphic artist, being told that today!

Some people like copies of paintings or musical instruments to have the "look of age," a vintage value. They would prefer, for example, a new "Baroque" violin with an artificial patina of age over its varnish. Given a choice, in other words, they prefer to see "old" things look like they look now (that is, old) rather than how they looked then (which would have been new).

Even Michelangelo passed off some of his statues as antique by artificially weathering or damaging them.[3] People who make fake paintings have to age them because being old is a condition of being original. And for his "Lefébure" harpsichord, Skowroneck used a simulated patina, original old dust, and artificial scratches to make experts think the instrument was old.[4]

I myself like a Baroque violin to look new, like it looked in the Baroque period; I like my music to sound new, as it sounded then. (In fact, I even like the idea of newly composed Baroque music, for the same reason.) Not that I want to be there then, with open sewers, plagues, and absolutist governments. I do want, however, to see the Baroque period as it saw itself when it was the present. When, in other words, all these objects were new. Most of the instruments in old paintings look brand new.

For me, the appearance of age is not what makes an instrument, a performance, or a score authentic. To borrow Harnoncourt's words:

> We must understand the genuine musical concerns of Monteverdi and understand how those concerns are reflected in living music. We must attempt as musicians to see with new eyes everything that was current for Monteverdi and *will remain current for all times*, to reanimate it, to render it with our feelings, our 20th-century mentality—for certainly we do not wish to return to the 17th century.[5]

The italics are mine. The only thing I can think of that "was current for Monteverdi and will remain current for all times" is the style he worked in. Style can jump centuries. It is the only relevant criterion for ascription and for replicating.

Of course, there are those who argue that we can't know what music and even violins were really like in the Baroque; our ideas about these things are always changing. This, we have to agree, is true; art fakes demonstrate that art is captive in its period and place. But if we wait to try to get it completely right, we'll never get it. First, we cannot know if we have succeeded. And whether it's right for all time is not the issue. All we want is to be confident we have realized the style as we perceive it at this particular moment.

Seconda Pratica

Four centuries ago, in 1605, Claudio Monteverdi announced his intention to publish a book called *Seconda Pratica, overo Perfettione della moderna musica,* in which he would explain the principles of a new, "modern music." "Seconda Pratica" was Monteverdi's name for a music in which priority was placed on the expression of the emotions of the text. Seconda Pratica radically rejected the mainstream and believed it was recovering a tradition that had been lost in antiquity.

The concept of a music in which "harmony is the servant of the words" had originated from research by "the Camerata," a group of poets and musicians in Florence, who for some years had been investigating the history of the Greek drama of antiquity. Their purpose was to revive it if possible, and their reading of the evidence indicated that the texts had been sung rather than spoken. Several members, including Giulio Caccini and Jacopo Peri, composed dramas entirely in recitative that carefully imitated the natural rhythm and melody of speech. As music, the new style was strange and shocking in sound.

There have been many turns in the road of performing style, but few of the degree these musicians achieved. Seconda Pratica (or *nuove musiche* as Caccini called it in his volume of solo songs) was invented by radical thinkers who were serious about reviving a form of earlier music. Their deliberate rejection of received tradition precipitated much argument and discussion.

In the then-mainstream approach to music, *Prima Pratica,* there was no attempt at realistic discourse or dialogue. The text was pretty much impossible to understand because voices, composed in imitation of each other, sang the text at different times.[6] Prima Pratica was the polyphonic Netherlandish style that flourished all over Europe, represented by composers like Ockeghem, Desprez, Mouton, Clemens non Papa, Gombert, and culminating in the work of Adrian Willaert (d. 1562). Prima Pratica was described and codified in the writings of Gioseffo Zarlino (d. 1590). Here is an example.

🔊 AUDIO SAMPLE: 45. Henry's Eight, 1997. Clemens non Papa: Ego flos campi

And here is another example of Prima Pratica by Monteverdi.

🔊 AUDIO SAMPLE: 46. Concerto Italiano, 1994. Monteverdi: Secondo Libro, "Non si levava ancor l'alba novella"

In putting priority on projecting the meaning of texts with complete clarity and great expressiveness, the composers of Seconda Pratica were willing to drop customary musical conventions; rules were changed or ignored so that the music could remain inconspicuously at the service of the text. In addition to Monteverdi, Peri, and Caccini, composers who experimented with Seconda Pratica included Gesualdo, Cavalieri, Fontanelli, Ingegneri, Marenzio, de Wert, and Luzzaschi. Here are two famous pieces by Monteverdi in Seconda Pratica style.

AUDIO SAMPLE: 47. Complesso Barocco, Curtis, 1996. Monteverdi: Lamento della ninfa

AUDIO SAMPLE: 48. Complesso Barocco, Curtis, 1996. Monteverdi: "Or che 'l ciel"

The Camerata unintentionally ended up inventing something quite new, like neither the mainstream nor the Classical past it had hoped to emulate. Perhaps it was opera, perhaps it was a base from which opera developed,[7] as well as the principle of animating spoken text. It inspired all the music prior to the Romantic era. We could call it the basis of Baroque music.

The Camerata were not purposely setting out to invent a new music, any more than modern-day players of Period style are; their idea was historical. The turning of the carousel of time is not a thing that is easy—or even possible—to resist, but there can be very interesting results by mixing ideas from the past (as we dimly perceive it) with assumptions of the present.

The parallel of Seconda Pratica to the subject of this book, our own HIP, is obvious. Like HIP, the Seconda Pratica was reacting from within a venerable tradition (the Prima Pratica).[8] It just might be possible, then, to see in vague terms where our own "Seconda Pratica" is going.

The vision of HIP as meaning something "beyond a dead past" and pointing to "an idiom not yet invented" has been talked about since the 1980s.[9] It would be pointless to force this analogy too far, but the general similarity between Seconda Pratica and HIP is striking: the rejection of the dominant style (Netherlandish polyphony in one case, Romanticism/Modernism in the other), the attempt to substitute a contrasting one (monody/Period style), the resort to history, even the fanaticism and the rules. The new style is invented not out of whole cloth, but is certainly a construct based on insufficient evidence. And finally, the effort ends up serendipitously producing something new and unimaginable in advance.

Of course, musical movements in those days involved more composing than now, but that will hopefully change. In any case, unless somebody can convince us that there is a real difference between performing and composing, the point is a minor one. And I can't imagine anyone at the time performing Seconda Pratica with the restraint and refinement that would have been normal for the pieces of Prima Pratica.

In the case of Seconda Pratica we know what happened; where our movement is presently leading will not be clear for a generation or two. We have a great deal more historical material for our case than the members of the Camerata were able to piece together for theirs.[10] What we are now creating has as yet no name, even if we hear it in varying degrees in many contemporary concerts. What we know for sure is that there is no escaping the carousel of time. As art fakes show, every imitation will unconsciously show signs of the epoch that produced it. The harder we work to imitate the past, the more personal and contemporary the results will be. As Paul Henry Lang writes, "it is always our present we are interpreting, but we are doing so by looking into the past."[11]

Monteverdi never finished his book, by the way, but through his other writings it is clear he was moving toward the principle of Rhetoric, an idea already in the air. This perception of music as oratory and musical performance as Eloquence continued to be appealing throughout the Baroque period. "And if it be sayd," writes Roger North in the 1720s, "that it is impossible to produce speech out of inanimate sounds, or give an idea of thought, as speech doth, I answer that whenever a strong genius with due application hath attempted it, the success hath been wonderfull; as when the great Corelli used to say [of the violin] *Non l'intendite parlare?* ["Do you not hear it speak?"]"[12]

The idea was still strong in Mozart's day. Mozart's correspondence with his father while writing *Idomeneo*, for instance, is frequently on the subject of the cut-off point between speaking and singing, very much the same issue that had concerned Caccini and Monteverdi.

Past Examples of Authenticity Movements

There were other HIPs, like the one that existed in England as early as 1726. Called the Academy of Ancient Music, it was "the first organization to perform old works regularly and deliberately." It had curious similarities to twentieth-century HIP, being at first mostly supported by musicians.[13] Roger North, writing in ca. 1726, might well have been describing it:

> And untill a set of musicall *vertuosi*, well weighed in a resolution, and capable to make the experiment, and of whom none, as thinking themselves wiser, shall put on the contemptuous frowne and seem inwardly to sneer, shall be mett together, with all things fitt for the same designe, there will be no reason to expect the antiquitys of musick should ever be understood.[14]

The Academy involved many prominent singers and players at the time, such as Tosi, Galliard, Haym, Bononcini, "Il Senesino," Dieupart, Loeillet, Geminiani, Pepusch, and Chelleri. Agostino Steffani acted as honorary president. Handel, interestingly, was not involved. The Academy remained a specialist circle defined by its interest in earlier repertoire that was not shared by the larger musical community.[15]

Despite the similarity of their names, the Concert of Antient [!] Music, which was founded a half-century later in 1776, had a very different purpose from that of the older Academy. Its members were not an isolated gathering of professionals but a modern concert society led by peers of the realm. The concerts were put on in grand style, and from 1785, the king regularly attended them.[16]

The Concert of Antient Music's repertoire crossed over the great changes from Carissimi and Purcell through Handel into Hasse, Jommelli, and Christian Bach. It defined its repertoire as "no younger than about 20 years," which meant that, in the minds of people in London in 1776, contemporary music extended backwards some twenty years, after which it passed into the category of "Antient." This sounds more like how we think of popular music.

Speaking like a true canonist, Roger North in 1728 wrote of "the works of the great Corelli" in England, which "became the only music relished for a long time, and there seemed to be no satiety of them, nor is the vertue of them yet exhaled, and it is a question whether it will ever be spent, for if musick can be immortall, Corelli's consorts will be so."[17] In England, as Weber shows, North was not exaggerating Corelli's position. Weber wrote of the concertos, "It was not so much that people necessarily thought them better than Vivaldi's, but that the works fulfilled a particular role as a model of taste that kept them in use well after their style had gone out of date."[18]

In Germany in about 1680 when, after the Thirty Years War, the nobility had gained the political upper hand, one way they re-enforced their status was by importing French and Italian music to fill the void in the country's musical infrastructure. Instrument makers began copying (exactly, apparently) the new designs of French woodwinds, and there was a great demand for instruction in the performing protocols of Italy and France.[19] We also have the descriptions of playing style by Georg Muffat, who had evidently worked with Lully in the 1660s and some years later went to Rome, where he was closely associated with Corelli. In 1695–1701, Muffat published accounts of his experiences.[20] The German musicians to whom these books were aimed must have been very much like us, concerned with replicating the major seventeenth-century performing styles.

In eighteenth-century France, too, there was an interest in *musique ancienne*. The Atelier Philidor at the court copied many volumes of earlier seventeenth-century examples of "musique classique française." Lully's operas continued to be performed for a century after his death (Le Cerf de la Viéville was of the opinion in 1704 that "the public should be given new [non-Lully] operas only for fear of making Lulli's seem old too soon because of being performed continually"[21]). One reason for Lully's longevity onstage was that the bylaws of the Opéra stipulated that one of his operas should always be kept in readiness should a new work fail. Revivals of Lully were consistently successful at the box office, however.[22] From the 1730s, Rameau's operas shattered many people's illusion that Lully could never be replaced. Lully (and Rameau as well) did eventually disappear in the late eighteenth century.

It is ironic to read Le Cerf de la Viéville's proud words, written in 1704, that "The overtures of Lulli have beauties that will be new and admirable through all the centuries."[23] As recently as 1970, practically no one then alive had heard a single note of his music; happily, that is now quickly changing.

The Difference between an Art Fake and a Period Concert

There have always been copiers, inspired by a sentiment expressed in 1607 by Annibale Carracci, the great Bolognese painter. Carracci was quoted as saying that if his pictures were mistaken for those of Titian and Correggio, which he often imitated, "the deception would be to his credit, especially since the painter's goal is to fool the eyes of the viewer, 'making appear to them as true that which is only feigned.'"[24] There is no hint here of a feeling of guilt for copying. And indeed in the eighteenth century, copies must have been viewed in a different light, otherwise William Topham would never have published his edition advertised as *Six sonatas . . . compos'd in imitation of Arcangelo Corelli* in 1709. Corelli was still alive at the time.

We know only the failures of forgers. Fakes that have succeeded are still undiscovered, and remain attributed to other, more famous artists. That is what a successful fake is, by definition. But experts argue that few fakes survive for long. What one generation will accept and spend considerable money for will leave the next cold. They are looking at, and for, different aspects of the work. As Kurz put it, "Every forgery will—unconsciously—show symptoms of the style of the epoch which produced it. Contemporaries may not discern it but, seen from a distance, the signs of the true period of origin gradually become apparent. Friedländer once said that the life of a forgery does not outlast thirty years, in other words its own generation."[25] As forgeries get farther away from the period in which they were made, they begin to betray the attributes of the wrong period. Werness observes, "Characteristics that mark an era may be those that are most universally appreciated at that time. They seem also to be the qualities that become 'dated' most quickly. The generation for which these qualities are in fashion tends to be blind to them, but to the next generation they may become painfully evident."[26]

Copies in Period style would presumably share this property of "shelf-life" with forgeries. I am thinking of performance styles, instrument copies, editions, and compositions, even replicas made as authentically as possible. Consider recordings of Period playing from the 1930s and 1940s—those of Landowska, for instance. They certainly sound dated. Instruments made in the same period that were called "copies" seem insensitive and too heavily built, and editions of music are (not always, but usually) difficult to use because of the intrusive additions and directives of well-meaning musicologist-editors. We cannot help it; our view of history is limited by our vantage-point and our imaginations.

Han van Meegeren's paintings are an example. Van Meegeren produced a number of paintings in the 1930s and 1940s in the style of Vermeer and de Hoogh.[27] He managed to fool all the Vermeer experts of his time. When they are viewed today, it is hard to understand how anyone could have thought they were by Vermeer. Werness comments in her article on the famous legal prosecution of van Meegeren, "Some of van Meegeren's beautiful figures curiously resemble Greta Garbo . . . that charm has faded with time."[28] We are indeed captive on the carousel, as Joni Mitchell demonstrated in her two very different recorded versions of "The Circle Game."

In music, a celebrated case is that of Fritz Kreisler, the "last of the violinist/composers."[29] For years, Kreisler played a number of "arrangements" which in 1935 he announced were actually of his own composition. Kreisler had begun using the names of then-obscure composers because he "found it impudent and tactless to repeat my name endlessly on the programs." Kreisler's confession was generally accepted in good spirit, and the predominant opinion was that he was "a paragon of modesty" or "a genius with a sense of humor who played a 'magnificent joke.'"

But Kreisler's confession did elicit a few accusations of "conscienceless forger" and "unethical imposter,"[30] and led to a bitter exchange with the chief music critic of the *London Times*, Ernest Newman, who questioned Kreisler's ethics and abilities. Ethically, Newman had a point; affairs like this undermine confidence in editors, and Kreisler could indeed, as Newman suggested, have just as well used fictitious names instead of real composers.[31] There is thus always the issue of honesty, even though Kreisler had made no effort to conceal the fact that the pieces were fakes. Here is Joshua Bell's recording of "Louis Couperin's" *La Précieuse*, an interesting overlay of style imitations. Kreisler in Romantic style imitates Couperin in Baroque style, and Bell in Modern style imitates Kreisler, with Period style (whether conscious or not) in the background.

🔊 **AUDIO SAMPLE: 49.** Joshua Bell, 1996. Kreisler: La Précieuse (alleged to be by Louis Couperin)

In the art world, the legal justification for prosecuting artists for imitating style is "fraud," that is, purposely misrepresenting the object to one's advantage when large sums of money are involved. Van Meegeren sold his fakes at very high prices (the prices had to be appropriately high to make his work credible). He himself claimed his motive was purely artistic, but he was convicted of fraud as well as forgery.[32]

One point worth underlining is that the question of fakes is separate from that of artistic quality. Forgeries are not necessarily bad art; quite the contrary. Forgers are deserving of considerable respect; not only are they artists of obvious ability, able to deceive experts on an æsthetic level, but are good enough as historians and craftsmen to be able to mislead curators on details of aging, technique, and materials as well. Haskell mentions a forger named Tobia Nicotra who "convincingly executed 'autographs' of Palestrina, Handel, Gluck, Mozart and others." That these were falsely attributed does not say anything about their musical merit; they could have been excellent.[33] Forgers beat both the experts and the artists at their own games. As Lessing observes, "Considering a work of art aesthetically superior because it is genuine, or inferior because it is forged, has little or nothing to do with aesthetic judgment or criticism. It is rather a piece of snobbery."[34] Thus van Meegeren, whose paintings were greatly admired when they were thought to be Vermeers, should have been honored for being capable of both pleasing and duping his contemporaries. What causes the historical replicas of musicians to be accepted as "authentic" (as we say) but those of artists and composers to be called fakes? (Imagine a concert of a well-known Period group billed as "fake performances!")

Having painted some of the best "Vermeers" in existence, van Meegeren concealed his name for years. In effect, he was pretending to be Vermeer. Musicians and instrument makers do just the reverse; they advertise their own names, worry about their reputations, and spend hours writing CVs (always putting them in the third person, as if someone else had written them) and being photographed in "artsy" poses. In revealing their identities, musicians get the kind of public approval that really should have been van Meegeren's.

How Historical Musicology and HIP Differ

Vertubleu, s'écria le Marquis, des sottises écrites! Ce sont celles qui durent le plus.

(Le Cerf de la Viéville)[35]

Henry Fielding once observed that in books of history "nothing is true but the names and dates," whereas in his own novels "everything is true but the names and dates." R. G. Collingwood also discusses this comparison:

> As works of imagination, the historian's work and the novelist's do not dif-
> fer. Where they do differ is that the historian's picture is meant to be true.
>
>   Genuine history has no room for the merely probable or the merely pos-
> sible; all it permits the historian to assert is what the evidence before him
> obliges him to assert.[36]

Collingwood's point is that a legitimate historical construction does not
involve creative additions or interpolations.

Performance practice and historical musicology are closely intercon-
nected, but they differ in one fundamental way. While performance practice involves the reconstruction of past common practice, musicology is
both less and more. It deals only in verifiable history—that is, evidence
that is "meant to be true" (as far as can be established). What is considered verifiable history almost never offers a complete picture; in the case
of music, not even recordings (if they existed) could do that. Performers
have to fill in that picture and transform it into coherent music. Music
historians may not, by the code of their profession, do it for them.

Like Pontius Pilate washing his hands, historians pass over undocu-
mented events in silence, or treat them neutrally, or (as a last resort) admit
ignorance of details that are unclear.[37] Somebody has to keep their hands
clean; fashions in performing style come and go (they come and go among
historians too, for that matter, as scholarly fashions change). "It is the
narrative impulse that brings the fictive element into history, for there is
both too much and too little evidence for continuous narratives; the historian must both fill in and weed out."[38]

It is not therefore unreasonable of music historians to try to distinguish truth from fiction.[39] Of course, that gives musicologists a nerdish
image, obliged as they are to be more concerned with mundane activities
like correctness than with the glamour of performing. "Art and Air come
seldom from under a Gown," as Roger North put it (referring to the academic robes that are still used in a limited way in universities).[40]

I remember my shock some years ago when attending an American
Musicological Society conference here in Montreal. The presenters dressed
like business people and were terribly serious (often about silly things). It
seems that whimsy and wit are not part of most academics' idea of how
to study seventeenth- and eighteenth-century music. I think they haven't
read enough Mattheson (the most important Baroque writer on German
music) whose style is so delightfully informal. Some day in the not-distant
future, I believe, students of music history will smile at the exaggerated
formality of their twentieth-century musicological forbears. Let us hope
the musicologists of the twenty-first century will learn to wear more comfortable clothes.

Because musicians perform concerts, they can't skip over the bits they
are not sure about. The musician is forced to assume "too much": that is,
more than can be proven.[41] "It is impossible," as Nicholas Temperley put
it, "to sing or play a piece of music using only historically established facts

as determinants of style."[42] Not many musicians can get away with a stunt like the one Toscanini is credited with: at the first performance he stopped Puccini's unfinished *Turandot* and announced to the audience, "At this point the Master set down his pen." The performance was left unfinished.

So Period style is more like a historical novel. Just as a novel must have a form/plot and characters, a successful concert performance of a piece of historical music must perform all the notes and make sense to a modern audience. Continuous narrative and coherence are obligatory for the historical performer.

Pontius Pilate, being an educated man (and apparently not inclined to religious absolutes), responded to Jesus' claim to speak Truth with the question "What is Truth?" (One can imagine Pilate hoping for a fleeting moment for some kind of real dialogue with another thoughtful person—the intellectual stimulus he probably sorely missed out there in a minor posting far from Rome.) Chapter 9 of this book touches on how truth and history interface. My conclusion, like that of most other people, is that when it comes to history, truth is relative.

First, there is the inadvertent fiction that can easily creep into history, created by that sense of narrative that is so tempting. Another obstacle is described by Daniel Leech-Wilkinson, writing about music of the Middle Ages:

> Often it's not easy to see exactly where this invention [the inadvertent fiction] happens, because each step that a scholar takes in forming and setting out their view is a small one, and necessarily fits well with views that colleagues already hold. Otherwise it could never be accepted, and scholars never propose views that have no chance of being taken up: there are market forces that limit what they may safely propose if they want any kind of career. But when you add all those small steps together, over a long enough time, a view of the subject gets built up that is far more specific and detailed than can possibly be confirmed by the small amount of hard evidence that survives. Each new step uses some medieval evidence as its basis, but the way that evidence is read is very largely determined by the nature of views already accepted.[43]

The end result, as Leech-Wilkinson explains, is theories "that look plausible but that could be wildly wrong."

As long as musicology communicates by words and not by acts, it can only go so far in helping musicians. There are innumerable details of music too subtle to be described in words that are nevertheless of decisive importance for the character and style of a performance. These nuances can only be investigated and communicated in the context of musical performance; musicologists who are not musicians will never find them. As Leech-Wilkinson wrote, "True, there was evidence brought together that would have been hard to ignore," but "it was music-making, not scholarship, that changed medieval music history."[44] Christopher Page writes of medieval music, "The dilemma faced by musicology has not changed:

either one works minutely, assembling fragments of evidence that some day in the future may accumulate to such an extent that a picture becomes visible; or one takes what one has and guesses the rest. Only the latter can lead to performances."[45]

I speak here of musicians and musicologists as separate people, but as time goes on, more and more individuals are full-fledged members of both groups. That is not surprising. In HIP, the two activities are part of the same subject.

Dolmetsch mistrusted musicologists, who in his day had little to offer him as a musician. The comments in his book are trenchant, and his impatience is amusing, "What avails it to know when the grandfather's uncle of a certain lutenist was baptized, or how many wives he had, if neither the lutenist's music nor a lute is procurable? We crave to hear the music itself in its original form, and this is what the 'musicologue' hardly ever thinks about."[46] And as Dreyfus points out, HIP has always had a platform that resists and undermines some of the goals of the musicology of the postwar generation as well. Musicologists like Frederick Neumann (with agendas not always fully explained) criticized players for their lack of rigor, and for using empirical methods (i.e., actually trying out historical notions in real music before they had been "proven" to be "true"). This latter is an argument of long-standing.

It has to be said that musicology has not always been HIP's friend. For most of musicology's own brief history it has been under the thrall of Romantic stylistic premises, through which it has systematically misunderstood certain aspects of seventeenth- and eighteenth-century music. It has ignored fundamental issues and argued over irrelevancies. As Fabian points out, "the scholarly preoccupation with 'local' and 'inessential' issues such as the execution of trills or the use of over-dotting fostered pedantry and diverted attention from the more significant matters of metre, rhythmic flexibility and the improvisatory character of decoration."[47] When it met in Los Angeles, the American Musicological Society twice had Sol Babitz, a distinguished violinist and one of the honored pioneers of HIP, physically thrown out of its meetings by the police. At the time, Babitz's historical discoveries were disconcerting, and his manner of presenting them may have been different from that of many musicologists.

There are also times when musicology turns up information that is awkward for performers, as, for example, Joshua Rifkin's conclusion that Bach's "choirs" were normally made up of only one voice per part (OVPP; the orchestra remains at standard Period strength). The rationale has been explained in a recent book by Andrew Parrott.[48] He suggests that being used to a large choir for Bach's works is like listening to string quartets played by an orchestra. In practice, the effect of OVPP depends on the quality of the specific singers; we have to learn how to make it work. Potential advantages include enhanced drama in the voices (as vocal parts can use much more expressive nuance) and more clearly audible instrumental lines. Here's the first OVPP recording of the *St. Matthew Passion.*

🔊 **AUDIO SAMPLE:** 50. Gabrieli Consort & Players, McCreesh, 2002. Bach: "O Mensch, bewein dein Sünde groß," *Matthew Passion*

It's typical of the Period music scene that while there have been great and profound discussions about OVPP, everybody involved—on both sides—makes recordings of Bach's cantatas that involve women instead of boys on the soprano and alto solo parts. That is manifestly not what Bach did, and the difference is musically more significant than if they were to use a piano instead of a harpsichord in the continuo, or a flute instead of a violin in an aria. The result is that more than 80% of Bach's cantatas have never been recorded with the original voice types Bach used![49]

When all is said and done, historical musicology is still meant to act as a foundation of verifiable history on which performance practice can be constructed. Without it, we easily drift away from Period style, as we are now drifting away from copying original instruments. Performance practice is to performing musicians what original instruments are to makers, and manuscript sources are to publishers: a fund of reliable historical information that can be periodically revisited and reconsidered as both we, and it, change with time.

Romantic and Baroque Audiences Compared

Professional musicians nowadays tend to look patronizingly at amateur performers. In our society, a "professional" is a certified expert, and those who do music for recreation are unlikely to have the same skills (if for no other reason than that they do not devote time enough to developing them). But in the Baroque period, the relationship between performers and audience was different.

First of all, there were many more amateurs who were excellent musicians. The leisured class had time to cultivate and become proficient in music. It is entirely possible (though history is unlikely ever to discover it) that in those days amateurs were sometimes better performers than professionals. Second, making music was not regarded by the upper class as a commercial activity; to make money from music would have been a bit like expecting a monetary reward for volunteer social work today. Accepting payment for music-making was demeaning and distancing; it made one a member of the "staff." Roger North, who was an accomplished amateur player of the viol, violin, and organ, referred to professional musicians as "mercenaries" and considered them "a morose, ungentile and unsatisfyed nation."[50] A good "professional" musician in those days was thus a servant, essentially an asset of the better sort, perhaps comparable to a head gardener or a racehorse. The point is they were on a lower level socially than their audience. Few musicians were of Corelli's status, able to count on the indulgence of a patron. "When he was playing a solo at Cardinal Ottoboni's, [Corelli] discovered the Cardinal and another person engaged in discourse, upon which he laid down his instrument; and being asked the reason, gave for answer, that he feared the music interrupted conversation."[51]

People going to a concert or the theater in the seventeenth and eighteenth centuries were often better heeled than the musicians or, for that matter, the theater owner. There was an element of "audience sovereignty" that is unknown now. Until about the first third of the nineteenth century, sovereign audiences considered themselves ultimately in charge of the event.

Obviously, many fewer Baroque concerts were public, that is, open to anyone who could afford a ticket. Among the private and public rituals of the ruling classes were hunting and shooting, balls, salons and dinners, and musical performances. "Much of the music we hear today in public concert halls was composed to adorn such events in the past, to which the public was definitely not admitted."[52] Nor for that matter were the parts the musicians played from in the public domain either. Music was usually privately commissioned and owned (like paintings still are today), and often existed—deliberately—in only one manuscript that was the patron's private property, just like the products of his court painter or pastry chef.

Musicians in the Romantic age were less concerned with an audience's humour, or how their performances influenced it. The new idea of autonomy, and the waning of Rhetoric, eclipsed the Baroque idea of music as *Klang-rede,* a discourse in notes that was meant to affect the mood of an audience. Nor (unlike their eighteenth-century brethren) were nineteenth-century musicians usually performing music conceived for the specific audience that was listening to it. The Romantic artist was not overly concerned with the taste and judgment of the public; geniuses owe more to their muses.

Being indifferent to the reactions of their listeners would have been unthinkable to musicians of the Baroque period. Musicians were, after all, (a) servants, and (b) writing music that was unlikely ever (they thought) to be heard again. Their listeners were their patrons, and sponsors of the event. The audience for this music consisted of invited guests, often connoisseurs, and the music was created for them only, to be enjoyed at that moment only. As servants to their aristocratic audience, musicians, dancers, and actors were there to divert and entertain, just as the entertainment media are today. They could as easily be ignored. With a snap of his fingers, a patron could have a piece or a movement repeated—or stopped. Like the CD now, a concert existed for the convenience of the user.

By the early nineteenth century, the new concert decorum of silent attention was being strongly advocated, as E. T. A. Hoffmann's writings document.[53] In 1803 Goethe also went on record as trying to regulate audience behavior. "'No sign of impatience is permitted to occur. Disapproval may draw attention to itself only through silence, approval only through applause,' and he meant applause that did not interrupt the performance."[54] In France, a periodical in 1802 advised its readers that it was improper at concerts to talk, yawn, sneeze, cough, or "blow one's nose [so as] to shake the windows."[55] Such information was evidently useful to readers.

Since the Romantic Revolution, when the idea of universal participation in the arts came in, audiences have tended to be "lowbrow" in relation to the Classical music they hear. There is a general understanding that it was not written for them, and that there are probably parts of it they cannot understand. Gay writes of Romantic audiences "virtually frozen in the seats as they revelled in the spell of sounds, scarcely breathing, consumed with guilt if they rustled with their program, good 19th-century listeners controlled their appreciation until the designated moment for emotional explosion [the applause] had arrived."[56] And according to Finnegan:

> The role of audience too is of greater significance than at first appears: their apparently 'passive' reception is in fact a positive convention of Classical music performance: it has to be learnt by the audience (a point which comes over clearly when inexperienced attenders, including young children, break the accepted norms and suffer consequential disapproval or rebuke), and is the culturally approved form of audience contribution without which a live Classical performance cannot be successfully enacted.[57]

Decorum had become a serious issue by Wagner's time:

> Patrons of the Wagner festival in Bayreuth proved notoriously militant in the suppression of applause. At an early performance of "Parsifal," listeners hissed an unmusical vulgarian who yelled out "Bravo!" after the Flower Maidens scene. The troublemaker had reason to feel embarrassed; he had written the opera. The Wagnerians were taking Wagner more seriously than he took himself—an alarming development.[58]

While this rigid etiquette may be regarded as more of a social issue than a musical one, the audience's level of comfort has a direct influence on its reception of the music. When "good listening" means "well-behaved listening," correctness becomes an end in itself. One of the more innocent examples of "bad" behavior is applause at "inappropriate" moments during concerts. Applause between movements, for instance, reveals that the individual who claps is not aware that the work is not finished; in other words, they have never heard the piece before or have not read the program (or may even perhaps be unable to read): these are all seen as serious blunders. While performers should in theory be grateful for signs of appreciation at any point during a concert, the usual reaction of musicians to such applause (which invariably stops rather quickly) ranges from patronizing tolerance to obvious disapproval. The depressing message this gives is that decorum is more important than the pleasure of the audience.

The architecture of a modern concert or opera hall is both symbolic of the prevailing idea of what a concert is and discretely implicated in channeling the behavior of the audience in ways that are considered correct. Christopher Small compares it to the theme park, like Disneyland. Modern technology is used to create an artificial environment, often associated with the past, but without the smells and dirt.[59]

The modern concert hall is normally hermetically sealed from the outside world and rarely even has windows; music is meant for contemplation and needs privacy and distance from the world.

Christopher Small makes some astute observations on concert halls. They usually separate strictly the ceremonies of socializing and listening, by providing a foyer for the former, often with a bar. The hall proper with its seats attached to the floor allows no convenient space for standing and chatting. The seats enforce immobility on the members of the audience, and they all face toward the conductor's podium, which is the center of attention. Priorities were evidently different in the eighteenth century. A French architect observed in the 1760s that, because of the angles of the partitions between the boxes, "one has to stand to see the stage in all our theatres."[60]

Communication among members of the audience is discouraged by the hall's design. That design also lets them understand that they are there to listen, not to "talk back." They are passive recipients, and the days when there were riots at musical premieres, like Stravinsky's *Rite of Spring* in Paris in 1913, are long gone. Concert audiences today pride themselves on being well behaved.[61]

One very powerful influence on the quality of a theatrical experience is the management of the lights. Darkening the theater during performances was not practical until the advent of electric lighting, developed at the end of the nineteenth century. House lights began to be lowered at La Scala, for instance, in Toscanini's time (1898). This was one of the moves initiated by theater managers during the middle of the nineteenth century, intended to moderate audience sovereignty and to prohibit vocal and rowdy behavior. Chairs began to be bolted to the floor, and the audience's actions and movements were restricted in various ways. The audience was not only fairly helpless in the dark, but contact between the audience and the performers was lost.

Baroque opera houses, by contrast, were normally lit throughout the performance, "a practice that permitted patrons to converse in an intricate social language spoken by the hand, the eye, the fan, and the lorgnette."[62] Patrick Tucker writes of keeping the house lights on for his productions of Shakespeare, "to make sure that the actors could see the audience."

> This has an extraordinarily powerful theatrical result. In our modern times, for most productions the audience sit in the dark, and the actors are up there on stage in the light—the event is very much divided into Us and Them. This is, however, quite a recent development, and for much of the history of theatre, audiences were very much seen by their actors. The effect is that the actors and audience share just one space. . . . This leads soliloquies to be debates between the character and the audience.[63]

A paradox of modern concert decorum is the contrast between the intensity of emotional experience and the seemingly reserved demeanor of the participants.

> Such passionate outpourings of sound are being created by staid-looking ladies and gentlemen dressed uniformly in black and white, making the minimal amount of bodily gesture that is needed to produce the sounds, their expressionless faces concentrated on a piece of paper on a stand before them, while their listeners sit motionless and equally expressionless listening to the sounds.[64]

Rhetorical audiences were evidently more expressive of their reactions. Bartel writes of the Baroque period:

> The audience for its part did not assume an aesthetic-reflective or distanced and critical stance [as in Canonic music]. The presented affection enveloped the listener, causing a direct and spontaneous reaction. He was not free to control himself; rather he was controlled by the realized affection, spontaneously breaking into laughter or weeping, sorrow or longing, rage or contentment. Numerous contemporary eyewitness accounts refer to the intensity and grand effect of such affection-arousing compositions, causing the entire audience to break spontaneously into sobbing and wailing.[65]

For modern audiences, even positive reactions are discouraged (except applause, but only at the end of pieces). "To boo at the end of a performance one has particularly disliked is possible, though a bit extreme." It is strictly against etiquette to show any visible or audible reaction in the course of the performance, of either approval or disapproval, the kind that is common and perfectly legitimate at the end of a jazz solo.[66]

In Mozart's and Beethoven's day it was not unusual to applaud after each movement, often with the purpose of getting a repeat. Mozart wrote to his father from Vienna in 1781 how pleased he was with an audience that shouted bravos while he was playing a piano solo. As Gay comments, "He would have taken unbroken silence as a sign of disapproval."[67] In some places, audiences of the nineteenth century applauded during movements; Brahms wrote in a letter that "Joachim played my piece [the

Violin Concerto] better at each rehearsal, and the Cadenza sounded so beautiful at the actual concert that the public applauded it into the start of the Coda."[68]

To us, the most shocking example of unseemly behavior was at the opera in the eighteenth century. Brought up as we are with the notion that an audience receives an opera with the same devoted absorption as a symphony or indeed a sermon, we are disturbed to discover that "people took for granted that they would socialize during parts of the performance; they had often made appointments to meet and would move between boxes or parts of the hall."[69] Smoke from the stage lights (a mixture of tallow candles and oil lamps) "filled the front of the theatre with thick, ill-smelling smoke," and spectators sometimes saw each other better than the stage.[70]

Burney wrote in the 1770s, "I shall have frequent occasion to mention the noise and inattention at the musical exhibitions in Italy; but music there is cheap and common, whereas in England it is a costly exotic, and more highly prized."[71] Burney elsewhere compared "the silence which reigns in the theatres of London and Paris" with "the inattention, noise, and indecorum of the audience . . . quite barbarous and intolerable" in Bologna.[72]

Well-to-do Italian families went to their box at the opera with their household staff and servants, so they could take meals, entertain guests, and generally carry on their daily business. Audiences, it seems, regarded the entertainment on the stage much like modern families think of television at home, as part of the routine of life (rather than as masterpieces by geniuses).

The Paris Opéra was apparently noisy as well. Johnson quotes the comment of a late eighteenth-century visitor that "a conversation as loud as it was continuous covers the voices of the actors."[73]

From contemporary descriptions, the atmosphere at eighteenth-century operas sounds like that of a baseball or soccer game today. Like at a modern ball game, the crowd may seem indifferent and inattentive, but are instantly focused when something significant happens; it may well have been the same for concerts in the past. Madame de Sévigné recalled that she was unable to hold back her tears at the "Plainte italienne" during Lully's *Psyché* (1678).[74] Le Cerf de la Viéville wrote in 1704 of the Paris Opéra,

> A number of times in Paris, when the duet of *Persée*, so learnedly written and so difficult, *Les vents impétueux*, etc., was well given, I have seen the entire public, similarly attentive, remain for the half of a quarter-hour without breathing, with their eyes fixed upon Phineus and Merope, and when the duet was finished, nod to each other to indicate the pleasure it had given them.[75]

The exceedingly formal behavior protocol in concerts of Classical music actually works to discourage the principal purpose of a concert of

Baroque music, which is to move the spirits of the listeners. Despite Arnold Dolmetsch's attempts to moderate this formality by putting on his concerts at home, talking with his audience, dressing in Period costume, stopping in the middle of pieces and trying again, and discouraging applause, HIP has not yet managed to differentiate itself from typical Classical concert decorum.

Period Musicians in Victorian Outfits

In the nineteenth century, normal concert decorum prescribed full evening dress for both musicians and audience. Nowadays things are less formal for the audience, who are hardly ever in full formal dress. The musicians are another story: they continue to preserve a custom that was standard a hundred years ago. Frozen in time, their late nineteenth-century clothes are entirely appropriate for the repertoire they usually play and the instruments they play it on.

I wish I could say that Period performers don't engage in Period costuming, but many of them do. What is pathetic is that they don't wear silly, artsy "Olde Englishe" outfits as Dolmetsch used to do, or authentic waistcoats and wigs. Instead, they imitate their Modernist brethren, and dress up as late nineteenth-century musicians. The message they send is that they are *wannabe* "Romantic" musicians too. I see it as no coincidence that the custom of wearing tails for Rhetorical music concerts became common in the 1980s, concurrent with the rise of Strait style and interpretive conductors for HIP ensembles.

8

Ways of Copying the Past

Emulation and Replication:
Two Renaissance Approaches to Imitation

Imitating art works of the past is what the Renaissance was all about. Writers, historians, sculptors, painters, and architects studied and copied the models of antiquity, and the same kinds of issues that occupy Period musicians today were discussed at length then. The subject of *imitatio* preoccupied thinkers and generated masses of writing.

The Renaissance principle of imitation was in fact two separate concepts. One was the imitation of Nature (Mimesis), the other involved imitating earlier works. It is the second type that interests us here. It is generally known nowadays as "the imitation of art."[1] When a Renaissance artist or writer copied an already-existing work, they might do it in different ways. The most common were:

- *translatio*, absolute copying, called here "replication,"
- *imitatio*, eclectic borrowing, and
- *emulatio*, emulation, copying with improvement or enhancement.

The Emulation Principle

The humanists who invented Seconda Pratica at the end of the sixteenth century were participating in a wave of thought that attempted to square their devotion to antiquity with confidence in their own creative powers.

"It was a general Renaissance view that present efforts could equal and perhaps surpass classical achievements."[2] Emulation—*emulatio*—was their paradigm.

"Emulation," according to the *OED*, is "to copy or imitate with the object of equalling or excelling." As a component of the word "emulation," the element of surpassing the model is unfamiliar to most of us today. But the idea is common enough. "Emulation" indicates the kind of copying that produced Stokowski's Bach arrangements, for instance, Pleyel harpsichords, and Mozart's reworkings of Handel's works.

Emulation was common in the Baroque period, as Peter Paul Rubens's retouchings of works by well-known artists indicate.

> It is not so much that Rubens was making the past live as that he saw himself as part of a living and constantly changing tradition, singing with new verses a song passed down from one generation to the next. Insofar as his work continued the progress of painting, the whole body of past art became identical in a larger sense with his own contribution. In his copies and retouchings, Rubens thus carried to a consistent end Quintilian's idea that each artist's work develops from and transforms the work of his predecessors.[3]

A good example of emulative mode in Baroque times was the stage costumes in plots involving antiquity: a Baroque actress playing a Roman queen did not dress in Roman style, as she would really have done in antiquity; she was completely "à la mode" in Baroque style.

Mendelssohn "emulated" Bach in 1829 in much the same way Wagner did later for Beethoven, and Stokowski did in the 1950s. Harnoncourt dryly suggests that, in the same spirit, a performance of Brahms today should really be emulated, or brought up to date, by someone like Stockhausen to be "worthy of the attention of a modern audience."[4]

The emulation principle motivated HIP performance as well. Wanda Landowska, who passionately embraced Period style as a principle and equally passionately flouted it when she had her own ideas, once wrote, "I am aware that the disposition of the registers in the harpsichords of Bach's time differed somewhat from those of my Pleyel. But little do I care if, to attain the proper effect, I use means that were not exactly those available to Bach."[5] Looked at from today's perspective, this statement is breathtaking in its "incorrectness." "Little do I care" is not good form for Period players, let alone the admission that the hardware was "not exactly that available to Bach." Avoiding such statements is probably the first thing a historical performer learns these days.

The French piano firm of Pleyel would not be such a notorious example of the emulation principle if Landowska had not made it famous. Pleyel's iron-framed "harpsichords" eventually became synonymous with instruments vaguely inspired by the past but accommodated to later taste in construction, sound, and feel (in this case, a taste presumably engendered by the piano). Pleyel's interpretation of a harpsichord can still be heard on recordings of Landowska and some of her students, made starting in the early 1930s.

That both the makers and players like Landowska were open and honest in discussing this difference between "what was" and what "should be now" suggests that they considered it normal and acceptable that these modes were not the same. The prevailing mentality seems to have allowed the Pleyel workshop to feel at ease making such an instrument, and Landowska to feel comfortable playing it.

What justified Pleyel's conviction that what they were making was a "harpsichord," even though they were perfectly aware that it differed in many important and obvious ways from any historical example? Despite the stylistic errors, it can be argued that disrespect for the past was not the issue. Early twentieth-century musicians were seeing history chronocentrally, in a different relationship to themselves from how we see it now in relation to us. This remains the mind-set of Modern style music-making, which looks on its main repertoire, written over a century and a half ago, as valid contemporary art.

Before the shift in the late 1950s and 1960s, when emulation was the principle in instrument-making, instrument makers must not have thought of making deliberate replicas as the central issue; even Arnold Dolmetsch, HIP's original conscience, was relatively free with his instrument designs (raising the pitch of his recorders to 440, for instance, and designing a harpsichord with the specific purpose of making it fit in a London cab). (Many recorders these days are still altered from their original pitches to play at A-415.) All the so-called historical instruments made before the 1960s, like organs, harpsichords, and gambas, were the designs of their makers: impressions and personal interpretations of the past.

The Replication Principle

It was in the mid-1960s that another, humbler mind-set became common in HIP: the principle of exact replication of instruments, their pitches, and musical notation; in fact, every facet of Period musicking. This new concern with the physical parameters of Period musicking, like the size of ensembles and the instruments themselves, became the issues that constituted the popular meaning of Authenticity.[6]

Record jackets began to announce the use of "ORIGINAL INSTRUMENTS" or "HISTORICAL INSTRUMENTS.") Those little proclamations were not there just for documentation. They were, as they say, "commercial"; they sold—or were thought to help sell—the recordings. They reflected a new curiosity in those days about original instruments—always during concert intermissions there were people on stage looking at the harpsichord (often from underneath). On the old Teldec Bach cantata recordings, for instance, the liner notes were in a strict hierarchy of font sizes. I'm looking at one as I write. Of the credits, the biggest font, in small caps, is the conductor (HARNONCOURT or LEONHARDT), followed by the name of the ORCHESTRA, then the **vocal soloists and choir** in bold, then, in the smallest font of all, the names of the musicians and finally, in the same font, the makers and dates of their instruments.[7] I always found it remarkable that the instruments were apparently regarded as of equal importance and status with their players, as if instruments were somehow transmitting the message of the past.

There are rewards associated with replication. Things become clear that were mysterious before, logic appears in what seemed mistaken courses, "new" discoveries and understandings emerge. This is the Serendipity effect at work.

Imitation in the Canonic System

Copying of any kind is strictly prohibited in the Canonic system. Although the great masterpieces might serve as general inspiration, imitation breaks the rule of originality. Hence the discomfort of music historians who find regular and frequent instances of *imitatio* in the mature work of "great" composers like Monteverdi and Handel (who had never heard of originality!).

"The present pejorative meaning of 'copy' is of relatively recent origin," writes Lowenthal. "During antiquity, copying was not distinguished from creative innovation; all works of art and architecture were viewed as copies. . . . Copying was common in late-Roman and Hellenistic times. . . . Throughout the Middle Ages, artists and craftsmen copied their own masters and other prototypes with no notion that originality was desirable." Humanist "architects and sculptors copied great works of antiquity (or more often their Hellenistic copies) and artists copied each other."[8] This attitude seems strange to us now, looking at it from the other side of the Romantic Revolution. As Wittkower put it,

> We witness a new approach to the whole province of art, an approach that eventually destroyed the belief in the value and virtue of imitation. The toiling scholar-artist was replaced by the genius who invents—to quote Addison— "by the mere strength of natural parts and without any assistance of art and learning." His work was regarded as the gift of a unique mind sovereignly dictating his own laws, and from this point of view any form of imitation appeared to be plagiarism.[9]

In the nineteenth century, imitation was replaced by *influence,* a concept that preoccupied critics and historians of the Romantic period.

> The curriculum at the [Renaissance] classical academies, which was based on drawing from Early and modern models, was seen as the necessary preparation for emulation, the step forward into creative self-realisation, as if in competition with one's antecedents. . . . the modern educational ideal has been to encourage self-determination from the start—and this encouraged even the student to think of imitation as shameful.[10]

Style-Copying and Work-Copying

A copy of an object or act from the past can be of two kinds. It can be a replica or facsimile—that is, a clone or reproduction of an existing work. Making such a copy implies the existence of an original. Let's call this *work-copying*. The other kind of copy does not reproduce something that already exists or once existed. Most fake paintings, for instance, do not copy a specific work already known; they copy the style (as it is perceived at the time), but the artist makes up new paintings. Skowroneck used this principle in making his "Lefébure" harpsichord (described below); there was no original. And we as musicians do not reproduce any specific performance, but apply our general knowledge of Period style to any piece from the given time and place. For this concept, I propose the term *style-copying*. In style-copying, the style is extrapolated from all the works of a particular artist, or even all the works of his period or country, and this style is applied when making a new performance.

This dichotomy extends to other disciplines. Collingwood made a similar distinction in studying history. He called the accumulation of the "outsides" of events (discovering what happened instead of why it happened) the making of chronicle rather than history. Chronicle is a simple organization of statements, or testimony, from received records of the past. Trill charts, for instance, and repertoire lists, and biographies. But history doesn't use just any kind of testimony, it looks for evidence. Evidence is testimony that answers a specific question.[11] The concept of evidence in history is analogous to style-copying, which in this case would consist of understanding style by using inference (if a trill is seen to work in one situation, generalizations can be made that allow one to deduce where else trills will be appropriate—or better yet, desirable). So, to play trills authentically requires that one understand what purposes they served. The ability to apply a style generally, to "get" it, and start using it elsewhere is not something that can be done by rote.[12] Linguists call this *linguistic competence:* the ability to extrapolate new but correct expressions in a foreign language and to reject unacceptable ones.[13]

M. J. Friedländer said in his well-known book *On Art and Connoisseurship,* "A forgery done by a contemporary is not infrequently successful . . . because the forger has understood, and misunderstood, the old master in the same way as ourselves."[14] Since style depends on current perceptions, style-copying is also based on current perceptions that are subject to change with the passing of time.

In the art world, the most famous example of style-copying is the work of van Meegeren. There is no difference in principle between how van Meegeren applied Vermeer's techniques (color, light, and materials) to new and original subjects and compositions, and a musician like Gustav Leonhardt playing a concert of Couperin's music, imitating Couperin's playing style or the playing style of the era of Louis XIV, on an instrument imitating the action and framing of the style of harpsichord Couperin would have used. The difference lies in how they are presented and marketed.

Style-copying is also used in the dubious enterprise known as the art market. It could in fact be blamed for its shaky foundation; the art market is based on the personal opinions of art critics. As in the violin market, which has the same dodgy feel to it, the problem is that sums of money out of proportion to the real values of the objects—are fixed on the attribution of artist to work. Art experts use two different strategies in attribution: the first is "style criticism" (recognizing a personal style; also known as "connoisseurship"). The other, called "source criticism," uses outside information, like dating the wood of the frame or using a history of ownership.[15] The problem with the first strategy, style criticism, is that it ultimately depends on the second: "If not a single work were attributed to Mozart in autographs, authentic copies, authorized prints and the like, there would be no 'Mozart style',"[16] with its unique traits, on which to base judgements.

Musical scholars being an objective, positivist crowd, connoisseurship appears undependable as a means of identifying composers. (Much of Bach's instrumental music, lacking source information, is still undated because Bach scholars argue like lawyers, and style criticism is incapable of convincing them.)

I've introduced here two sets of dichotomies: replication/emulation and work-copying/style-copying. Are the two pairs one and the same? Replication and work-copying are very close, as you have to have the "work" in order to make a replica of it. But emulation and style-copying are almost in opposition. Where emulation can casually use a group of works as inspiration (as neoclassicism did, for instance), style-copying is concerned with authentic and accurate imitation. Style-copying is replication, but not of specific works.

Style-copying is what most Period musicians do in performing. They aren't reproducing some specific past concert, which would be work-copying. So (as I'll discuss below) although it's true that we musicians and listeners are different from the original auditors and do not have "Period ears," it's not particularly relevant; it is the style as we now perceive it that is important, not the literal re-enactment of some historical event.

"Talking to Ghosts" and Work-Copying

One of Richard Taruskin's more memorable sentences is the following: "To put my thesis in a nutshell, I hold that 'historical' performance today is not really historical; that a specious veneer of historicism clothes a performance style that is completely of our own time, and is in fact the most modern style around."[17]

Majestic as it is, this declaration bobs rather ignominiously in the wake of Harnoncourt's many statements on his relation with the past, such as this one: "It would be absolutely senseless to come to know and understand this music, to want to perform it as 'early music,' from the point of view of musicologists or musical archivists. We are contemporary, living musicians, not scholars of antiquity."[18] And Wanda Landowska's honest statement of a hundred years ago: "If Rameau himself would rise from his grave to demand of me some changes in my interpretation of his Dauphine, I would answer, 'You gave birth to it; it is beautiful. But now leave me alone with it. You have nothing more to say; go away!'"[19]

Critics of HIP often have the mistaken idea that Period musicking is meant to clone an actual concert that once took place: a work-copy, in other words, of some specific musical event. Piers Adams of the ensemble Red Priest attributes this idea to HIP, "There is a paradox at the heart of the whole 'authentic' movement—the very act of re-creating some hypothetical past performance is in itself 'inauthentic.'"[20] Harnoncourt, who has been doing Period musicking longer than most of us, cites Nietzsche, "The really historical performance would talk to ghosts."[21] Nobody has time or interest for that. Harnoncourt writes: "Ich tue das nicht, und ich habe das auch noch nie gemacht" ("I don't do that, and what's more have never done it").[22] Back in 1954, the British Period style pioneer and teacher Thurston Dart wrote, "It is impossible for anyone living today to hear early music with the ears of those who first heard it, and it is idle to pretend otherwise."[23]

Nostalgia is not the subject of this book. I'm not talking about the wistful yearning for some past period or irrecoverable condition; that's more appropriate in a book about Romanticism. The past may be very good material for inspiration, but it's gone now. Here is a typical remark by Harnoncourt on the Concentus Musicus's first performance of the *St. Matthew Passion*, made in 1970, "What we accomplished was not the revival of an historical sound, not a museum-like restoration of sounds belonging to the past. It was a modern performance, an interpretation thoroughly grounded in the 20th century."[24] Landowska, unashamedly incorrect, wrote further, "At no time in the course of my work have I ever tried to reproduce exactly what the old masters did. Instead, I study, I scrutinize, I love, and I recreate . . . I am sure that what I am doing in regard to sonority, registration etc., is very far from the historical truth."[25]

The Kon-Tiki Observation

As Bernard Sherman put it, "Music historians try to find out what happened in the past, performers try to make something happen now."[26] One method they use helps keep their project practical: instead of studying and reproducing individual events (which would be work-copying), they keep things general, concentrating on style.

Piers Adams writes, "[Red Priest] are not claiming that our performances are 'authentic' in the sense that the music might actually have sounded like that, nor, strange as it may seem, are we even especially concerned whether or not the composers themselves would have enjoyed our take on their music."[27]

Thor Heyerdahl, in *The Kon-Tiki Expedition* (1951), told the story of the raft he and his colleagues built and sailed across the Pacific.[28] They did it to show that Incas could have done the same. Heyerdahl wrote that "we did not mean to eat aged llama flesh or dried kumara potatoes on our trip" because *Kon-Tiki* was meant to reconstruct one aspect of the past, not to pretend "that we had once been Indians ourselves. Our intention was to test the performance and quality of the Inca raft, its seaworthiness and loading capacity."[29]

In my experience, very few historical performers are interested in pretending "that we had once been Indians ourselves." After all, neither costumes nor postures can be transmitted over the radio or on a CD, while musical style can. The nature of Bach's audience is no more relevant to what Period performers are doing now than aged llama flesh or dried kumara potatoes would be—or wigs and candles.[30] These elements are not part of the project.

In his new book, Peter Walls even assembled a list of Period practices that we have—until now—rejected as "obsolete," like beating time with a large wooden staff.[31] He does note that the line between useless and usable is being constantly reevaluated. As an example of an ambiguous case, he cites Quantz's advice about touching the traverso's headjoint to one's powdered wig to stop slipperiness on the embouchure due to perspiration.

"What Really Happened" in History

Daniel Leech-Wilkinson writes, "We hear what we believe; we cannot know what it is that they heard."[32] He is right to be skeptical, as he is writing about medieval music, the most extreme form of historical music. The problems in trying to recover seventeenth- and eighteenth-century music are magnified in medieval music. "We know almost nothing with certainty of the sound of music prior to 1500," Harnoncourt writes, "Everything achieved up to the present in this area is hypothetical in nature, and will remain so forever because this music in its true form has died away once and for all."[33]

In his perceptive new book, *The Modern Invention of Medieval Music*, Leech-Wilkinson comments:

> There is nothing against which to measure or check the correctness of one's conjectures. They may be strengthened or weakened by the chance discovery of more evidence, but there are no 'controls'. Too many things might have happened at any point for one to know what did. . . . It is very tempting to say that despite all this we can come to some understanding of 'how it was'. But realistically we cannot, and if by chance we did we couldn't know that we had. To do musicology honestly, therefore, one has to let go of any claim

to, or any belief in, being right when one offers a hypothesis as a result of one's research.

This means accepting that all our research into "how it was really played"—performance practice—amounts to theories that, though plausible, cannot be proven. (Not that they are less interesting or less usable for being unprovable!)

Historians talk about the idea of *wie es eigentlich gewesen* (what really happened—or, as Dulak calls it, "the one true past").[34] They are obliged to accept that, as Collingwood put it, "The past is simply non-existent; and every historian feels this in his dealings with it."[35] Leon J. Goldstein writes:

> In terms of what, after all, are we to decide that something is evidence for something else, or that of two somewhat divergent accounts of what purports to be the same occurrence one is better than the other? It is clearly not in terms of what really happened when the past was present, since that is not available for the historian's inspection. And this leaves only the discipline itself, the principles and criteria in terms of which it assesses the cogency and acceptability of putative historical evidence.[36]

It follows that the past is not somehow *there*, fixed and unchanging, *wie es eigentlich gewesen*, seen by an ideal observer, while our knowledge of it is *here*, "approximating, more or less closely, to the independent reality of historical fact."[37] Goldstein writes of the "ideal observer":

> Some writers seem to think that . . . the full meaning of a description of a past event is precisely what would appear to an observer, or ideal observer, witnessing the event. But a God's-eye view of the course of human events would not be an historical view of it, nor would an account certified as true by God, *i.e.*, a work of divine revelation, be an historical account. An historical account is one which is the outcome of the application of the methods and techniques of historical inquiry, and these do not include the reports of ideal observers.[38]

This being true, the hard conclusion is that history needs to be rewritten on a regular basis as, with the passage of time, our points of view and perspective on the past modify, and other evidence appears.

Beyond History: The Shelf Life of Historical Evidence

Indeed, the very definition of historical facts is subjective; as Collingwood formulated it,[39] "evidence is not evidence until it makes something evident." And what we may want to be "made evident" will also change with time. This means, logically, that the evidence itself will alter along with our changing perceptions of it. Thus, historical evidence can have a "pull-date," and with it, every aspect of musicking that depends on that evidence.

An example is Stokowski, who may sound funny today, but can be respected for his contributions to the music of his day; we can even perceive some of his greatness and that of the musicians who played for him.

While we are appalled at the style of some early recordings, we can appreciate how they might have been effective for an earlier audience with different expectations.

Leech-Wilkinson takes the example of an esteemed medievalist of a half-century ago, Gustav Reese. Nowadays, much of his work is regarded as out of date. But, as Leech-Wilkinson points out, in its time Reese's teaching was of great use to many people; "the fact that it now looks 'wrong' need not invalidate it." To say this would be "to fall into exactly the same trap that medievalists so often warn against, that of reading a text anachronistically, measuring it against values of another time. Read according to the æsthetic premises and beliefs of his own time, Reese was of course right."[40]

This is my thought when I read Ton Koopman's idea of a new generation of "hipsters too cool for authenticity" that skips the study of sources:

> Younger players . . . go off and make music, relying on what the earlier generations have taught them. I think that's dangerous because, if we are wrong, the next generation should find out our mistakes, and correct us. . . . I'm certain we made mistakes, especially in unresolved problems like rubato, where we have very few sources to go on. I hope the next generation will discover new sources and reveal new answers in them.[41]

Seen from the perspective of a pull-date, if history is forever changing, it would be remarkable if these young hipsters didn't regard many of our solutions as mistakes. M. J. Friedländer, writing of art fakes, remarked, "We laugh at the mistakes of our fathers, as our descendents will laugh at us."

With the existence of musical recordings for over a century now, the ability to hear details of performance from another style period is ours. The capacity to step outside our present style and look at it with a degree of objectivity is a great gift. I love Robert Philip's comparison of old recordings to "a telescope outside the earth's atmosphere—less local interference."[42]

Speaking of circumventing "local interference" and managing to reach the unadulterated historical sound, accurate original recordings of musical performances do exist in the form of mechanical musical instruments from the eighteenth century and before. These instruments recorded contemporary performances of pieces by composers like Handel, Emanuel Bach, Haydn, Mozart, and Beethoven. As David Fuller writes, these are "real recordings from the past, completely free of any ideas about performance conceived since the 18th century." Mechanical instruments had reached a high degree of accuracy by the early seventeenth century. These instruments conserve valuable information on some of the subtlest and most controversial mysteries of performance history, including tempos, articulations, gracing, notes inégales, and other rhythmic mannerisms, not to mention rubato. They have been largely ignored until now. Fuller observes, "When and if all the data come in that are hidden away in mechanical instruments, the performance books are going to have to be rewritten."[43]

One very precise form of automatic musical instrument was developed by Père Engramelle, who explained his discoveries in his book *La tonotechnie* (1775). Engramelle's technique involved the conversion of keyboard performances to pins and staples on a cylinder and required him to analyze musical technique in a uniquely detailed way. Mechanical instruments were able to communicate rhythm very precisely, and the schematics in his book are easily transferred to computer. His book included charts for pinning twelve pieces of music. Here is an example, a reconstruction by computer based on an Engramelle diagram:

 AUDIO SAMPLE: 51. Balbastre: *Romance* (1779)

Schmitz and Ord-Hume comment on Engramelle's charts:

> From this can be drawn several interesting observations: all tempos are strikingly fluid; endings are clearly retarded; the inequality of *notes inégales* ranges in proportion from 3:1 to 9:7; staccato takes precedence over legato; there are minute gradations of staccato (which is, however, normally extremely short), and there are similarly fine shades of differentiation for legato; grace notes are short and invariably fall on the beat; no trills maintain the same rapidity throughout.[44]

Rewriting the performance books, indeed! Early twentieth-century recordings can be of use as well, as Philip points out: "The recordings have preserved the general performance practice of the period in great detail, and the detail includes habits which are scarcely mentioned, if at all, in written documents. The recordings therefore shed light on the limitations of documentary evidence in any period, not just in the early twentieth century."[45] In other words, what do we not know about eighteenth-century performance, since we only have written information, and lack recordings?

Regardless of how different it sounds to us now, if a performing style is successful today, it must share the basic—and often unspoken—components of our contemporary musical culture. Our modern Period style surely shares our present æsthetic. A good case can be made for the idea that all the music of a given period, regardless of its genre, is connected by a deep underpinning of similar style. Church music from the 1930s, for instance, has a certain resemblance to popular songs of the same decade: they share, happily or not, a similar conception of performing style; the container is similar even if the contents are different. As Sorrell suggests, it is quite possible that an eighteenth-century musician, were they to travel forward to our time, might more easily notice the difference between jazz and Classical styles than the superficial differences between what we call "Period" performing style and what is normally considered "modern."

If the spirit of improvisation is so important in Baroque music, then only an expert improviser can come close to its essence. Although wildly irreverent of the letter, the improvisations of Django Reinhardt, Eddie South,[46] and Stéphane Grapelli on Bach may communicate more of the spirit of his age, despite all the mannerisms and paraphernalia of the 20th century, than the self-consciously learned accounts by some of the more inhibited groups on the authenticity bandwagon.[47]

🎧 **AUDIO SAMPLE: 52.** Eddie South, Stéphane Grappelly (!), Django Reinhardt, Paul Cordonnier, Paris 1937. Bach: Double Violin Concerto (swing version).

What an eighteenth-century musician would think is not something we can know, or need to know. We can only act on our own best knowledge; as long as we think our Period style sounds like the real thing, it achieves its purpose. "We hear what we believe." This, despite our definition of the "real thing" as a performing protocol that we *think* the composer's contemporaries would have accepted as normal (and even—we venture to hope—pleasant).

What's Wrong with Anachronisms

If it's true that nothing in history can be proven definitively, how can we talk meaningfully about anachronisms? If all of history's so-called facts are merely provisional hypotheses based on evidence and plausibility that are accepted by the majority of experts until they are replaced with better ones, what's wrong with anachronisms? Plenty, as far as I'm concerned.

First of all, about history, provisional as it indeed is. It may not be ideal, but it's the best we've got and we still depend on it for our ideas of the past and the traditions of our culture. It's like the dictionary. We all know that it's impossible to define words except with other words that cannot themselves be defined except with other words, and so on. That doesn't stop us from finding dictionaries useful. Nor do we need to throw history overboard; we do need to keep the idea in the back of our minds that it's a house of cards, not a house of concrete.

Our "Period Bach" style, for instance, is carefully honed by music historians and performers, and constantly compared to historical evidence and new ideas. Period Bach style is not Bach's style, of course. It is ours, using Bach's as an ideal. We accept its criteria provisionally, since we know updates are on the way. We are in the same position as historians who are only able to take the evidence available and draw the most complete possible information from it; they neither can nor do claim to know what really happened.

We can know no more than our cleverest minds deduce. As Collingwood wrote,

> We can easily conceive the work of medieval history as being done better
> than it was done in the 18th century; but we cannot conceive it as being done
> better than it is in our own times, because if we had a clear idea of how it
> could be done better we should be in a position to do it better.[48]

We have little choice but to act on what we know now; our other option is to ignore history completely.

9

The Medium
Is the Message

Period Instruments

The Instrument Trade-off

Instruments can be seen in terms of Darwinian adaptation. They are constantly changing in small ways to make it easier for musicians to perform the music currently in fashion. There is an immense pressure on instruments to be as well-adapted as possible to the music of their time. Instrument makers are very receptive to the demands of players, and these demands are the immediate cause of mutations. The natural result, as Harnoncourt has written, is that "Each period has precisely the instrumentarium best suited to its own music. In their imagination, composers hear the instruments of their own time and often write with certain instrumentalists in mind."[1]

The years 1760 to 1840 are usually associated with the Industrial Revolution. They also encompassed a series of significant musical developments that led from Galant music to the Romantic/Canonic æsthetic. During that period every kind of musical instrument underwent a fundamental transformation from the Baroque type to the Romantic. String instruments were rebuilt, mainly in order to make them louder and reduce the overtones, giving them a rounder, thicker sound. Woodwinds were redesigned so that each semitone was played with its own dedicated tone hole; this meant adding keys to close those holes when they were not used. Wagner (1873) writes about the brass and how since Beethoven's time they had become chromatic. The general system of tuning changed fundamentally, as leading tones became high rather than low and a new simplifying universal tuning, equal temperament, became common.[2]

This sounds like progress. And no doubt for people alive at the time it felt like it too. But in absolute terms, instrument-making does not operate that way. There are no free lunches. You gain something only by giving up something else. By making one thing easier, another thing gets harder. Keys on woodwinds, for instance, made it easier to play in extreme tonalities by eliminating cross-fingering and making every chromatic note similar in timbre; but this gain was offset by

- the greater difficulty of scales with few accidentals,
- thirds and leading-tones that were less well in tune, and
- the loss of individual character between tonalities.

The instruments of one period are not "better" in some absolute sense than their counterparts in other periods. The traverso, in other words, is not "better" than the Boehm flute except in one way: it is much easier to play eighteenth-century music in eighteenth-century style on an eighteenth-century instrument. Fabian writes, "The dynamic nuances and uneven tonal timbres that are second nature to the baroque flute or baroque bowing have a crucial bearing on articulation as these delineate rhythmic or ornamental groups almost automatically, while a modern flute or violin can only imitate the effect by substitute means such as accenting and agogic inflections."[3] Advances in instrument design are always relative, reflecting demands in the music being played; they are in fact trade-offs, a question of adapting to changing priorities.

In the early nineteenth century, at the height of the heated debate on adding keys to woodwinds, things must have looked different. Louis-Auguste Vény wrote in his oboe method of ca. 1828 that "The common hautboy (the traditional two-keyed "Hautbois ordinaire") is a defective wind instrument; it uses irrational fingerings, uneven tones, and cannot be played in all the keys."[4] Obviously, what is an advance in instrument design depends on your priorities. For playing Corrette or Couperin, the "Hautbois ordinaire" beats Vény's new model hands down. "Irrational fingerings" means cross-fingerings, which do indeed produce an uneven scale and limit the tonalities in which one can play. But when the cross-fingerings were replaced by a key system, many musicians and listeners were unhappy with the homogenized equality of the oboe's sound.

Because of this relativity, it is pointless to consider one phase of an instrument's mutation better or worse. "Better" really means "best-adapted" to the demands of the music, and invariably, that means that matching up music to contemporaneous instruments will offer the best chance of success. (This assumes we fallible musicians can play all these models of instrument competently, of course, which is assuming a great deal.)

The Influence of Instruments on Performing Style

After a generation of playing them, it is clear that while Period instruments can serve to encourage experiment, they have little *direct* effect on a player's stylistic approach to the music.[5] The fact is, as Taruskin writes (paraphrasing the National Rifle Association—or did they get it from him?), "instruments do not play music, people do."[6] What we have discovered is that authenticity is not a product of the instrument being played, but of the musician's sense of style. Style originates, of course, in the player's head (and/or heart). This is where musical "restoration" takes place.

A number of interesting players have discovered how to project Period styles using Romantic hardware. This is wonderful. But it doesn't mean that players of Romantic hardware have suddenly *en masse* started playing Rhetorical music in Period style. Why should they? Nor does it mean that there is any less difference between Period style and Modern style.

While style crossover is possible and desirable, there are real and significant differences between Period and Romantic instruments. These differences do make it easier to play music of a given period on that period's instruments. Baroque style demands quick changes of dynamics, for example. Dynamic change happens more slowly on Romantic instruments, making it problematic to engage the short gestures in the Rhetorical repertoire—these are instruments designed to do long-line phrasing. That is why Romantic instruments, when they play Rhetorical repertoire, often run phrases together, or fail to give them sufficient shape to be completely understandable. Gestures are often difficult, and not usually practicable, whereas long-lines feel natural to play. On the other hand, certain attributes of Period instruments do clearly encourage traits of Period style, such as the way they blend in sound, the inflection of notes using early bows, and the ease with which lines can be articulated with the lower pressure of early wind instruments. As a broad generalization, it could be said that less tension and pressure allow for smaller, subtler gestures and more frequent starts and stops. A bicycle compared to a freight train—each has its advantages and disadvantages.

Back in the 1960s there was an element of motivation involved as well. It seemed obvious that if a musician played a Period instrument, that constituted a guarantee of their commitment to playing in the style that went with it. Why else would one have gone to the trouble of locating a Period instrument, equipping it with the appropriate strings, reeds, mouthpieces, and so forth, and learning to play it? To have done all that would have been pointless if one simply played in Modern style. More logical was to play in Modern style on a mainstream instrument, with an infrastructure in place (teachers, instrument makers and repairmen, schools, method books, jobs in orchestras, etc.).

Conductors who work with both Period and Romantic instruments talk about appropriate and inappropriate instruments. "There is really no substitute for the real thing," comments Koopman, even if that by itself is not enough. Brüggen has said, "When I conduct the Bach B Minor Mass with a modern orchestra, even though we always give our best possible performance, something is always lost, since the musicians play instruments which weren't conceived for that music, especially the strings."[7]

Angela Hewitt, playing Bach on the modern piano, does her best to play lightly, but there is no escaping the soloistic, dominating presence of the piano in small ensembles. (As Joseph Kerman observed, "it is almost impossible to play Mozart emotionally on a modern piano without sounding vulgar."[8]) The Romantic bow does not as willingly shape each note, the Romantic reed does not allow sudden and extreme changes of dynamic, the Romantic key system eliminates the options of alternate fingerings and finger-vibrato.[9]

Helmuth Rilling uses Romantic instruments in his recordings. He thinks they sound better. For many, like me, hearing Bach on these instruments means we have to translate back into the sounds we are used to (i.e., instruments of Bach's time). That probably has to do with our backgrounds and habits; Rilling is used to the sound of Romantic instruments, as I also was when I began my career. My teacher, Raymond Dusté, was a master at playing Bach's oboe solos on his keyed oboe, and I still remember them. I sometimes wonder what the more creative and experimental oboists of the generation before mine would have done with the hautboy (that is, the "Baroque oboe") had it been available to them. They were the teachers, or teachers of the teachers, of the hautboists who are now playing and recording.

Romantic instruments sound at A-440 (more or less), at least a semitone higher than Bach's *Cammerton* instruments,[10] so that Rilling's choir and soloists have to sing everything higher than Bach wrote it. As any singer will confirm, a semitone sometimes makes all the difference.

Rilling also uses adult females on the soprano and alto solo lines, also presumably because they sound "better." Added together, these are factors that probably produce a very different sound and character than those heard by Bach and the fellow members of his congregation.

There are also differences in technique. John Butt talks of how Period instruments "alert the player to historical difference. . . . [they] will force the player to rethink his techniques . . . [and] the repertory will have to be seen in a new light."[11] There is also the related element of "pushing the envelope." "One reason for returning to original instruments (apart from the sonority itself) is that so often they restore the sense of moving out to a technical frontier."[12] Period instruments are often more difficult to play than Romantic ones; like sports cars, they offer more control but must be approached on their own terms. Consciously or unconsciously, one is aware that players are closer to their technical limits when playing difficult pieces on a Period instrument. That is part of the effect; what is intended to sound difficult should not sound easy and glib. Playing Bach, one has the feeling the music "fills up" the instrument, using all its capacities.

The Violins of Autumn

HIP can be seen as a rejection of the idea of Absolute Music—that music exists independently of how or when it is performed, and with which instruments—and the acceptance of the more modern theory of arts as "form-based" or "content-based." At least part of the experience of music is the sound of the instruments. Davies offers an interesting perspective: "In literature, the work cannot be replaced by a paraphrase in modern-speak because the story told is not separable from the manner of its narration. One can paraphrase Jonathan Swift, say, but one loses his work of art in doing so. What goes for literature applies yet more clearly to music."[13] "The medium," Davies suggests, "is the message" (or at least part of it). Here, for example, is music that is "harpsichord-specific."

🔊 AUDIO SAMPLE: 53. Skip Sempé, 2004. Louis Couperin: Pavanne in f#

Helmuth Rilling, as we know, speaks of translating Bach into modern language. A problem with such translations is that there are some things that do not survive the conversion. An essential element of much poetry, for example, is how it sounds. Paul Verlaine's famously evocative "Chanson d'Automne" is an example:

> Les sanglots longs des violons de l'automne
> Blessent mon coeur d'une langueur monotone,
> Tout suffocant et blême quand sonne l'heure,
> Je me souviens des jours anciens, et je pleure;
> Et je m'en vais au vent mauvais qui m'emporte
> Deçà, delà, pareil à la feuille morte.

Autumn Song

> A voice that sings
> Like viol strings
> Through the wane
> Of the pale year
> Lulleth me here
> With its strain.
>
> My soul is faint
> At the bell's plaint

> Ringing deep;
> I think upon
> The days begone
> And I weep.
>
> And I go'
> Where the winds know,
> Broken and brief,
> To and fro,
> As the winds blow
> A dead leaf.
>
> Translated by Gilles de Seze[14]

The poem's meanings can be approximated in translation, but the sound and general effect cannot be duplicated in another language. I'm suggesting that the same is often, perhaps always, true in music as well.

Period Instruments: Hardware and Software

The extremist position on original instruments is probably best known in the form of Malcolm Bilson's notorious remark in an article in 1980 on performing Mozart on the fortepiano. Bilson was no longer able to accept the idea that it is better to hear a great artist on the wrong instrument over a mediocre player on the right one. "Perhaps it is wrong to put the instrument before the artist," Bilson writes, "but I have begun to feel that it must be done. . . . [Using a modern instrument,] there is simply no way that the greatest, most sensitive artist can ever come close to a true Mozartean sense."[15] This same principle is true of Bach's cantatas; no performance on Romantic instruments or with singers using operatic style can approach the original conception and sound of these pieces.

Charles Rosen argues against old instruments. He speaks of "a living and unbroken musical language from the past to present has enabled us to translate the sound of the past into the new sounds of contemporary instruments."[16] What does Rosen mean by "contemporary instruments"? Real "contemporary" instruments are fairly rare. As I discussed earlier, the symphony orchestra does not use them. The so-called modern instrumentarium is, like the music for which it was created, 120–150 years old. Instrument mutation came to a standstill when the repertoire iced up. What Rosen really means when he speaks of translating the sound of the past "into the new sounds of contemporary instruments" is translating the sound of Baroque instruments into the sounds of Romantic ones.

I have to say that Rosen's own instrument, the piano, is something of an exception to this generalization. The piano has continued to evolve during the twentieth century, moving since World War II ever closer to the sound of the psaltery and dulcimer, a colder, clearer, more crystalline sound than pianos made before the war. In historical music, the modern piano's status has seen a dramatic change in the last century. Since the late 1960s, contemporary taste and the musical establishment tolerate the use of the piano in Rhetorical music only if it is particularly well played.[17] Now that Bach's own instruments are readily available, any keyboard piece of Bach played on the modern piano is in fact an arrangement, as much so as if it were played on the saxophone, or the kazoo. As Peter Walls puts it, "Playing baroque works on instruments their composers could not have known but which audiences are expected to accept as modern equivalents is a form of unacknowledged transcription."[18]

Glenn Gould had an answer for that. He thought that Bach (like Gould himself) was indifferent to the instruments he wrote for, that he was thinking in "pure music."[19] And yet pianists who play harpsichord music are forced to make many decisions that are irrelevant to the music: long crescendos and decrescendos, dramatic gestures quite foreign to the style, and for clarity's sake, non-legato playing that sounds silly on the piano, an instrument built to play legato. The added dynamics are often distracting because they are unnecessary and suggest meanings that were not originally there.

Consciously or not, Gould too was influenced by his instrument, as indicated by what he did (or rather, did not do) when he had occasion to record on a Wittmayer "harpsichord" (or what passed for a harpsichord before the revolution in instrument copying in the 1960s).[20] He ended up playing it just like his piano. In his own words (from the liner notes), "On the harpsichord, it's very easy to achieve the sort of secco, pointillistic *détaché* line that I've always tried to produce on the piano with varying degrees of success." Gould needed a fortepiano for the sound and touch he was trying to get. A pity none was available to him.

> On the other hand, having achieved it, you can't influence [the harpsichord] dynamically and you're left, so to speak, beholden to the generosity of the ear which is sometimes prepared to read dynamic implications into rhythmic alterations. But this introduces another set of problems, because, on the harpsichord, you have a choice between rhythmic inexorability and its converse, which is infinite rubato, a kind of sound world which really never comes to rest on any bar-line. I was determined to try and find a way around that problem. And I thought, well, the best solution would be to pretend that I'm not playing the harpsichord at all.

This seems an accurate enough description of what he did, although there are some very attractive experiments with harpsichord sound from time to time. Here is a track where he is obviously experimenting with articulation.

🔊 **AUDIO SAMPLE:** 54. Glenn Gould (harpsichord). Handel: HWV 426

When Gould is playing, regardless of the instrument, he catches and holds one's attention, and there is no choice but to listen.

 AUDIO SAMPLE: 55. Glenn Gould (harpsichord). Handel: HWV 428

As an hautboist, I know Bach valued the distinctive qualities of each instrument. He was not indifferent to instruments, but wrote with friendship and affection for all of them. That is why he was able to create such a rich gamut of effects using instruments.

Frans Brüggen is no doubt right that in the end, the choice between Period instruments and Romantic instruments is "a question of taste: either you like it or you don't." If you don't like Period instruments, Stan Godlovitch's comment is worth considering. He suggests that if you want the best possible tool, you need the Compleat Synthesizer; that really is a modern instrument.

Measuring the Makers

I have often seen makers of Period instruments try out antiques and immediately speculate on how they could be altered to "fix" this or that "problem."

Come to think of it, of all the various branches of HIP musicking, I don't know a single maker these days who claims to be copying original models without changes. An honest colleague of mine who has been making hautboys for 38 years recently wrote, "In case anyone is wondering: no, I do not build exact copies. I just think we ought to drop the word."

Martin Skowroneck, the distinguished harpsichord maker, calls his instruments "historical," but he does not believe in replicas either. Skowroneck recently published a book on his work. Here is a passage from it:

> For my taste, the 8' bridge was a little too close to the bentside in both [original] instruments. So I altered the form of the case somewhat. The result was, as I had to repeat far too often, an instrument close to Dulcken, but far from a copy. It did not help much: the more this instrument became known through the recordings, the more in vain was my defense against the word "copy".[21]

Skowroneck first became widely known for making harpsichords for the early Concentus Musicus recordings, and the series of legendary Dulcken models he made for Leonhardt and other players in the 1960s.[22] I have always thought that Skowroneck is one of those rare makers capable of catching in his copies the essence of an original recorder or a harpsichord (he makes both), while sometimes ignoring the exact dimensions of the originals. But after reading his words, I realize it isn't specific instruments he copies, but rather a sound and character that is convincing; that is, as we imagine instruments of the time to have sounded, and even more, pleasing to hear. Skowroneck's condition is surely the ambition of every player: to make their audience glad they are hearing them, and convinced that what they are hearing has a recognizable *cachet* of oldness. Skowroneck is the paragon of the style-copy maker. Nor is he a defender of replication. "In no other field," he writes, "whether in the Arts, mechanics, economics or any other subject, the term copy is thought of as highly as in instrument making. . . . To copy as "correctly" as possible . . . not only hinders the creativity necessary for good results, . . . faults in an original (and these exist!) might be copied along with the rest."[23]

"Faults" in an Original

He raises an interesting concept here. What is a "fault" in an original source—whether notes on a page, too-light bracing on a harpsichord, tuning on woodwinds, or a seeming casualness about marking articulations in old manuscripts?

On one side, it is only realistic to assume that there must have been mistakes and accidents in the work of Period musicking in the past. We could go too far with duplicating the past unthinkingly. Without exercising any judgment, we could reproduce some characteristic that hampered players at the time—using their equipment with their expectations. (Charles Rosen implies this in the title of his article, "Should music be played 'wrong'?")

But in this field, how do we differentiate an original fault from a deliberately made feature whose usefulness we are not yet able to appreciate or recognize?[24] To comprehend the purposes of such apparent mistakes often takes years of playing, combined with reflection. If we "correct" them, we may inadvertently eliminate differences between the present and the past the way nineteenth-century editors used to bowdlerize out the cross-relations in Purcell scores.

Collingwood cited Croce: "When [Neolithic man] made a certain implement, he had a purpose in mind; the implement came into being as an expression of his spirit, and if you treat it as non-spiritual that is only because of the failure of your historical insight."[25] Just as there was a purpose behind the implement, there is brilliance hidden behind what look on paper like banal musical figures in Vivaldi, for instance (Vivaldi's music often doesn't make sense until the audience is present).

The Lefébure: More Than a Style-Copy

In a fascinating and amusing article, Skowroneck describes how he created a "fake" harpsichord, which he ascribed to Nicholas Lefébure and dated to 1755.[26]

The Lefébure project was inspired, it seems, over a bottle of good French wine and a wager with Gustav Leonhardt; the object was to make an instrument that "would appear as an original" even to harpsichord restorers. This could be called a "correctly attributed fake." Skowroneck subtitled his article "Forgery without Intent to Defraud," and indeed as soon as he had succeeded in his claim that his instrument was antique, he announced his ruse. His work might better be described by other words than "forgery." He was copying style, after all, not $20 bills.

What he did, in fact, was a brilliant example of style-copying as applied to instrument making. There was no original, so in making the Lefébure harpsichord, Skowroneck was using the same principle van Meegeren had used in his fake Vermeers: he was not copying a specific model (which would be work-copying) but rather a general style.

Skowroneck describes how he changed his usual building methods for the Lefébure. The differences in his procedure were of two kinds: those that merely made the instrument appear antique (like artificial scratches), and those that represented earlier techniques of making that he normally omits (like special hinge designs, the exclusive use of hand instead of power tools, and paintings of flowers that are now extinct on the soundboard).

Skowroneck notes that he taught himself some new techniques that he has subsequently taken over for his "signed" instruments. Above all, he writes, the sound "was clearly 'older', or riper than my ordinary production."[27] Why, we might ask, should Skowroneck's normal models sound different from this instrument that was purposely built to sound original? Why not make every instrument sound original? This probably goes back to a question about vintage I discussed in chapter 7: should a newly made violin look old or new? Skowroneck needed to make the "Lefébure" appear to be old and perhaps a little tired. His regular instruments are of course new.

Old or new, it is a magnificent-sounding instrument, and has a seasoned maturity that resembles the mellow fatigue one associates with antique harpsichords and that distinguishes them from the crispness of new instruments.

🔊 **AUDIO SAMPLE:** 56. Gustav Leonhardt, 1991. Forqueray: La Morangis. Uses Skowroneck signed "Nicholas Lefébure, Rouen, 1755"

A Plea for More "Correctly Attributed Fakes"

The idea behind the exact copies or replicas of original instruments in the 1960s was that since we were trying to learn the basic principles of both the music and the instruments, the sensible thing was to follow every original indication as literally as possible. How could we understand Period playing techniques or style if we began with instruments that were already adaptations and compromises?

Using original instruments is impractical, especially winds. They are hard to find, prohibitively expensive, and risky to use regularly (they are easy to crack, and often wear out after a while). We have an obligation to save them for future musicians to have as models. So—except some of the string players—everyone needs a facsimile of an original.

With instruments, however, it isn't realistic to talk about a literal duplicate; wood grain and density already give every instrument its own special character. Even modern factory instruments made in series differ from each other. Again we meet the "head thing," a question of attitude. A replica in instrument-making terms is not necessarily a clone of an original. It is one on which the maker does not make intentional changes; there are no deliberate differences and no compromises to modern taste.

At this early stage in our understanding of both performing style and instruments of the Baroque, I believe what we need is copies of specific originals, work-copies. Not even generic style-copies. We don't need an instrument designed and built to play as "well" as possible, without "faults." For learning the musical ecosystem of the Baroque, I'm not helped by an "improved instrument;" the improvements are based on criteria that can easily change. The only constant is the original. So what I want is a blind duplicate of an original, "warts and all." This is the concept of a stylistically authentic copy that would have pleased its original maker's contemporaries (to the best of our present knowledge), and that fools modern experts into thinking it is original. Any maker who can do that gets my respect; it takes talent and hard work.

I think Period instrument makers are there basically to compensate for the lack of original instruments in the world. For craftsmen, originality should be a minor issue. And they should be wary of fixing "problems" in original designs.

"Don't Fix It if It Ain't Broke"

There are compelling reasons for continuing to refer to originals for guidance. For a start, although copies can sometimes play as well as originals, they usually don't. Original instruments, string, keyboard, and woodwind, play better, as a rule, than modern copies. Many HIP players are not even aware of the difference in quality, because they have never played an original instrument—or even, in some cases, a faithful copy of one. In short, our generation of makers needs to get better (which they are certainly doing), and the original instruments are the only teachers they have.

Second, the process of learning from these instruments is far from finished; they have already shown us how to do many things that were unimaginable or unnatural on Romantic instruments.

Third, because makers these days tend to work more toward the principle of emulation (i.e., improvement) rather than replication, we have a situation where makers (and therefore players) are cast loose from original instruments as a reference point, from which it is all too easy to gradually drift away. Remember the Pleyel harpsichord!

Being physical objects, instruments that survive from the past seem less ephemeral than music or styles of playing. But these elements are closely linked. As our idea of music of the past changes, so does our way of playing it, and our expectations from instruments. Our images of instruments and what they can do with this music mutates. One generation's beautiful turning may appear gross and vulgar to another generation—especially one later by two or three generations, when the objects are not yet "antique enough." The makers who copy them also change their minds, gradually, about what is important to copy, and even what it is they are seeing when they examine original instruments.

Back in 1971 when I was a maker myself, I made a tour of European instrument collections. In just over a month I played some 174 hautboys, or an average of five new instruments a day. Never before or since have I examined, played, and measured as many original hautboys in so short a time. Of course I was looking for a fabulous model (which I found), but my larger goal was to learn what original hautboys were like "in the wild." I partially succeeded but was limited by my lack of experience with other kinds of instruments than the ones I already knew, by a lack of appropriate reeds, by the crankiness of instruments unused to being played, and so forth.

Those original models are still lying in their cases in the museums. I have no doubt I would see and understand them differently now after 35 years of playing. I imagine it would be the same for anyone else. Those instruments are like a dictionary one can go back to, and if you bring new questions they will give answers you never dreamed of. We need to keep referring to them.

Some people think we know enough now to make our own models that do what we want to do. I would remind them that many non-musicians can now explain to you the difference between seventeenth-century Flemish and Italian harpsichords, while the woodwind player nowadays who can distinguish the playing qualities of French and Italian traversos, or late seventeenth- and mid-eighteenth-century hautboys, is rare. It seems premature to claim we know much yet about how most Period instruments originally played, or were originally played. What we don't know about those instruments is vastly more than what we do know. And with such a limited appreciation of what already exists, it seems hasty to be thinking already of improving and adjusting the instruments. Imagine music editors, instead of restoring early manuscripts, fixing the "faults" in the music. "Don't fix it," as they say, "if it ain't broke." We don't even know if it *is* broke or not.

IV

WHAT MAKES BAROQUE MUSIC "BAROQUE"?

10

Baroque Expression and Romantic Expression Compared

I am Musica. *With my sweet accents I can make every restless heart peaceful and inflame the coldest minds, now with anger, now with love.*

(Monteverdi, the Prologue to *Orfeo*)

Musick and oratory aggree strangely in principles.

(Roger North, *The Musical Grammarian*, 1728)

Rhetoric: Beyond Communication

Good expression in music, Quantz declared, "can be compared to that of an orator. The orator and the musician have the same objective, both in the composition of their productions and in their performance itself." The ultimate aim of good performers, he writes, is "to win over the hearts of their listeners, to arouse or still the movements of their spirits, and to transport them first to this Passion, then to that."[1] Quantz is describing Rhetoric, or oratory, originally the art of speaking eloquently in public. "Older than the Church," the detailed Rhetorical treatises of Greek and Roman writers, including those of Aristotle, Cicero, and especially Quintilian, were rediscovered during the Renaissance and soon permeated European culture.

It was only in the early twentieth century that music historians rediscovered the importance of rhetoric as the basis of aesthetic and theoretical concepts in earlier music. An entire discipline that had once been the common property of every educated man has had to be rediscovered and reconstructed during the intervening decades, and only now is it beginning to be understood how much Western art music has depended on rhetorical concepts.[2]

What Windows is to computers, Rhetoric was to Baroque and Renais-

165

sance musicians; it was their operating system, the source of their assumptions about what music was and what it was supposed to accomplish. And although it was applied to music from the outside, in a sense it would be more accurate to describe music as one form that Rhetoric took.[3] With the rise of Romanticism, Rhetoric was swept away again, which is why it is only in the last few years that we have begun to appreciate its significance in our current pursuits.

Rhetoric is remarkably adaptable. It can be applied over a spectrum from writing style to dance. In music it has several facets. Since it serves as a framework of form (with sections like *dispositio, pronunciatio,* etc.), it is useful in establishing and analyzing structure, both large-scale (like whole pieces) and small-scale (like figures). As I will show later on, it reinforces the partnership between composers and performers, which was seriously damaged by Romanticism. Rhetoric also acts as a kind of hermeneutics or narrative, providing handles for understanding music's meaning, in ways parallel to discursive thought, stories, and descriptions of emotional states. And it provides performers with a rationale for making emotional contact with their listeners. This is potentially far-reaching because—since the revolutionary days of the 1960s—Baroque music has been constrained by the simplistic idea that expressive performance is Romantic. Rhetoric offers an alternate discourse and validates expressive performing in "Early music."

In our own time, musical Rhetoric was first resuscitated by Period musicians of the mid-1960s who developed a new style of playing based on figures and gestures, with the goal of projecting Affections that I will call *Eloquent style* (it can be heard on recordings from the decade 1965–75 by a number of players, including Leonhardt, Brüggen, and Harnoncourt). Harnoncourt, early in his recording career, started to underline the importance of the speaking qualities of music, and his books use the words "*Klang-rede*" and "dialogue" in their titles. It is a curious fact that despite the vigor of Eloquent Style, the theoretical study of Rhetoric as a rational explanation and guide for musical performance remained dormant for another generation.

All five traditional elements of the "processes of creation" in Rhetorical thinking are of interest to performers. Musicians have been discussing how to apply these elements to music for centuries, and most recent studies tend to look at them from the point of view of composers (a bias inherited from Romanticism, no doubt). Looked at from the performer's angle, my reading of Cicero and Quintilian would organize the five divisions like this:

1. *Inventio* (invention): inspirations and "inventions" in the form of figures and gestures; the essence of a piece
2. *Dispositio* (arrangement; syntax): organizing inventions into a composition

3. *Elocutio* (technique; style): precision, accuracy; being together and in tune; projecting style
4. *Memoria* (memory; getting off the page): gracing and passaggi, improvisatory elements
5. *Pronunciatio/Actio* (effective, moving performance; delivery): declamation; *Vortrag;* eloquence (i.e., affecting the mind and heart of the listener)

From the early years of the twentieth century, starting with Albert Schweitzer, German music historians gradually developed a systematic theory of Affections, an *Affektenlehre* or Doctrine of the Affections. After World War II, the subject was not generally picked up by anglophone musicologists, whose discourse was dominated at the time by positivism and the doctrine of Absolute music, neither of which had room for it.

It was only in the closing decade of the twentieth century that writings connecting Rhetoric to musical performance began appearing in English. The concept of musical figures came into focus more clearly with the appearance of John Butt's *Bach Interpretation: Articulation Marks in Primary Sources of J. S. Bach* (1990), one of a series of books he has written that have changed our view of Baroque performance.

Subsequently, beside a growing list of interesting shorter studies, three books have appeared that I would recommend to any musician. The first is Dietrich Bartel's *Musica Poetica,* based on his German dissertation. This appeared in 1997. It has been indispensable since its appearance. It includes much original German material in translation and gives a systematic item-by-item discussion of figures. Patricia Ranum's *The Harmonic Orator* (2001) gives a perspective on French musical eloquence; it too provides a wealth of source material translated into English. Judy Tarling's *The Weapons of Rhetoric* (2004), the most recent book to appear, is an excellent introduction, and concentrates especially on musical delivery, "the issue," as she sees it, "most directly relevant to the performing task."[4] Tarling manages to convey the growing realization among historical performers that Rhetoric encompasses and addresses much of what is of concern to.them.

Once More, with Feeling: The Affections

In about 1715 Roger North wrote up a list of what amounts to various Affections. An Affection is "a frame of mind or state of feelings; one's humour, temper, or disposition at a particular time."[5] It can be an emotion, a state of mind, an attitude, even a physical state; as in North's list:

> Grave, reasonable, merry, capering and dancing, artificiall, malencholly, querolous, stately and proud, or submissive and humble, buisie, in haste, frighted, quarrell and fight, run, walk, or consider, search, rejoyce, prattle, weep, laugh insult, triumph; and at last, perhaps, vanish out of sight all at once;

or end in very good temper, and as one layd downe to rest or sleep. There is no end of the varietys of imitation in musick, so I leave that to imagination.[6]

Affection might be called the meaning in music. Whereas a Romantic musician was chiefly concerned with generating beauty, a Baroque performer's job, first and foremost, was to understand what "humour" they wanted to evoke (the French called them "Passions"), and to convince their audience of its presence. For a musician to play or sing a piece without perceiving its meaning would be like learning to speak a foreign language by rote, imitating sounds without understanding words. Keith Hill writes:

> Even when players play music without an affect in mind, normal ordinary listeners like myself hear and feel the effects that result from not having a clear affect . . . such as wandering, jerky, stilted, perfunctory, inane, bored, tired, get it over and done with as fast as possible, reluctant, and so on. I do not consider these affects worth my time, since I experience them too often on a daily basis.[7]

John Neubauer, in *The Emancipation of Music from Language: Departure from Mimesis in Eighteenth-Century Aesthetics,* describes the Affections as "freezing complex and fluid psychological processes into a few fixed categories."[8] Neubauer's wording shows how difficult it is for us, from our historical vantage point behind Romanticism, to access or admire—or even understand—the philosophy that accommodated the Affections. As North's list attests, there were a good deal more than "a few fixed categories" of Affections, although, compared to the complexities of real emotional states, the number is no doubt limited. But the Affections were not intended to be taken as a description of reality, any more than a contemporary audience watching a play or opera thinks they are seeing actual events. The Affections, like theater pieces, were conventions, leaps of the social imagination, collective constructs. Their interest was their ability to isolate emotions, offering the opportunity to consider them in their undiluted, extreme forms. Looked at negatively and without historical imagination, they have been described as "the abrupt change from one static passion to another, which is all that the Cartesian model allows . . . a series of static depersonalized passions."[9]

This comment breathes the air of the Realist movement that arose at the beginning of the nineteenth century in theater and literature;[10] in modern terms, Realism attempts to give fiction the illusion of being true. A degree of realism is necessary in any theater performance, to allow the imagination to work. The "mimetic illusion" was strong in the seventeenth-century; actors made every effort to create the semblance of reality, giving audiences the impression of being "authorized witnesses" to the events on the stage (and occasionally participants, as audience members sometimes intervened for the sake of one character or another).[11]

It is Realism that gives us Shakespeare plays with dialogue that sounds modern in intonation and pronunciation—interesting (as Shakespeare always is), but essentially non-historical or even anti-historical. No one living today has had occasion to observe Baroque theater and thus be in a position to describe it as "static, depersonalized, and limited," as Neubauer does. We could substitute "fixed, commonly understandable, and specific" as more productive possibilities. The sudden and absolute transformations of Affection noticeable in French chamber pieces, for instance, would not otherwise have been possible. Just as Baroque theater lighting displayed a stage director's skill, such abrupt and extreme changes of Affection between movements displayed a musician's talent at evoking and intensifying Affections clearly and convincingly.

Dealing with emotions as separate elements, taken in suspension from real life, had another use. As in the theater, "actors do a service in playing a kind of game with relationships so that the spectators can imagine those relationships and the Affections to which they give rise and even possibly experience them, without having to commit themselves to them."[12] In this way they can test and consider the effects of various emotional states or attitudes hypothetically ("in the lab," as it were).

Neubauer's phrase "stock affects" does contain an insight, though. Affections, like symbols, could be evoked because they would be recognized, at least in an approximate way. They did represent tenderness of some kind, or anger, or confusion. They could be compared to the "tag" music we all know in movies—such music is instantly decipherable (common moods are fear, pride, weirdness, courage, and of course love—usually with an oboe); indeed some scenes in films would be unintelligible without their "background" music evoking emotional associations.

Music like jazz and opera seria, that includes improvisational freedom, has of necessity to operate in a conventional framework of familiarity. The framework acts as a medium so listeners can understand what the performer is trying to say with the unfamiliar, improvised components—thus, the presence of common, everyday elements, like Adagio and Allegro movements, the Da capo aria, and of course the standard inventory of Affections.

Mattheson was apparently the only eighteenth-century author to actually use the word *Affektenlehre*,[13] the Science/Doctrine of the Affections. George Buelow has argued that "a concept of stereotyped musical figures with specific affective connotations never existed in the Baroque composer's mind or in theoretical explanations."[14] I doubt that musical figures had the same connotations for different composers, but I am amazed and totally convinced by Albert Schweitzer's demonstration, in his book on Bach (1905), that many gestural shapes had associations with specific Affections. Schweitzer's arguments are especially effective when he uses the Cantatas and other vocal works as examples, since texted music usually indicates or even explicitly states the Affection of the movement.

The *stile rappresentativo* going back to Monteverdi could not last forever, and the way it mutated was by becoming less focused and specific.

Where early on, a single Affection was treated for an entire piece, as time went on Affections began to be contrasted in a single movement. Sebastian Bach remained for the most part faithful to the single Affection in his vocal works, though not in his galant instrumental pieces. Mattheson's comment on "one specific Affection" in the *Vollkommene Capellmeister* of 1739 was old-fashioned for the time: "Actually, since instrumental music is nothing else but a tone-language [Ton-Sprache] or musical discourse [Klang-Rede], it must always be based on one specific Affection, and a great deal of care needs to be taken to choose expressive intervals, to proportion skilfully the phrases, the appropriate progressions, etc., in order to arouse it."[15]

By the late eighteenth century, Affections were succeeding each other in quick order. Quantz writes, for example, "At each bar you should adopt a different Passion, so to speak, being now melancholy, now gay, now serious, &c.; such changes are most necessary in music. They who can master this ability is not likely to want applause from their listeners, and their playing will always be *touching*."[16]

Eventually, Affections became so changeable and evanescent that the entire system ceased to be meaningful; listeners were no longer sure of seizing clearly defined Affections in a piece. More than one narrative could be going at the same time. Hence the sense, by the time we get to Romantic music, that communication is intuitive and changeable, that the same piece could mean different things to different people, even on different hearings.

Persuasion: Winning Over the Listeners

As a Chinese fortune cookie once informed me, "The object of rhetoric is not truth, but persuasion." Seventeenth- and eighteenth-century writers were generally agreed about the remarkable ability of music to move the heart and spirit.

An Affection is quite different from a subjective and individualistic Romantic emotion; it is a change in one's spirit that is induced from outside. The origins of the word "Affection" indicate this. Derived from the Greek *pathos*, "Affection" designated an emotional state induced by an external cause.[17] The Latin translation of *pathos, affectus*, is based on the verb *adficere*, meaning to work upon or influence (like the modern English "affect," as in "That change will *affect* all of us").

An interaction between the performer and the listener was thus implicit in the word "Affection"; Affections affect us. As Mellers put it, "Amerindian, African or Eskimo shamans never ask whether the songs they sing are intrinsically 'good', but rather how far they are efficacious— do they do good things?"[18]

To re-quote Bartel, "Numerous contemporary eyewitness accounts refer to the intensity and grand effect of . . . affection-arousing compositions, causing the entire audience to break spontaneously into sobbing and wailing."[19] Burney's description of a concert he heard around 1770 has the intimacy and spontaneity of a jazz performance:

> All who had any share in this concert, finding the company attentive, and in a disposition to be pleased, were animated to that true pitch of enthusiasm, which, from the ardour of the fire within them, is communicated to others, and sets all around in a blaze; so that the contention between the performers and hearers, was only who should please, and who should applaud the most![20]

That Rhetorical music should be, as Leonhardt suggests, "if anything, *more* expressive than Romantic music,"[21] may surprise some people. Gluck inspired considerable weeping, loud and open, from the time of his première at Paris in 1774.[22]

Neubauer seems unaware of such historical reports. He does not think that seventeenth-century music was yet designed to "'pierce' listeners and engender in them a desired feeling" because the Affections in use were too conventional. Curiously, Thomas More in 1516 used that very word when he wrote of melodies that "wonderfullye move, stir, *pearce,* and enflame the hearers myndes."

In a sense, then, Modernism is the precise contrary of oratory. While Rhetorical musical performances could provoke open and noisy weeping, a modern concert can prompt prim comments like "[His readings] are all cautious, all most commendably planned, all well laid out in detail, but they present little that kindles the ardour of the listener."[23] Most of us have probably experienced concerts with atmospheres that could have been described as "a chaste boredom . . . raised to the highest virtue."[24] Persuasion is definitely not on the Modernist agenda.

Declamation / Expression / Vortrag

An Oration is so far eloquent as it affects the Hearer's Mind.[25]

Declamation that can grip a listener by the scruff of the neck lives on. Among politicians and trial lawyers it may have become a pale shadow, but in a powerful form it is still practiced among southern Baptist preachers in the United States. An example known by many Americans is the Reverend Martin Luther King Jr.'s speech "I have a dream," which, with its sense of timing, tremors in the voice, and energy, is in its delivery much more powerful than the words it used.

If you have ever heard Aretha Franklin sing gospel songs like "Oh Happy Days" or "Amazing Grace," you will hear echoes of her father's legendary sermons that one of his listeners wrote "still make the hair on my head stand." Here is part of one of the Reverend C. L. Franklin's sermons, recorded in 1955:

🔊 AUDIO SAMPLE: 57. Rev C. L. Franklin. Sermon "Pressing on," 1955

A measure of how far we have gotten from declamation as a performing model is the word "harangue," which has distinctly negative vibes these days. In the old days, though, it was a literal synonym for declamation and still has that status in English dictionaries. Mersenne in 1636 used the word "harangues" in speaking of music as oratory, and in 1738 Louis Riccoboni, in his *Pensées sur la déclamation,* used "harangue" interchangeably with "declamation." As a musician, have you ever imagined yourself haranguing a crowd? (One never seems to harangue anything but crowds; never audiences.)

"Declamation" itself once had a more positive tone, and it still calls to mind its original intensity and sense of purpose. The style we have all embraced in the last couple of generations is the reverse of declamation; it is as natural and everyday as possible. "In the staid concert world of today," it is said, "the musician who gestures too broadly is considered to have something of the charlatan about him."[26] Declamation, on the contrary, is speaking in an emphatic manner that uses exaggerated enunciation and precision. Bacilly wrote that "Familiar language and the language of vocal music are two entirely different things."[27] Baroque declamation is not normal street-talk; it is exaggerated in clarity, in pronunciation, in the rising and falling cadence of the voice, in the timing of pauses indicated by punctuation, and so on. The difference might be compared to British and American English, the latter displaying fewer pauses and variations of tone. How did instruments do this, one wonders? Declamatory playing must also have been emphatic, using exaggerated articulation and precision; the musical equivalents would have been agogics, rubato, pauses, inflection, dynamic nuance, articulation, and so forth. We can only try to imagine it now.

Here is an example of what it may have been like: this is Cecilia Bartoli showing us the intensity that music can carry:

🔊 AUDIO SAMPLE: 58. Il Giardino Armonico, Cecilia Bartoli, 1999. Vivaldi: "Qual favellar?"

Like the Rev. Franklin's sermon, Bartoli's performance was not made with reference to the old Baroque tradition of declamation, but it gives us an idea how powerful it must once have been.

Delivery (eloquence or *pronunciato)* is what Quantz and Emanuel Bach called *Vortrag,* a subject they each considered important enough to merit a separate chapter in their books.[28] In German, *Vortrag's* meaning has shifted since the eighteenth century. Nowadays it just means a performance, even a bad one. Then, it meant something more compelling and persuasive. In the French version of his book, Quantz called *Vortrag* "la bonne expression"; according to him, the two most essential elements of music were "de toucher & de plaire" (to touch and to please).[29]

Here is another example of declamation in an old recording of Rameau's *Castor et Pollux,* one of the most important operas in French history. When Harnoncourt recorded it in the early 1970s, it was a daring venture to make the attempt to revive so many lost aspects of performance. The result was not entirely satisfying: fascinating and unforgettable because of the beautiful music trying to emerge, but not sung in anything like Eloquent style. First, let's listen to one of *Castor et Pollux*'s most beautiful pieces, "Nature, Amour." Here is a performance from the 1990s that is fairly good, if predictable, done by Jérôme Corréas with Les Arts Florissants playing in a competent but musically mediocre way.

🔊 AUDIO SAMPLE: 59. Les Arts Florissants, Corréas, Christie, 1992. Rameau: *Castor et Pollux:* Act II, Scenes 1 and 2: Pollux's aire "Nature, Amour" plus recit

Now let's listen to the recording by Harnoncourt, in which he hired singers of the "old school," and one can hear them, like their acting colleagues at the Palais Royal, doing a style not unlike early twentieth-century melodrama, which I take to have some connection to the old dramatic tradition of declamation. Gérard Souzay as Pollux is clearly from an older stylistic convention, with a wide vibrato, mannered pronunciation, and an inflexible ponderousness like a diesel 18-wheeler. Here is his "Nature, Amour:"

🔊 AUDIO SAMPLE: 60. Concentus Musicus, Souzay, Harnoncourt, 1972. Rameau: *Castor et Pollux:* Act II, Scene 1: Pollux's aire "Nature, Amour"

The recit (II/2) sounds absurd and affected in the style of Souzay and Jeanette Scovotti, and yet it probably has more in common with the dramatic conventions of the eighteenth century than the readings of the later recording.[30]

🔊 AUDIO SAMPLE: 61. Concentus Musicus, Souzay, Harnoncourt, 1972. Rameau: *Castor et Pollux:* Act II, Scene 2: Pollux's recit

The contrast between these two productions is extreme. "Tristes apprêts," probably the best-known aria in the opera, is sung in Harnoncourt's recording by Scovotti in a style that brings to mind those recitals by singers with flowers in the bosom and their hand on the piano. The 1990s recording is sung with many of the attributes of popular music (the use of vibrato at inopportune moments, slides, and a detached, "whatever" air).

It is far from certain that a performing protocol based on declamation would be accepted nowadays, in either singing or playing. The Modernist æsthetic confuses declamation with Romanticism (in other words, with what seems in "bad taste"). A remark in Judy Tarling's book, for instance, draws the line at what are termed "unlimited expressive effusions," which, she writes, "were always considered to be in bad taste, and I hope that the control of these according to good rhetorical style will encourage an appropriate level of expression in good taste without inhibiting the more extrovert performer." Taste is subjective, of course; the boundary between good and bad taste is not the same for everyone.[31] Tarling goes on to say, "Making every phrase sound 'like an epigram' is just as faulty a rhetorical style as playing in a dead-pan manner, and is quite tiring for the listener, who needs to be refreshed with simple unemotional musical information from time to time."[32] This sounds amazingly like the famous "No sex, please, we're British."

Commitment: The Baroque Performer "Himself in Flames"

> *This above all: to thine own self be true,*
> *And it must follow, as the night the day,*
> *Thou canst not then be false to any man.*[33]

Jean Poisson, well-known actor at the Dresden court, wrote in 1717, "All the rules of Cicero, of Quintilian, and of the Illustrious Moderns who might have written on declamation, are useless to the orator, if he does not follow the first, which is, to clearly understand what he is saying and feel it strongly himself, in order to make it perceptible to the Listener."[34] Quantz (who was also at the Dresden Court in 1717) urged performers to cultivate a calm and almost melancholy Affection when playing an Adagio, "for what does not come from the heart will not easily touch the heart."[35]

Quantz is following Cicero here, who argued that the orator "must himself achieve a state of excitement if he is to evoke emotions in his auditors, for 'no mind is so susceptible of the power of eloquence, as to catch its blaze, unless the speaker, when he approaches it, is himself in flames.'"[36] Roger North describes how the violinist Nicola Matteis, "flaming, as I have seen him, in a good humour he hath held the company by the ears with that force and variety for more than an hour together, that there was scarce a whisper in the room, tho' filled with Company."[37]

Collingwood associated (what he called) "representational" art with a lack of sincerity because it was intended to manipulate the Passions of an audience. "A person arousing emotion sets out to affect his audience in a way in which he himself is not necessarily affected. . . . A person expressing emotion, on the contrary, is treating himself and his audience in the same kind of way; he is making his emotions clear to his audience, and that is what he is doing to himself."[38] Collingwood's point is valid, but he misrepresents Baroque performers, who did not distinguish the goal of moving an audience from being moved themselves. Indeed, as Quantz saw it, if musicians "are not themselves moved by what they play, they cannot hope for any profit from their efforts, and he will never move others through their playing, which should be their ultimate aim."[39]

Insincerity or hypocrisy, even pretense, were the opposite of what musicians like Quantz and Emanuel Bach meant by declamation.[40] Quantz spoke of the "inner feeling—the singing of the soul,"[41] and Emanuel Bach uttered the sentiment that "Aus der Seele muß man spielen, und nicht wie ein abgerichteter Vogel"[42] (one should play from the soul, and not like a trained bird). Bach, echoing Quantz, wrote that "musicians cannot move others unless they themselves are moved; it is essential that musicians be able to put themselves in each Affection they wish to rouse in their audience, for it is by showing their own emotion that they awaken sympathy. In languishing, sad passages, they languish and grow sad. That is visible and audible."[43]

Charles Burney, who visited Bach at his home in Hamburg in the early 1770s, wrote that

> After dinner, . . . I prevailed upon him to sit down again to a clavichord, and he played, with little intermission, till near eleven o'clock at night. During this time, he grew so animated and *possessed*, that he not only played, but looked like one inspired. His eyes were fixed, his under lip fell, and drops of effervescence distilled from his countenance. He said, if he were to be set to work frequently, in this manner, he should grow young again.[44]

Such emotional involvement from the performer was not, apparently, uncommon. One eyewitness gave the following famous description of Corelli's playing: "it was usual for his countenance to be distorted, his eyes to become as red as fire, and his eyeballs to roll as if in an agony."[45] Le Cerf de la Viéville cites Raguenet's quite serious description of Italian musicians whose instrumental pieces "affect the feelings, the imagination, and the soul with so much strength that the violinists who play them cannot prevent themselves from being transported and seized with fury because of them; that they torture their violins and their bodies, that they are agitated like those possessed, etc."[46] He comments that "our [French] violinists are more calm." Mattheson compares French and Italian musicians, remarking on the "gesticulations and mannerisms" of singers, though he finds the Italians carry this even further. "They frequently have tears in their eyes when they perform something that is melancholy."[47] Charles Avison, discussing the charge of church organist, wrote "Yet, if he feels not this divine Energy in his own Breast, it will prove but a fruitless Attempt to raise it in that of others."[48]

John Mason, writing on Rhetoric in 1748, states categorically, "It is always offensive to an Audience to observe any Thing in the Reader or Speaker that looks like Indolence or Inattention. The Hearer will never be affected whilst he sees the Speaker indifferent."[49] To sing or play as if you're delivering someone else's message—as Quantz writes—or as if everything is planned out in advance and already written in score form is a recipe for a performance that will not engage an audience.

The Baroque musician's relation to a score resembles that of an actor to a role. The audience knows the actor is not the character they represent. The musical score also describes a character, and for the moment that the musician performs it, they "act" that Affection or feeling with as much conviction as they can. Only a few kinds of musicians (piano-lounge players, who specialize in a repertoire of styles, opera singers, and jazz players) have regularly to switch styles, so for most musicians, training and tradition in changing styles are missing. Assimilating styles deeply enough to be convincing to an audience is very difficult, and the number of performers who can project several styles is small; most orchestral players are limited to Modern style plus a mild and generic Eloquent style. Also, musicians often perform in a single style out of personal conviction; to make the kinds of switches that are daily work for an actor will seem insincere to a musician. It does not bode well for Eloquent style that many musicians move back and forth between gigs in Modern style. Few of them can make differentiations of any depth.

To succeed, the musician, like the orator—and unlike the actor—has to convince the audience of the reality of their emotions. On this question, a good piece of advice comes from Quintilian, translated for us by John Mason in 1748,[50]

> Above all Things then *study Nature;*
> avoid Affectation;
> never use Art, if you have not the Art to conceal it.

Romantic Expression: The "Autobiography in Notes"

The overriding purpose of Rhetorical music was to move an audience emotionally: summoning, provoking, conjuring, and kindling Affections of the social kind, Affections that were shared.

The autonomous music of the Romantics, on the other hand (however beautiful), was not on the whole concerned with sharing. It expressed—or seemed to personify—abstract ideas like the divine in nature or the infinite. It also concentrated on a single individual, the genius-creator of the piece, the "artiste." In poetry, for instance, Abrams writes, "According to [John Stuart] Mill, 'Poetry is feeling, confessing itself to itself in moments of solitude . . .' The poet's audience is reduced to a single member, consisting of the poet himself. 'All poetry,' as Mill put it, 'is of the nature of soliloquy.'"[51]

Abrams may be right that the most distinctive feature of this new approach was that it was centered on the artist and tended to invalidate the audience.

> To pose and answer æsthetic questions in terms of the relation of art to the artist, rather than to external nature, or to the audience, or to the internal requirements of the work itself, was the characteristic tendency of modern criticism up to a few decades ago, and it continues to be the propensity of a great many — perhaps the majority — of critics today. This point of view is very young measured against the twenty-five-hundred-year history of the Western theory of art, for its emergence as a comprehensive approach to art, shared by a large number of critics, dates back not much more than a century and a half.[52]

Abrams was writing in 1953. It is not difficult to guess which movement he is describing, which in the next sentence he calls a "radical shift to the artist."

The Romantics developed the idea that the expression of *individual* feelings constitutes the creation of art. They praised themselves for inventing the first music that could truly be called "art" because it was the first to be "expressive," embodying the ultimate language of the emotions. To the Romantic, expression depicted subjective states of mind and heart; it was a kind of report on what the individual artist-composer himself was feeling. This is a conception many people today still hold. Dahlhaus called the new Romantic concept of music an "autobiography in notes."

Romantic music is not even necessarily written for an audience; it is, after all, "autonomous." The process of unique artistic discovery may or may not be witnessed by a public. Noël Carroll writes, "Whereas arousing emotions is audience-directed, expressing an emotion is a matter of self-clarification on the part of the artist."[53]

It is not unusual to see "artists" (and this goes even for some performers of Rhetorical repertoire) seemingly indifferent to the effect of their performances. They seem to think they are there to be observed, and their public are like *voyeurs,* scarcely different from the clientele at Mme. Tussaud's.

Mary Hunter has gone into the early Romantic performance discourse in detail. One of the points she brings out is that the performer was expected to undergo a profound spiritual transformation; "that the job of the performer was understood to be about developing and displaying a unitary consciousness that merged his own subjectivity with the composer's."[54] In comparing Rhetorical and Romantic performance, she observes that in Rhetorical performance "the notion of the fully conceived and essentially self-sufficient work waiting to be rendered into sound through a communion of souls is barely evident."[55] It would seem to have been a Romantic creation.

Berlioz wrote of the musician forgetting the world when making music, "He listens to himself, is his own judge, and when he is moved and his emotion is shared by those artists near him, he no longer concerns himself with the reactions of the distant public." And Wagner vouchsafed to a correspondent in 1860, "You must know, my child, that those like myself look neither to the right nor the left, neither forwards nor backwards. Time and the world are nothing to us. Only one thing matters to us and determines our actions, namely, the necessity to release what is within us."[56] Salmen points to many other passages that indicate the Romantic concept of the self-perceived superiority, and loneliness, of the Romantic artiste.

Baroque musicians had not concerned themselves with depicting subjective states of mind and heart. "The 'doctrine of the affections' does not, strictly speaking, preclude the possibility of psychological self-portraiture on the composer's part; but it does declare it to be æsthetically irrelevant, a private matter of no concern to the public."[57] Evoking Affections does not involve describing feelings that are personal, but ones that were mutual and could be recognized and understood. As Bartel put it, "The necessity of a personal and subjective experience as an inspired source for composition was foreign to the Baroque mind. All irrational, indefinite, or inaccessible musical thought was considered unworthy."[58]

"A personal and subjective experience" was, of course, essentially Romantic. "The romantics' infatuation with the self was a mental aphrodisiac," writes Peter Gay. "Decades before Oscar Wilde observed that to love oneself is the beginning of a lifelong romance, they proved that the re-enchantment of the world often began with self-enchantment before the mirror." Fascination with the individual personality of the artist-composer manifests itself today in film stars, publicized by fan clubs and supermarket tabloids.

By contrast, Sebastian Bach, on being complimented on his organ playing, is said to have replied, "There is nothing remarkable about it. All one has to do is hit the right notes at the right time, and the instrument plays itself."[59]

Romantics obviously came in different colors, and the many flamboyant personalities frequently disagreed among themselves.[60] But what united them—the "largely irresistible" Romantic message—was a fascination with individual feelings.

Collingwood writes that expressing a (Romantic) feeling "is not done with the intention of arousing a like emotion;"[61] it merely allows others, he says, to understand how we feel. Romantic musicians did also reach out to their audiences and as they became transparent vessels, they spoke of trying "to transmit to the soul of the listener the feeling that the composer had in his soul."[62] This is one of Baillot's descriptions of performance in 1803;

quite different from Quantz's in 1752, which characteristically makes no mention of a composer ("To win over the hearts of their listeners, to arouse or still the movements of their spirits, and to transport them first to this Passion, then to that."[63])

In his article on expression in the *New Grove,* Roger Scruton puts the Romantic view in a nutshell by saying that "to describe a piece of music as expressive of melancholy is to give a reason for listening to it; to describe it as arousing or evoking melancholy is to give a reason for avoiding it."[64] The distinction is between the Romantic artist "expressing" an emotion that is observed by an audience but not necessarily shared, and the Baroque craftsman "arousing or evoking" an emotion in the hearts of their listeners.[65]

Christopher Small speaks of the Romantic idea of musicking as "a one-way system of communication."

> The listener's task is simply to contemplate the work, to try to understand it and to respond to it . . . he or she has nothing to contribute to its meaning. That is the composer's business.
>   . . . Music is an individual matter . . . composing, performing and listening take place in a social vacuum; the presence of other listeners is at best an irrelevance and at worst an interference in the individual's contemplation of the musical work.[66]

People talk of the meaning of Beethoven's Ninth as definable in endless ways; as a work that each individual meets on their own terms. This is good Romantic talk, centered, as usual, on the self. Eighteenth-century Affections, by contrast, conveyed what Taruskin has called *"public* meanings." The heroism of a Baroque piece was communal, shared by all; it would have seemed pretentious if it had been autobiographical. Pretentiousness— or what seems like it to us now—did not seem to bother Romantics.

Romantic feelings were different from Baroque Affections, then, in being individual, unique, and possibly unrepeatable. Here is an early Romantic attempt by the poet Ludwig Tieck to describe a poetic impression of a piece of music:

> Like magical seeds, how rapidly the sounds take root within us, and now there's a rushing of invisible, fiery forces, and in an instant a grove is rustling with a thousand wonderful flowers, and with incomprehensibly rare colors, and our childhood and an even more distant past are playing and jesting in the leaves and the treetops. Then the flowers become excited and move among one another, color gleams upon color, lustre shines upon lustre, and all the light, the sparkling, the rain of beams, coaxes out new lustre and new beams of light.[67]

This style of writing is typical of the Romantics (Berlioz—as we saw above—has a similar style). It strikes us now as a description of random associations, and the flower theme conjures up the psychedelic experiences of the 1960s (with the addition of religious allusions). But, for all its fervor there is an aleatoric quality, as if the listener's reaction could well have been different if they had heard the same piece again.

By contrast, Charles Avison in 1753 gives a portrait of his distinguished colleague Francesco Geminiani, writing that "he was always peculiarly happy in his various Expression, well of the *tender,* the *serene,* the *solemn,* as of the *joyous* and *rapid;* and, with a ready and proper Execution, always entered into a true Feeling of the Spirit, or softness suitable to each of these *styles.*"[68] The tone and character of Avison's description contrast strongly with Tieck's, although both authors are discussing passionate expression.

The real distinction that E. T. A. Hoffmann and other literary figures of the early years of the nineteenth century were making was between the old idea of music as enhancing the power of words (in the Seconda Pratica sense), and a new vision of music as a medium for expressing feeling (any feeling) without using conventional language.[69]

An enthusiasm for heightened emotional states, using music as a vehicle for rapture, as an art expressive of infinite and insatiable longing and indefinable feelings leading to ecstatic mystical revelation, is seen in the writings of numerous artists, poets, composers, and critics of the period, notably in Herder's *Kalligone* (1800), in E. T. A. Hoffmann's novels, stories, and music criticism, in the music journalism of Weber, Berlioz, and Schumann, and in the novels of Jean Paul. Music was elevated to an art-religion and was seen as the ultimate language of the emotions.[70]

Rhetoric Abandoned by the Romantics: An Art "Broken to Service"

Two developments in the Romantic movement tended to marginalize the Rhetorical approach. One was the Romantic vision of an "absolute music," an unattached medium, disdaining "every aid, every admixture of other arts." By contrast, the Baroque performer had had agendas, things to accomplish. In that earlier time, music had been "pragmatic," as M. H. Abrams called it, looking at the work of art "chiefly as a means to an end, an instrument for getting something done, [tending] to judge its value according to its success in achieving that aim."[71]

That was the reason many Romantics rejected Rhetorical works as "Representational art," art created for calculated goals—art "broken to service."

For a Romantic, the idea of music used as a way to influence people's emotions was vulgar, like using art for propaganda and advertising. We may not share this distaste, but we can understand it, because there is still a lingering sense, inherited from the nineteenth century, that musicians (indeed, "artists" in general) are above questions of money, and so on, and that to use one's work for an ulterior purpose, to provoke and awaken reactions, both "commercializes" it and disqualifies it as art. Modern-day equivalents of music with an agenda would be hymn tunes, national anthems, and of course TV jingles, definitely not your disinterested art for art's sake.

Reacting in the 1830s to the idea of "eloquence" (i.e., Rhetoric), John Stuart Mill writes disparagingly:

> [When the poet's] act of utterance is not itself the end, but a means to an end—viz. by the feelings he himself expresses, to work upon the feelings, or upon the belief, or the will, of another,—when the expression of his emotions . . . is tinged also by that purpose, by that desire of making an impression upon another mind, then it ceases to be poetry, and becomes eloquence.[72]

Abrams comments on this, "The purpose of producing effects upon other men, which for centuries had been the defining character of the art of poetry, now serves precisely the opposite function: it disqualifies a poem by proving it to be rhetoric instead."[73]

As Mill's statement shows, there was a shift in the understanding of words like "Rhetoric" and "eloquence," once noble concepts, but consigned in the nineteenth century to the artistic dumpster.

Hence the often derogatory overtone of the term "Rhetoric" nowadays; Rhetoric is what you use when you argue your own cause, even if it's unashamedly partisan. "[In literary style,] grand and confident poses seemed dishonest, or fraudulent, or merely ridiculous. 'Eloquence' seemed artificial; men and women were described as 'waxing eloquent' when they couldn't quite be believed."[74]

Rhetoric Overwhelmed by Beauty (= Æsthetics)

Another reason Rhetoric was marginalized in the nineteenth century was the new association of art with the Beautiful.

Beauty was not an invention of the Romantics, but the ecstatic contemplation of it was. This became standard Romantic behavior at concerts, as many pictures from the first half of the nineteenth century show. The contemplation of beauty eventually became a branch of philosophy and was given the name "Æsthetics." Immanuel Kant was one of the first to use the new word "Æsthetics" in the 1780s; by 1798 it had appeared in English (although it did not become common until the 1830s).

Laurence Dreyfus writes that in the Romantic period "critical theory abandoned oratory in favour of aesthetics, replacing the perfectible art of invention with the godlike realm of creativity."[75] Nowadays, "æsthetics" is often used to mean the philosophy or theory of art, probably because Romantic ideas of art have predominated for so long, most people buy the Romantic idea that art is exclusively beautiful.

But in the Baroque period, musicians were concerned to evoke a wide range of Affections that wasn't limited to the Beautiful. As Collingwood pointed out,[76] to the Greeks like Plato and Aristotle the concept of beauty had no connection at all with art. Baroque music actually featured certain kinds of negative emotions; sadness, anger, doubt, and so on. North in ca. 1726 wondered what kind of music could be written to correspond to Rafael's "famous Pest House," a melancholy painting on the plague.[77] Looking for only the beauty in Baroque art is to miss part of what it is trying to communicate.

It is true that Bach's friend Abraham Birnbaum, professor of oratory in Leipzig, discusses at some length the beauty of Bach's music.[78] At the same time, there are numerous cases where Bach purposely wrote disagreeable sounds by exploiting technical weaknesses in instruments, which seem to have built-in possibilities for ugliness as well as beauty. There are the out-of-tune 7th, 11th, and 13th partials on the natural trumpet, which Bach regularly used to represent terror, dread, and evil. He used the very flat 7th partial of the trumpet in aria number 7 in Cantata 43 on the word "Qual" ("torment" or "agony"). In his setting of the aria "Zerfließe, mein Herze, in Fluten der Zähren" ("Melt, my heart, in floods of tears") in the *St. John Passion,* the traverso is in f minor, a very weak, "tragic" sounding key regularly using several cross-fingerings, corresponding to the desperate, suffocating emotion of the aria.

Taruskin discusses another aria, BWV 13/5, that deliberately evokes unpleasant Affections. The text is "Groaning and wailing pitifully will not cure sorrow's sickness." Besides the usual slurred descending half-steps, appoggiaturas, chromatic melodies, and diminished seventh chords, Taruskin draws attention to "pungent" progressions. He indicates parallel sevenths in bar four, which he considers

> a solecism, a mistake. The writing [like the subject of the aria] is diseased. The effect on the naivest ear, all the more on a schooled one, is almost literally nauseous. This kind of direct analogy goes beyond Handel's ingratiating ways of representing horror. There is no way this passage could be described as pleasant or entertaining. That is not its purpose.[79]

🔊 AUDIO SAMPLE: 62. Amsterdam Baroque Orchestra, Mertens, Koopman, 2001. Bach: Cantata 13/5

Taruskin doesn't mention the text of the other half of this piece, which turns it into an *antithesis* aria, reversing the theme:

> But one who can to heaven look
> And strives to find his comfort there
> Can easily discover a light of joy
> In his grieving breast.

Bach didn't gratuitously evoke sorrow's sickness, as Taruskin's incomplete report implies. Still, the worse Bach could make it out to be, the more attractive heaven would seem. This was propaganda, music in the service of the Church.

It is possible that the ascendancy of the Beautiful—the exclusively Beautiful—was actually the most decisive element of the Romantic Revolution; in any case, it left little room for Rhetoric and declamation as understood by Baroque musicians. Rhetorical assumptions were too deeply ingrained to have completely disappeared, but there are many signs of the rejection of its principles at the beginning of the nineteenth century. What we now call Rhetoric is a faint shadow of the original model. Rhetoric is not a part of the values of either Romantic or Modern style of performance (even if modern writers on Romantic music sometimes misleadingly use the word for its buzz-value). To recognize its former importance, and to cultivate it once more and benefit from its inspiration, would represent the discovery of something new in our culture.

11

The Rainbow and the Kaleidoscope

Romantic Phrasing Compared with Baroque

Romantic and modern phrasing is seldom based on small units, but is an integral element of legato style. The Romantic long-line or "climax phrase" is traditionally the length of a singer's or wind player's breath. Also called "the overarching phrase," the "sweeping melodic line," the "*sostenuto,*" the "grande ligne," the long-line phrase is essentially a dynamic shape, starting softly and building to one or more notes, often high and usually somewhere in the middle of the phrase (these are the "goals" or "climaxes"), then diminishing to the end. This kind of phrase is performed in a single curve into which subsidiary tonguing, bow changes, or the words of lyrics are (as it were) inserted. One learns to minimize these articulations so they do not interrupt the long arch but are incorporated into it, almost as graces. Another way of thinking of it is that the notes of the phrase are superimposed over a long-tone or *messa di voce* (crescendo-diminuendo). This creates a *sostenuto* effect, one of the hallmarks of Romantic style.

Long-lines go together naturally with legato playing. "One must make legato a special study" is typical Romantic advice. "They who cannot play legato cannot play well." Because of the energy and pressure involved, players of Romantic-type instruments are often reluctant to disturb or interrupt the air-flow or bow-stroke by stopping. Listen to the incredibly long phrases of Mengelberg's violin soloist in "Erbarme dich."

🔊 AUDIO SAMPLE: 63. Concertgebouw Orchestra, Durigo, Mengelberg, 1939. Bach: "Erbarme dich," *Matthew Passion*

It is difficult to say where the phrase ends (if it ever does); at the end of each bar, the violinist gives the standard signals for continuation: crescendo, legato. He thus manages to spin the entire first ritornello of eight bars into one great overarching form: a "rainbow phrase."

The long-line phrase is so generally accepted and assumed nowadays that it is often applied by Period performers to seventeenth- and eighteenth-century music. The tradition is so strong that it is often superimposed on the music unconsciously, I believe. Here it acts as a "Procrustean Bed," since it rarely fits the smaller structural units of the gesture (which I will discuss immediately below). The result is many gratuitous, meaningless crescendos and diminuendos that are misleading to the ear, since they don't confirm the logic of the music—in fact, they often conflict with its meaning. Here is an example by a Period group in a recent recording of Cantata 172/4 by Bach. Bach elaborates an unusually legato line in this aria. In this recording, especially in the Da Capo and the passages when the voices are singing, the crescendos and diminuendos are irrelevant and unnecessary.

🔊 AUDIO SAMPLE: 64. Amsterdam Baroque Orchestra, Prégardien, Koopman, 1995. Bach: Cantata 172/4

The piece is unusually good even by Bach's standards; an invention that almost dances, worthy of Rameau. Here is how the Leonhardt Consort recorded it, succeeding in discovering this dancelike character through their phrasing.

🔊 AUDIO SAMPLE: 65. Leonhardt Consort, v.Altena, Leonhardt, 1987. Bach: Cantata 172/4

The long-line's purpose, like that of all phrasing, is to clarify structure. It works beautifully for music written in the nineteenth century when it was developed. But the structure it looks for in Rhetorical music, especially the climax, is simply not there. Seen from the point of view of the gesture, climax phrasing seems slightly absurd. To quote Anner Bijlsma, "Pianists and conductors, especially, love the expression 'phrasing-slur,' combining many small and different motives into one witless line. It sounds like talking—and all the while keeping one's mouth open."[1] (This from a cellist who is a master of the long-line when he wants it, which is obviously not all the time.)

Harnoncourt credits the successful spread of the long-line phrase to its adoption at the Paris Conservatoire in the early nineteenth century.[2] In the case of the hautboy we know it took place in the 1820s to 1840s at the hands of the Conservatoire's head professor, Gustave Vogt.[3] I assume its development is documented in the new methods commissioned for every instrument taught there.

But already a half-century earlier, in 1770, Burney seems to have been describing something like it; he commented that Quantz, whom he had just met, did not play in "the modern manner . . . of gradually enforcing and diminishing whole passages, as well as single notes."[4] Larger more sustained dynamic shapes seem to have come into vogue fifteen to twenty years after Quantz published his book in 1752.

Figures and Gestures

Melodies in Baroque pieces tend to be complicated, with twists and turns, and this is because their basic structural unit is smaller than the Romantic phrase. Many of these units or motifs derive originally from the spontaneously improvised embellishments and diminutions of seventeenth-century singers, placed on the accented syllables of emotive words in the text. By the end of the century, these motifs and short melodic ideas were being called *figures,* a term borrowed from the "figures of speech" in an oration. Instrumentalists had meanwhile taken them up, and without the connection to text, melodic figures became formulas for constructing tunes, like building blocks. Baroque melodies were constructed as a series of figures, some with names and some generic.

A number of figures were described and given names. For our purpose in talking about phrasing, we will be considering the *melodic* figures. But there were other kinds of figures: a fugue was a figure, as was a retrograde repetition of a phrase. Many figures were characteristic harmonic progressions or rhythmic patterns. Bartel classifies figures into seven categories:

1 Figures of melodic repetition
2 Figures of harmonic repetition; fugal figures
3 Figures of representation and depiction
4 Figures of dissonance and displacement
5 Figures of interruption and silence

6 Figures of melodic and harmonic ornamentation
7 Miscellaneous figures

As I mentioned before, John Butt's *Bach Interpretation* is useful in clarifying for modern performers what musical figures are and how they might influence performance. Butt chose Bach's music as the subject of his book for a good reason. Bach, "to the astonishment and annoyance of his contemporaries,"[5] marked performing details—slurs in this case—very thoroughly when he had the time. This was unusual, because musicians in the eighteenth century were expected to know where to slur. Since these habits and formulas were common knowledge, they were rarely put down on paper. For us now, without the knowledge of these habits and formulas, Bach's markings are uniquely helpful.

Butt systematically studied Bach's autograph scores and parts, and was able to show how Bach tended to slur specific figures consistently; they are the most common slurs in his music.[6] It was normal to slur figures because they had originally been graces, elaborations of a single note.[7] In the sources, certain figures are shown slurred, like the *groppo* and *tirata* (see examples 11.10 and 11.12). Butt suggests that Bach's slurs may have served as warnings against emphasizing unimportant notes within a figure through misplaced articulation.[8]

The connection between slurs and figures provides a handle to modern musicians performing Baroque repertoire, helping them orient their articulation and phrasing to the units in which composers of the time thought. Using this knowledge, it is possible to infer other places where slurs would normally have been placed (and marked by Bach, had time been available).

Although Bach added many of his slurs in later editing, some of them were part of the original inspirations of the pieces when he first wrote them down. These built-in slurs would have been integral to his original invention, essential to the character of the movement.

Butt suggests the possibility that any recognizable figure in Bach's music—indeed, that of his contemporaries as well—is susceptible to slurring. And considering what a slur implies, this can be important for creating variety in expression.

In chapter 6 I mentioned the role of the slur in the Baroque period as an indication of emphasis with a diminuendo. In Baroque treatises, slurs were normally discussed in the section on graces. Later, slurs gradually lost their expressive role as a form of accentuation and (as down- and up-bowing became more equalized) developed into a technical instruction for legato playing. For Bach, marking a series of slurs, as in example 11.1, is a way of writing a chain of accents, one at the beginning of each slur; not the modern single impulse with superimposed articulation, but three independent thrusts, like short pickups (see ex. 11.2). Playing this way creates a piece with a somewhat different meaning.

Example 11.1 and 11.2   Paired slurs and effect

Examples of Melodic Figures

Many musical figures in Classical Rhetoric have strange names that sound like diseases—*parrhesia,* for instance, or *subsumtio.* Familiarity comes quickly, however, and in fact some of the melodic figures turn out to be familiar Baroque ornaments , like the appoggiatura (ex. 11.4). Ornamental figures like these usually had Italian names rather than Greek or Latin ones.

In 1739, Mattheson commented that

> Many might think then that we have used figures and suchlike for so long now without knowing their names or meanings, we can be content to put rhetoric on the back burner. These seem even more absurd than *Le Bourgeois Gentilhomme* of Molière, who had no idea it was a pronoun when he said, "I," "you," "he;" or that it was an imperative when he said to his servants, "Come here!"[9]

We are in the same position today. Most of us don't know the names of the figures we play all the time. Part of the reason for this is that the names of figures were never consistently or regularly used. Nor were the same patterns considered to be figures by everyone.

In practice, figures are malleable and can have multiple meanings depending on how they are performed—fast, slow, loud, soft, sinuous, abrupt—each conveys a different Affection. Figures are thus performance-sensitive, so that composing does not by itself fix unchangeably the choice of figures. As Vickers writes, "The paradoxical difficulty of writing its history is that rhetoric was meant to be done, not contemplated."[10] Still, the best way of learning to recognize figures is probably by analyzing pieces looking for them (in which case they will temporarily have to have a single arbitrary form).

Here (abstracted into notation) are a few examples of some standard melodic figures, taken from various German sources like Bernhard (ca. 1660), Printz (1696), Walther (1732), and Mattheson (1739).[11]

> *Accent, accentus.* An upper or lower neighboring note that precedes or follows a written note (exx. 11.3, 11.4). When it precedes, it is accented.

Example 11.3 *accentus*. First example. Upper neighboring note follows ("graced" version above, with four figures in first bar, for instance)

Example 11.4 *accentus*. Second example. The first three bars show different ways of notating the effect of the fourth bar; the *accentus* is the second eighth-note

Acciacatura. "An additional, dissonant note added to a chord, which is released immediately after its execution."[12] Not notated.

Anticipatio. "An additional upper or lower neighbouring note after a principal note, prematurely introducing a note belonging to the subsequent harmony or chord"[13] (exx. 11.5, 11.6).

Example 11.5 *anticipatio*. First example. Without syncopation

Example 11.6 *anticipatio*. Second example. Syncopated version in first three bars of the notes in second three bars

Circolo mezzo. A four-note motif with a common second and fourth note. The *circolo mezzo* is half of a *circulo,* which is "a series of usually eight notes in a circular or sine wave formation"[14] (exx. 11.7, 11.8).

Example 11.7 *circolo mezzo*. First example. Four "half-circles"

Example 11.8 *circolo mezzo*. Second example

Corta. "A three-note figure in which one note's duration equals the sum of the other two."[15] Very common (ex. 11.9).

Example 11.9   *corta.* Six versions

Groppo. A *groppo* is the reverse of a *circolo mezzo*, being "a four-note motif with a common first and third note"[16] (ex. 11.10).

Example 11.10   *groppo.* Applied in first bar to plain version (shown in second bar)

Suspirans. Similar to a *corta,* but the longer note has a pause half its duration before it[17] (ex. 11.11).

Example 11.11   *suspirans.* Two examples, first as *corta*, second as *suspirans*

Tirata. "A rapid scalar passage, spanning a fourth to an octave or more"[18] (ex. 11.12).

Example 11.12   *tirata.* Two examples

Tremolo / trillo. The definition varies between:
- wavering pitch or vibrato;
- a rapid (slurred) reiteration of one note;
- a trill.

The inconsistent terminology goes back to the early seventeenth century. From the 1690s, the *tremolo* was associated with the rapid (slurred) reiteration of one note, and the *trillo* with the trill.[19]

Gestures as the Antiphrase

The number of figures was in principle unlimited. As Lamy wrote in 1675 in his *L'Art de parler,* "I have not attempted to speak of all the figures . . . there is no better book for that than one's own heart."[20]

For all the figures that can be found in written sources, there are many more that might be called unofficial or generic. The original writers on Rhetoric considered figures exceptions, something "other than the obvious and ordinary." In that case, the other "ordinary" melodic units comparable in size to figures must have had a separate identity. I call these generic units of meaning, of which phrases are made up, *gestures* (or more properly, *audible expressive phrasing gestures*). Baroque melodies consist of a continual series of gestures: brief melodic events, structural cells of one to several notes in length. Each gesture expresses or emphasizes a single independent idea, sentiment, or attitude. The characteristic that defines a gesture is meaning, however slight. Gestures have been called "the hieroglyphics of speech."[21]

I notice people using the word "gesture" in this same approximate sense nowadays, but I should immediately say that as far as I know they were not identified by this name in original sources. There is no question that the concept existed, first of all because the music is demonstrably built on it. Second, figures are gestures, and there is no lack of documentation of them. And third, the modern performing style that is in general use today for playing Baroque music, a style that grew out of the music itself, is based on gestures. A hundred years from now, musicians may decide we got it all wrong, of course, and then gestures will hit the recycle bin, but for now, although seldom identified by name, they are the essence and core of current practice.

Quantz called the smallest units of musical meaning "pensées" in French and "Gedanke" in German (he also occasionally used the word "Sinn"). These words mean ideas / thoughts / senses / feelings / meanings.[22] An alternative, more modern term for gestures is *"motifs."* The NG2 defines motif as

> a short musical idea, melodic, harmonic, rhythmic, or any combination of these three. A motif may be of any size, and is most commonly regarded as the shortest subdivision of a theme or phrase that still maintains its identity as an idea. It is most often thought of in melodic terms, and it is this aspect of motif that is connoted by the term "figure".[23]

Motifs are frequently expected to recur, however, unlike gestures. Another problem with the word "motif" is that it did not enter the English language in any of its meanings until the mid-nineteenth century at the earliest.

In her famous article of 1980, Ursula Kirkendale wrote,

> Music of renaissance and baroque composers, who had been immersed in the study of Latin rhetoric while in school, cannot be adequately understood on the basis of our twentieth-century curricula, where rhetoric hardly exists any longer as an academic discipline and where instruction in music theory is too often limited to mere descriptive analysis of sounds in a vacuum. Because of this, Bach's instrumental music has come to be regarded (and performed) as "abstract," its rhetorical basis and function no longer understood.

To comprehend earlier composers we must try to reconstruct *their* educational and intellectual environment, restore the priority of humanistic methods, and perhaps even systematically exclude narrow and anachronistic modern attitudes which were unknown to them.[24]

In a similar vein, Laurence Dreyfus argues in his book *Bach and the Patterns of Invention,* that "historical propriety means avoiding explanations for a piece of music that one can assert to have been utterly inconceivable to the composer." This would include the imposition of long-line phrasing so often heard in performances of Baroque pieces. "Pragmatically," he continues, "this means being suspicious of terms that collide with well-established concepts and assumptions current in Bach's day, while at the same time daring to theorize beyond what can be reconstructed from explicit statements of 18th-century music writings."[25] I take courage from these views in my use of the concept of gesture.

Here is an example, the 1st movement of the "Septième Concert" by Couperin. It will be easier to communicate the idea of gestures with the help of recordings. I take the liberty of including here some of my own because it is more efficient to explain by playing than by writing. The extract is given in notation, with the gestures marked, in example 11.13.

Example 11.13   F. Couperin, Septième Concert, 1st movement

AUDIO SAMPLE: 66. Haynes, Napper, Haas, 1998. F. Couperin, Septième Concert, 1st movement

When the end of a gesture, often the last note, serves also as the first note of the next gesture, the "overlapping meaning" that results amounts to a musical pun.[26] Here is an example of overlapping: a short movement from one of Castrucci's sonatas (he was the leader of Handel's opera orchestra in London); it contains many overlapping gestures (ex. 11.14).

Example 11.14   Castrucci: Sonata, G major, 1st movement, gestures and phrases marked

Gestures can be situated next to each other, yet have completely different meanings and characters. Nothing can be assumed; each gesture has its own independent tempo, articulation, and dynamic shape, and is often in contrast with what precedes and follows it. This produces a complex line with constant variety and unevenness. As Quantz described it:

> Light and shadow must be constantly maintained. . . . a continual alternation of the Forte and Piano must be observed.[27] . . . In the majority of pieces one Passion constantly alternates with another, the performer must know how to judge the nature of the Passion that each idea [pensée/Gedanken] contains, and constantly make his execution conform to it.[28]

To illustrate the possibilities of separating gestures, here is a recording of the opening ritornello of an aria for alto and hautbois d'amour by Bach on the text, "Ach, unaussprechlich ist die Noth" (Ah, inexpressible is our distress). Bach made the instrumental part quite difficult technically, and its faltering incoherence and tongue-tied frustration is built-in to the part (ex. 11.15).

Example 11.15   BWV 116/2, opening ritornello, bars 1–12, Hautbois d'amour, gestures only marked

AUDIO SAMPLE: 67. Haynes, Taylor, Napper, Poirier, 1998. Bach: Cantata 116/2

The first three notes (bracket A) form a standard *corta* (see ex. 11.9). Bach has slurred them, probably to warn the player that they are a unit. The next four notes (bracket B) are less abrupt and are connected by logic (= harmony) to the three beyond that (bracket C, also a *corta*). Bach also slurred bracket C (the first time it occurs), as well as the written-out mordents in bars five and six.

Although these first three gestures connect with each other, each has a different character, and the melody gains in depth and richness if these differences are made audible.

About deciding where to place the divisions between the gestures, this is somewhat arbitrary and I think there are many ways to do this. The same player might even change their mind and place them differently at different times.

I originally learned to phrase by long-line, so it has been a revelation to me to recast Rhetorical music into the smaller units in which it seems originally to have been conceived. To phrase by figure/gesture is to go from two to three dimensions, to endow Baroque music with depth and relief, a natural calmness and an assured sense of timing.

Orders or Levels of Meaning: Gesture and Phrase

Let's go up the hierarchy of phrasing one level. This next level, which usually involves binding several gestures together in small groups, is a *phrase*. The phrase creates another order of meaning, communicating something that could not have been expressed except by combining gestures. Phrases were not seriously written about until the late eighteenth century, but the concept was obviously in use long before that. The phrase, like the sentence in language, has more individual character and makes a more decisive statement than the gesture. A phrase often represents a complete harmonic progression, finishing with a cadence.

A practical outcome of thinking in phrases as well as gestures is that fragmentation is avoided, and gestures give the impression of leading somewhere. Phrasing also increases the options for timing. Timing is waiting or not waiting just the right amount to get the maximum of meaning from the music.

Like gestures, phrases are continuous (that is, when one finishes, a new one begins). They share with gestures the attribute of being defined by their meaning, and they have no fixed length. Here is the Bach again (ex. 11.16) with the gestures as marked in example 11.15; the first phrase includes three gestures, the second the same, the third 6, and so on.

Example 11.16 BWV 116/2, bars 1–12, Hautbois d'amour, with gestures and phrases marked

The first phrase of this aria, made up of the combined effects of the first three gestures, begins with an Affection that seems to be searching (trying, actually, to find a way to express the text's "inexpressible" distress); in phrase two the search is repeated in another key (changing key is a statement in itself). The written-out mordent of the third phrase conveys frustration (at a later point the mordent is executed by both voice and instrument together); in phrase four the frustration is repeated. In phrase five a last desperate breakout is attempted, and finally, in phrase six this introductory ritornello ends in defeat and resignation.

The vocal entry confirms this phrasing. The word "Ach" is spoken on the first *corta*, and Bach sometimes writes it to be sung or played by itself, being cut off with an *abruptio*, a figure of interruption, a breaking off or rupture of the musical line; in some cases (like the voice's first two entries, both aborted) the phrase, broken off after the *corta*, is finished by the instrument.

Inflection (Individual Note-Shaping)

The difference between Romantic long-line or climax phrasing and gestural phrasing also affects the dynamic shape of single notes. In the long-line phrase, a note is a segment of a larger shape and goes essentially in one direction (toward, or away from, the climax note, in the form of a crescendo or decrescendo). On this subject, Harnoncourt writes, "The individual tone in music after about 1800 appears to me two-dimensional in its *sostenuto,* while an ideal tone in earlier music had a physical, or three-dimensional effect because of its inner dynamics."[29] Individual note-shaping or dynamic inflection has been a controversial subject among Period musicians. Quantz writes, for instance, "Each note, whether it is a quarter, eighth, or 16th, should have its own Piano and Forte, to the extent that time permits."[30]

Agricola, who in 1757 published annotations to his translation of Tosi on singing (1723), writes under the rubric *Mezza di voce,* "Each note, no matter how short its duration, must be given its crescendo and decrescendo."[31] Leopold Mozart observed that "Every tone, even the strongest attack, has a small, even if barely audible, softness at the beginning of the stroke; for it otherwise be no tone but only an unpleasant and unintelligible noise. This same softness must be heard also at the end of each tone."[32] Tartini's description of note-shape, similar to Mozart's,[33] inspired David Boyden to comment:

> What Mozart and Tartini seem to be saying is that there is a small initial 'give' to the old bow which has to be taken up before a good tone can emerge; and this remark is perfectly consistent with the character of the old bow. The same 'give' also occurs in the modern bow, but it is much less because the concave construction of the modern bow stick does not permit it; and this fact, combined with a modern technique that cultivates the smoothest possible initial attack and bow change, makes this 'small softness' practically imperceptible to the ear in modern playing.

Even the harpsichord does a subtle inflection; each note has a discrete shape, with a peak and "decay." Fabian comments on note-shaping:

Echo- and sigh-effects and paired slurs might [can in principle] be produced on modern instruments by conscious control of dynamics or by strong accents (e.g. Dart, Menuhin, Marriner). However, these methods never create those slight, 'living' nuances inherent in the physical characteristics of a baroque violin or transverse flute. The early bow's almost constant fluctuation of volume was, and to some extent still is, so foreign to modern musicians' aesthetic ideals that they seem to have fought against the effect, striving to neutralize this 'flaw' of their instruments for quite a while (e.g. Wenzinger, Harnoncourt 1964, Collegium Aureum, Newman). Even today, albeit less so since the second half of the 1980s, groups may be scorned for being 'mannered' in using 'too much' *messa di voce*. Among the recordings [of the Brandenburgs] only Leonhardt/Kuijken et al. (1976–77) and Harnoncourt (1982) explore the potentials of these 18th-century playing techniques. The result is a far more articulate, locally nuanced, rhythmically flexible rendering, providing a new kind of expression, one that highlights the speaking quality of Bach's music.[34]

Note-shaping and complex dynamic inflection are shown quite spectacularly in Quantz's famous Adagio (ex. 11.17), designed to demonstrate the "continual alternation of the Forte and Piano" that he advocated.[35] The average number of dynamic changes per bar is probably between 5 and 10 (it's 11 in the first two bars).

This extreme use of subtle amounts of dynamic inflection probably represented the general practice of the period prior to the appearance of Quantz's book. Mattheson wrote in 1739, "[The singer] should cultivate a wide range of dynamic control (since the innumerable degrees of softness and loudness 'will also move the emotions [Gemüthern]' of his listeners)."[36] But by 1770, when Burney met Quantz, he implied that Quantz was by then out of date (evidently an easy thing to be in the eighteenth century).

There was a good deal of experiment with dynamic inflection in Holland from the late 1960s, especially by Frans Brüggen on the recorder. But the long-line and modern taste gradually prevailed on this issue (popularly known in England as the "Dutch swell"), and it has gradually disappeared.[37] Today, dynamic inflection is definitely out; along with rubato, it is rarely heard in orchestras playing in any style. Combined with a rejection of beat hierarchy, it is little wonder that performances in Eloquent style are sometimes described as using "self-conscious downbeat bashing" and "distracting *messa di voce*."[38] Fuller speaks of "a kind of generalized rubato intended to clarify the metre and highlight important notes or events. . . . Its salient characteristic is an exaggerated lengthening of the downbeat. . . . Further rhythmic distortions may emphasize dissonant or climactic notes. . . . Sometimes all sense of the beat, far from being clarified, disappears in a fog of nuance."[39] One person's "fog of nuance" may be another's "more articulate, locally nuanced, rhythmically flexible rendering," and we are fortunate to be able to choose. Here is a most impressive example of what Fuller probably means: Susie Napper playing

Example 11.17   Quantz Adagio

Corrette. Personally, I love it, and the sense that it could be entirely different the next time she plays it.

AUDIO SAMPLE: 68. Susie Napper, 2005. Corrette: 3d movement from the Sonata in d minor from *Les délices de la solitude*

Example 11.17 Continued

* Each note of this phrase with a crescendo.
** In a "flattering" manner.

And for comparison, another excellent version of the same movement by Nadina Mackie Jackson on bassoon.

AUDIO SAMPLE: 69. Nadina Mackie Jackson, 2005. Corrette: 3d movement from the Sonata in d minor from *Les délices de la solitude*

V

THE END OF "EARLY" MUSIC

12

Passive and Active Musicking

Stop Staring and Grow Your Own

No matter how well and sensitively they can play or sing,
a musician who's not at home [with the art of composition] is
hardly better than birds that chirp their little songs so finely
and neatly.

(Johann Kuhnau, *Der musicalische Quacksalber*, 1700)

The Cover Band Mentality

Piers Adams of the ensemble Red Priest ponders the idea that once all the good Baroque pieces have been performed and recorded, what do we do? Should we then, he wonders, "all stop at that point and put our feet up with a glow of self-satisfaction? Surely if music is to remain a living art then the concept of performer as arranger/co-composer must be revived."[1] That seems right to me as well. Surely we should share the sense of freedom that musicians felt at the time. Not just in arranging their own and other people's compositions, but in writing new ones. But I know it will be something of a miracle to overcome our habitual Canonic thinking, which constrains us to play the same pieces over and over again, like cover bands.

The modern cover band typically imitates one of the famous rock groups of the late 1960s, like the Beatles or Led Zeppelin. Cover bands may wear the same clothes and hairdos, or act the same way as their models. The basic attribute of cover bands, however, is that they play someone else's music.

The groups they imitate weren't themselves cover bands, except maybe when they were just getting started. The original bands wrote their own songs and rarely did anyone else's. In this way they were like their forefathers: Vivaldi didn't often play Albinoni; if he was in need of another piece for his show, he wrote one (maybe in imitation of Albinoni, stealing his best ideas). Nor did Handel produce the operas of his rival in

London, Porpora. He created new ones to the taste of the town, each aria showing off perfectly the strong points of the singer who would perform it.

Why is this no longer happening in Baroque music? To be sure, we have concerts of Venetian violin concertos. Yes, we are getting Baroque operas. But there are no newly-composed Baroque operas to be heard, tailor-made to the production's cast. Our Baroque concerts only "cover" music already written. That surely would have struck Baroque musicians as very odd.

The eighteenth century had a word to describe musicians who only performed but did not compose. They were called "*Musikanten.*" "Hirelings," Bach's friend Abraham Birnbaum called them, "paid to . . . bring into sound pieces composed by others."[2] They were on the bottom end of the musical hierarchy (unless they were very clever on their instrument and could claim the title of "virtuoso").

A cover band (Rock or Baroque) pretends to be making it up, but in fact *they* know that *we* know it has happened before. How many of their performances are work-copies, duplicates of specific events from the past? Christopher Hogwood, in a notorious recording, actually tried work-copying the first performance of Beethoven's *Eroica,* including an "original" lack of rhythmic and dynamic nuance (many of the players were amateurs, but in those days that didn't necessarily mean they were less good than professionals—or "mercenaries," as North called them).

But in this chapter I'll try to frame the activities of most Period musicians in terms of style-copying—not bringing back the past, but taking inspiration from it.

Playing in the Wind

Still on the same basic subject, I'd like to talk for a moment about notation, which, although a magnificent tool, sometimes has its disadvantages. As Christopher Small points out, "it is a limiter, since it confines what can be played to what has been notated, so the player's power of self-directed performance is liable to atrophy."[3] For many modern musicians, the ability to improvise is at best undeveloped, and I believe it is not an exaggeration to say that many of them are quite unable to function without a written page in front of them (or in their heads).

The historical progress from orality to literacy has been gradual. The centuries prior to the Industrial Revolution saw the two elements in some kind of balance, so that musicians thrived in both worlds simultaneously.[4] Baroque parts and scores bear this out, leaving many decisions to the performers.

Plato believed that writing destroys memory. Some improvising musicians agree. Derek Bailey writes that there is a general suspicion among improvisers that to be able to read somehow blunts the inspiration to improvise.[5] But reading does not appear to have reduced the improvising skills of Baroque musicians. They wrote down "charts" (of sorts) and read from them, and at the same time were also trained like jazz musicians; they could fake and improvise both treble lines and continuo realizations in elaborate and sophisticated ways. They were in the enviable position of being both "literate" and non-literate musicians at the same time. If the wind accidentally blew their notes off the stand, they could keep playing.

Among organists, the art of improvising coherent, structured pieces of music still exists, and there are even improvisation contests like the one in Haarlem on the great St. Bavo organ. In the Baroque period, certain musicians like Sweelinck, Frescobaldi, Buxtehude, Bach, and Handel were famous for their public performances of improvisation. Handel's organ concertos, Opp. 4 and 7, have a number of movements marked "Adagio ad lib" or "Fuga ad lib." with no written solo part. That Handel could create such pieces on the spot is already impressive to us, but the fact that these pieces were published implies that Handel expected other soloists to be able to do the same. Not everyone was at that level, but improvisation was evidently in the air in a way it is not today.

Gracing: The Border between Composing and Performing

In Baroque times, it was generally agreed that the essential graces, in their appropriate places, were, well, essential—that is, indispensable. A melody without them was a mere skeleton, devoid of beauty.

If one wished to combine written and improvised music together in the same piece, something like the gracing symbols of the Baroque period would probably be the eventual solution. This kind of notation permits both types of music to coexist. The composer writes the plain air, providing the performer with inspiration and material, and the performer contributes unwritten additions on the spot. Gracing symbols were at a halfway point; they signaled that "this place needs the addition of a stylized reinforcement, or moment of concentrated intensity." The performer decided how to realize the effect.

The event was only described approximately, with a coded sign of some kind, the most common being a little "+" above a note. The graces were approximate because it was generally felt, especially in the seventeenth century, that they were too subtle to be captured on paper. Peri spoke of essential graces "that cannot be written, but if written, cannot impart any coherent meaning."[6] The first French source to take the time to explain the graces, Bacilly in the mid-seventeenth century, scrupulously refrained from marking them in his Airs, so the performer could demonstrate their abilities, and because he believed that graces were too subtle to be reduced to standard notation.[7] Lully, at about the same time, took a strong stand against the larger passaggi, though not the smaller graces.[8]

Graces are the ultimate test of a performer's musicianship and grasp of style. From the simplest trill to the cadenza, they immediately reveal the sensitivity and imagination—even the basic personality—of the musician. Is the trill automatic or does it fit organically into the movement's Affection? Is the cadenza gracious, learned, impressive, surprising, overflowing with ideas that might produce another movement? They are a window into the performer's heart and mind.

Rameau's comments on the essential graces are interesting, of course:

> No matter how well a grace is rendered, it will always lack a certain something that it deserves, if it is not guided by feeling. Too much or too little, too early or too late, suspensions or swelled notes held too long or too short, or the right number of repetitions of a trill (commonly called a *cadence*)—expression, and the context, require this perfect timing, without which an ornament becomes merely trite.[9]

Gracing symbols are a good example of indeterminacy in notation, the sort of subject that attracted writers.[10] With their ambiguous role, graces could be varied as the musicians saw fit, and others that were not written could be added. In notating Baroque gracing symbols, it was the overlap between exact placement and inexact manner that produced discussion in written sources. Graces can be seen as a balance between the composer's control (i.e., the placement) and the performer's (the manner). Couperin requested in one of his prefaces that all the essential graces he marked be "observed to the letter, without addition or subtraction."[11] That he needed to mention this is an indication that the reverse was occurring.

No wonder, then, that with the greater authority composers began to assume in the early nineteenth century, a reaction against gracing developed. The status of gracing in the Baroque period might roughly have corresponded to that of vibrato now: a technique inspiring emotion, not universally appreciated, but hardly seen as fundamentally affecting the composition. By Mendelssohn's time a century later, however, gracing was frowned on and was regarded as changing the written melodic line.

Predictably, the status of graces went steadily downhill from 1800 on, along with that of performers. Gracing and passaggi have had a rough time over the last two centuries. With E. T. A. Hoffmann's words in the early nineteenth century, we are witness to the transformation of the trill from a grace into a melodic attribute under the exclusive control of the composer: "Is it not wonderful that a tradition has been established concerning the precise embellishments of the song . . . so that today no one would dare introduce a foreign embellishment without censure."[12] Brown comments, "With Beethoven's work, for example, the traditional forms of embellishment—trills, grace notes—have become part of the basic musical structure; they now figure among the work's motifs, and nothing more can be added by the performer. Remember Beethoven, upset when performers added trills.[13]

By the 1830s and 1840s a reaction had developed to the elaborate *decoratio* indulged in by opera singers, and it came to be generally regarded as abusive. Gracing continued to be common into the middle of the nineteenth century but was reserved for lighter pieces with simpler harmonies. More serious pieces (at the time, generally Germanic) were not embellished. Hunter observes that "in the number of examples taken from the increasingly sacrosanct chamber music of Haydn, Mozart, and Beethoven" in Baillot's *Art du violon* of 1835, it is clear that "no ornamentation was to be added."[14]

By Victorian times Edward Dannreuther, founder of the London Wagner Society, was writing in his *Musical Ornamentation* (a book that remained a standard reference for many years), "No one will care to advocate the revival of a host of obsolete curlicues and twirligigs, or the resuscitation of a habit of improvising facile variantes or running into division. Divisions and graces have had their day and have served their purpose."[15]

Improvisation: The Domain of the Performer

A master [i.e., professional musician] can tell by the plaine notes, and the course of the air, how to grace with advantage, as well as he that made the composition.

Roger North, The Musicall Gramarian, ca.1726

North wrote in the 1720s that "the practice of Gracing [improvising passaggi] is the practise [!] of Composition, and without skill in the latter, the other will never succeede."[16] Quantz tells us the same thing. The French essential graces, he writes, were actually only the tip of the iceberg, because they could be learned without understanding harmony. But, for the more elaborate Italian passaggi, including preludes, divisions, and cadenzas, one had to have knowledge of composition. Quantz wrote, "You will have to do like many singers, and keep a master constantly at hand from whom you can learn variations for each Adagio."[17] This custom has not yet been revived, which accounts for the dismal cadenzas of most singers nowadays—cadenzas being commonly expected in vocal solos.

Modern performers (including many HIP performers) tend not to be very interested in extemporization. Although we all improvise with language for hours every day, most of us have had the child's delight in improvising music trained out. The natural ability to play "off the page," to fake it when necessary, is drummed out of us nowadays before we're half finished with conservatory training. Where seventeenth- and eighteenth-century musicians had a casual view of written music, and no doubt "improved" pieces regularly, a modern performer usually feels a definite constraint about altering anything.

This seems quite remarkable to musicians who play by ear; in the sardonic words of one:

> In the Straight world the performer approaches music on tiptoe. Music is precious and performance constitutes a threat to its existence. So, of course, he

has to be careful. Also, the music doesn't belong to him. He's allowed to handle it but then only under the strictest supervision. Somebody, somewhere, has gone through a lot of trouble to create this thing, this composition, and the performer's primary responsibility is to preserve it from damage. At its highest, music is a divine ideal conceived by a super-mortal. In which case performance becomes a form of genuflection.[18]

The least a singer could do nowadays is use the trick of Mme Mara, a famous prima donna of the late eighteenth century. In her performance of an aria by Gazzaniga in Venice in 1790, "She wrote out four different ornamented versions. By memorizing the different versions and employing them on subsequent nights during the run of the opera, Mara was able to give the impression of improvisation, which, she boasted, secured her triumph that season in Venice over her rival Brigida Banti."[19]

That the ability to embellish overlapped into composition shows the ambiguity that existed at the time between performing and composing. At one of his Saturday soirées, Rossini asked the singer Adelina Patti, after she had given a particularly florid rendition of one of his more famous arias ("Una voce poco fa"), "Very nice, my dear, and who wrote the piece you just performed?"[20] (A good question!)

Dennis Libby wrote of late eighteenth-century Italian *opera seria*:

> The composer determined the general character and structure of the composition and filled in its main outlines, leaving the surface detail to be supplied spontaneously by the performer in the heightened state induced by performance. This division of function was conceived of as complementary, with the contributions of composer and performer both essential to the final result.[21]

Composers usually wrote for specific musicians, with their techniques and capabilities in mind. In their turn, performers were highly sensitive "to the character of the music as the composer had determined it, for it was the performer's task to intensify that character." To quote Libby:

> The performer's contribution to a piece of music in performance was not regarded as post-compositional but as the final stage in the act of composition itself. It follows that it was not the composer's score but the performed music that embodied the finished work of art, one that was both fluid—varying with each realisation—and ephemeral, not directly recoverable. The concept of performance as work of art can be seen as the central principle of this musical practice.

In such an atmosphere, something else emerges: no longer the composer's score, but the entire company's (built, of course, on the genius of the official composer). This principle would apply especially to a musical genre like opera seria, where:

> 'What is to us the "work",' he [Strohm] writes, 'was 250 years ago only the "production",' and that was dominated to such an extent by singers that, as reconstruction, 'a revival of an opera seria today should really concentrate

less on what Handel or Hasse wrote than on what Senesino or Farinelli did with the chief role.' And if we had a Senesino, 'it might not matter so much that some of his arias were by Harnoncourt and not Handel. In fact they could even be by Penderecki.'[22]

In recent concerts, Matthias Maute improvised over original orchestral material in a Vivaldi recorder concerto. Playing without music, he extemporized parts of the outer Allegros, a completely new Adagio, and a cadenza of close to ten minutes. He wrote me recently, "The improvised Vivaldi cadenza was okay, though a little shaky—I grew nervous. It is such an uncommon situation to improvise a musical/technical exhibitionist piece . . . but it is part of the 'métier', that's why I absolutely want to go down that road." I hope other musicians will have the courage to follow Matthias.

Some improvisers believe it is impossible to transcribe improvisations. But then, the best performers of written music give the illusion that they are improvising (since to read mechanically is the kiss of death). Besides, composing is often a matter of repeating a good invention often enough to be able to remember it and get it down on paper. The act of writing down the notes is actually a mechanical process that consists of documenting an idea that already exists. The creative moment has already taken place when the invention or inspiration occurred to the composer while performing or practicing. Often, of course, this will be followed by a structural organization that can sometimes be achieved only on paper.

In the relationship between composer and performer, the two extremes of the spectrum were improvisation and Canon. Improvisation entirely eliminated the need for a separate person to produce musical inventions and write them down (the composer). In Romantic playing, the reverse was true, so that a recent writer like Peter Kivy could ask, "Composing is one kind of skill, performing another. Why should anyone think that talent or expertise in the one should imply either in the other?"[23]

It isn't surprising, therefore, that improvisation declined in the Romantic period, while the role of the artist-composer increased. By the twentieth century, improvisation was virtually purged from Classical music, and "untouchability" was the rule. Bailey writes bitterly of Modern style:

> The petrifying effect of European classical music on those things it touches—jazz, many folk musics, and all popular musics have suffered grievously in their contact with it—made the prospect of finding improvisation there pretty remote. Formal, precious, self-absorbed, pompous, harbouring rigid conventions and carefully preserved hierarchical distinctions; obsessed with its geniuses and their timeless masterpieces, shunning the accidental and the unexpected.[24]

Style-Copying in Composing

Let's test the principle of style-copying with the example of Period composing. I presume it is clear what I mean by the term "Period composing."

I'm not thinking of pieces that are essentially modern but tip their hat to past styles, citing them as references. Nor do I mean Modernist pieces written for Period instruments. What I have in mind is in the same spirit as Skowroneck's Lefébure harpsichord—a style-copy, which I defined in chapter 8 as "a copy, not based on any specific original, that is so stylistically consistent that experts cannot discover anachronisms or inconsistencies in it; a correctly attributed 'fake.'"

This would also be a good definition of newly composed Period music. The particular work is quite original, but the vessel in which it is contained, that is, both the genre and the style, is fixed and constant—new wine in old bottles. This is the way Baroque composers composed their pieces: within the conditions of a shared convention.

And this runs directly into a diametrically opposed starting point of New music. Most modern composers are involved in *inventing* a system, a style as it were, for every new piece. Actually writing the notes can be less interesting than developing the new medium. New and unique bottles, wine unspecified.

Roll over Beethoven

Talking over the idea of Period composing with friends and colleagues while writing this book, I've been surprised to see that it inspires controversy, sometimes even from people who have devoted their lives to HIP. Naturally, I've tried to find out why, but I have yet to get a complete answer. Subjects that elicit strong emotional responses like this usually touch on basic issues, though it may not be immediately obvious what the issues are. Thinking about them can act like an X-ray machine, showing HIP's basic values, and where it—or part of it—will not go.

Period composition gets all kinds of disparaging names like "mimicry," "parody," "plagiarism," and "spuriosity." These words are not normally applied to any of the parallel musical activities of Period musicking. Nobody accuses Period musicians of playing "plagiarized" or "fake" concerts, for instance. Period recordings are never called "spuriosities." Nor is a careful replica of a recorder called a "parody" of an original, or an Urtext edition a "mimicry" of the original manuscript. But as soon as the idea of composing in Period style comes up, one begins to hear these words.

The objections to Period composing seem to revolve around four issues:

- Period performing is alright but Period composing is not;
- the continuing force of the imperative of originality and the cult of genius;
- the question of copying;
- chronocentrism: composing should be exclusively in Modern style.

I've heard people say that to compose in a Period style would not be speaking with one's true voice. The implications of that are disheartening:

that *performing* in a consciously old style is also putting on a false voice; acting, in other words. As if the whole of HIP was a kind of theoretical exercise. Yet I wonder how composing in the style of twenty-five years ago is any different—any truer—than composing in the style of three hundred twenty-five years ago.

I'm beginning to realize that, just as all concert music—even that of last night's New music concert—is music of the past. Whether we use the style of three hundred years ago or the style of ten years ago, or ten days, it is some kind of tradition we are using; the only difference is the age of the tradition. A style ten years old has to be self-consciously learned exactly like a style of three hundred years ago. The issue, it seems, is a matter of how far back you feel like going.

Ton Koopman recounts his own experience as a conservatory student, for instance:

> I wanted to study composition as well, but I always composed in 17th or 18th century style. The teacher at the conservatory felt that I should change, that I should write in a modern style. I said to him, "but I'm not interested in doing that", and he replied, "then I'm not interested in teaching you". So occasions like . . . my reconstruction of the St Mark Passion, where I composed the missing recitatives, are welcome.[25]

Among those who are New music adherents or composers themselves, there is a general feeling that New music is in trouble, audiences are small, and if it were not for "artificial respiration" (universities and government grants), it would succumb. One way out of the impasse is to look at the music doing well in concerts these days, as that is what people seem to want to hear. If one has to choose a style in which to compose, why not choose a Period one? Like building seventeenth-century houses (see the beginning of ch. 7). And a performing infrastructure is in place!

Thoughts on the Genius Barrier

Historically, composing wasn't done by a distinct person with the unique role of "artist-composer," but rather by performing musicians as one of their jobs. Performers who didn't compose at all, like nowadays, or who performed only other people's music, were much less common in former times than they are now.

When Fritz Kreisler announced that he himself had written most of the "early" repertoire he played, Ernest Newman, the influential London music critic, bitterly questioned Kreisler's ethics. He also commented that it showed "how easy it is, and always was, to write this kind of music."[26] Newman wrote,

> Anyone with the least bit of music in him and the least knowledge of the period could produce this sort of thing [the overture to Handel's *Acis and Galatea*] any morning with the hand he did not require for shaving. . . . When

music becomes a less generalised and formalised and more personal matter
as it did in the 19th century, imitation becomes more difficult, because there
is no formula to exploit.

This seems to be a natural attitude among humans. Landowska called it
"Le mépris pour les anciens" (condescension for one's elders). And Roger
North, also probably thinking of the same attitude, commented, "The
grand custome of all is to affect novelty, and to goe from one thing to another, and despise the former. And it is a poorness of spirit, and a low
method of thinking, that inclines men to pronounce for the present, and
allow nothing to times past."[27]

It seems the Romantic obligation to produce "great works" is still a
factor. The word "masterpiece" is commonly heard. Light and easy music
is not in this club. But things were different in early times, when composers were not yet under this obligation to be profound and sublime.
Burney in 1773, for instance, describes compositions he likes as "very well
written, in a modern style; but neither common, nor unnaturally new."[28]
It would be good for composers if they did not feel required to make every
piece they wrote—or played—a magnum opus. Roger North's description
of a piece in 1728 contrasts revealingly with the impressions of the early
Romantic, Ludwig Tieck. North wrote about his piece, "It was a happy
thought, and well executed, and for the variety, might be styled a son-
nata; onely, the sound of bells being among the vulgaritys, tho' naturally
elegant enough, like comon sweetmeats, grows fulsome, and will not be
endured longer than the humour of affecting a novelty lasts."[29] By contrast, here is Tieck in the nineteenth century: "With its angelic presence,
it enters the soul immediately and breathes heavenly breath. Oh, how all
memories of all bliss fall and flow back into that one moment, how all
noble feelings, all great emotions welcome the guest!"[30]

Two Examples of Present-Day Period Composing

Among the more striking examples of present-day Period composition are
pieces by two German woodwind players, Winfried Michel and Matthias
Maute (the work of another very interesting Period composer, Hendrik
Bouman, did not come to my attention until too late to discuss here).
Michel explains that his original inspiration for trying his hand at writing in plausible Period style was a comment he once heard from Gustav
Leonhardt to the effect that we are not able to achieve perfect mastery of
composition as Baroque composers did.[31] Michel wondered why not and
proceeded to produce a number of good pieces, several of them now published and recorded, which are in quite credible eighteenth-century style.

Michel writes in his "Simonetti-Manifest":

> Ornamenting a solo line and realizing a figured Bass are right on the
> threshold of the act of composition. Small wonder every really good player in
> the "Baroque" period was a composer. I don't understand how it is possible,

the swarms of (technically good) ensembles nowadays, always playing the same pieces. It's a kind of vegetating in the past.[32]

Michel has published his remarkable pieces under several different names. Those by Giovanni Paolo Simonetti are in mid-eighteenth-century Berlin style and later German styles.

🔊 AUDIO SAMPLE: 70. C. Huntgeburth and W. Michel, 1982–85. Simonetti: Adagio ma non tanto, Sonata II/3

Michel also composes pieces by Giovanni Paolo Tomesini, playing with the possibilities of moving between the melodic idioms from Sebastian Bach to Beethoven. I find "Tomesini's" pieces not only interesting but particularly touching.

🔊 AUDIO SAMPLE: 71. Ludger Rémy, 1992. Tomesini: Andante in D, 2d Clavierstuck

Matthias Maute is a recorder virtuoso now living in Montreal. He's written a number of pieces in two general categories: style-copies (early eighteenth-century German),[33] and mid-twentieth-century styles.

🔊 AUDIO SAMPLE: 72. Ensemble Caprice, Rebel, 2001. Maute: 3d movement, Concerto detta la Sammartini

As this was going to press, I learned of the existence of a guild of "composers of the contemporary Baroque revival." They are located at www.voxsaeculorum.org.

Designer Labels

During the time it was thought to be by Vermeer, van Meegeren's *Disciples at Emmaus* was admired and praised by many thousands of people and was described by one of the world's experts as "*the* masterpiece of Vermeer."[34] Presumably, real Vermeers were compared to it to determine proper attribution. If it had been known to have been by van Meegeren, it would never have been given such respect and attention.

Fakes in the art world involve deceptive attribution, by definition. It can be argued that, in writing or painting in an old style, deception is sometimes useful or necessary. That is because of the factor of snobbery. Everyone, including the experts, has to believe the fake is (or could be) original or it won't be judged with the same æsthetic standards as works that are believed to be original. Even Skowroneck, who did not set out to make a "permanent deception," had as his stated purpose the production of a harpsichord that could pass as antique.

This same dilemma faces the Period musician who composes. The only way their pieces are likely to be accepted at face value by audiences is if he identifies them as the work of some musician of the appropriate period—one preferably not too famous. But if, on the other hand, they use their own names, it inspires an automatic uncertainty. One Period composer told me that going through an unmasking routine (disguising a newly composed piece as an antique in order to get it taken seriously and later confessing the deception) annoys many people and he has stopped doing it.

Winfried Michel has developed a clever way of dealing with this problem. Michel adopts the pseudonyms mentioned above, Simonetti and Tomesini, and publishes them in the standard context and format for Baroque pieces edited by musicologists. While giving a general impression that his "sources" are old, he is scrupulously honest in his tongue in cheek description of them: "handwritten score . . . used for the present edition. Formal, melodic, and harmonic particularities . . . enable a likely dating of the work at between 1730 and 1740. Our edition follows the very carefully written source exactly; a few additions by the editor are given in brackets."[35] He uses the historical jargon despite the fact that the pieces are announced on the title page as being "composed and edited [!] by Winfried Michel" in 1978–79.

Our Own Music

Period composing is the most profound use we musicians have yet made of Period styles, applying them to our imagination and our dormant sense of improvisation. Composition, particularly in Period style, is a very small step from performing and improvising. Still, it demands knowledge and the practice of new techniques, as well as trust in ourselves that we have at last completely taken these styles on board.

This, even more than performing music from a page, is a testimony to how well we have engaged Period styles. Far from reproducing a work already done, we will have thoroughly adopted a style and a manner of work from another time, while making music in the present—our own music. Matthias Maute writes in his new book, "Anyone who invents music themselves goes beyond the habits and customary role of 'interpreting' music."[36] As José A. Bowen puts it, "The point of learning a new language is that we can eventually speak for ourselves. When we are fluent, we can create expressions never heard before, but still understood."[37] When composing in Period style becomes common, we will have graduated from being cover bands to being creators of a contemporary music. We will have achieved self-sufficiency, and no longer be a colony of the past.

13

Perpetual Revolution

My students read Harnoncourt's writings from the 1970s and 1980s and wonder why he seems so angry, why he makes so much fuss about style and instruments. They were not there in the 1960s, of course, and to them it may seem as if we had always played these flutes without keys, and had always played them at A-415. Scarcely any Period players who are now in their twenties and thirties have even heard of Landowska and Dolmetsch.

They're right, the sixties are gone, and with them that revolutionary ethos. And yet, if they think we have achieved what the 1960s dreamed of, they are the dreamers.

There is still much to be done. We are only just aware of the possibilities of Rhetoric (including the permission it gives us to reach out emotionally), we are only now beginning to "get off the page," our singers need help, and many clever composers have still to discover their talents.

But we have made a beginning.

"The Musick of Fools and Madd Men": Limits to What Taste Will Accept

If the conoiseurs of musik in the proper [antique] time were raised up, and brought to hear some of our famed consorts, they would lye downe againe saying it was the musick of fools and madd men.

(Roger North, *Notes of Comparison*, ca. 1726)

215

José Bowen reports that authentic Grieg and Elgar are intolerable for some modern listeners: "All of the mountains of written evidence pale beside the recordings of Grieg and Elgar; we simply can't bring ourselves to prescribe what so clearly appears to be their bad taste."[1] Mellers writes the same thing about Elgar. "We have recordings that tell us how he wanted his music to go, and some people can't take it."[2]

There are probably limits to how far we can go today in giving up our tastes, and they no doubt vary depending on the individual case. The most difficult examples may be the historical markers: historical techniques that have no equivalents in Modern style and are therefore unfamiliar—the *messa di voce*, for instance, dynamic inflection, phrasing based on gestures rather than "long-lines," articulation syllables on woodwinds, and *flattement* (finger vibrato). These are not the subtle mannerisms that can overlay a basic modern technique: on the contrary, they negate many things musicians learn in Modern style, and they are immediately conspicuous in performance, probably even to non-musicians. To incorporate these techniques convincingly means rethinking the music because at first they often seem illogical, distasteful, unmusical—at odds, in other words, with our "taste." They approach the extreme limits of what twenty-first-century ears can accept, and we begin to wonder if Period style is really what we want to be doing after all (that in itself might be reason enough to experiment with these techniques, if perceiving this music from a "new" angle interests us).

In thinking about the past, Collingwood commented that "whenever [a historian] finds certain historical matters unintelligible, he has discovered a limitation of his own mind; he has discovered that there are certain ways in which he is not, or no longer, or not yet, able to think."[3]

This could be transferred over to our subject as "the pieces we don't like are ones we don't yet understand; that is, ones we don't yet know how to perform."

There are certain composers I've personally never appreciated, like Loeillet, Croft, Dall'Abaco, Devienne, Grétry, Heinichen, Naudot, Quantz, Shield, Stulichi, and Zelenka. I'm suggesting that the problem is not the music; it's my inability to put myself in the place of listeners who once appreciated those composers. I am bringing inappropriate expectations to their music. There are "certain ways in which I am not, or am no longer, or am not yet, able to [hear]." (I have learned to appreciate Boismortier and even Corrette, for instance.) I (and perhaps many of my contemporaries) need to discover the questions this music once answered.[4]

Not only does taste change, it is also subject to influence. Knowing that something was once stylish could influence our present regard for it. As Butt quite reasonably suggests, the original listeners had to learn the symbols and connotations of the music just as we do in the present.[5] Historical elements that seem at first distasteful might become interesting and eventually agreeable if we were disposed to see them that way and had time to get used to them.

Taruskin reproached one Period player with the idea that "your determination that the tempo was authentic was what gave you permission to like it,"[6] as if liking it was somehow not completely sincere if informed by the brain. Yet it seems we all allow our sense of suitability to influence our taste. As Peter Walls frankly commented, "I am at a loss to pinpoint exactly when an intellectual acceptance of a musicological argument has become metamorphosed into a way of listening but I assume that the process that has gone on here is one with which readers of this book will be familiar."[7] Walls's point is that we do indeed seem to be willing to allow our discoveries about performance practice to shape what we like to hear. Forensic musicologists are likely to find this appalling, but in fact it is a precious attribute, a sign of the optimism that permeates the Movement. It is part of the process of constructing this new style, which grows in a positive (not positivist) atmosphere, expecting the best—or at least hoping for it—even in doubtful cases.

Are Period musicians optimists? The question brings to mind that passage from Roger North I quoted in chapter 7:

> And untill a set of musicall *vertuosi*, well weighed in a resolution, and capable to make the experiment, and of whom none, as thinking themselves wiser, shall put on the contemptuous frowne and seem inwardly to sneer, shall be mett together, with all things fitt for the same designe, there will be no reason to expect the antiquitys of musick should ever be understood.[8]

Robert Philip comments on the recordings from the beginning of the last century:

> It may strike the modern reader as eccentric to suggest that performances on early recordings represent some sort of unpolluted pre-industrial purity. But it is a great deal more plausible than the notion that what sounds tasteful now probably sounded tasteful in earlier periods, which is an assumption behind many modern reconstructions of earlier performance practices and much writing on the subject.[9]

That we react to a piece of music as people did in earlier times is not given to us to ever know with certainty, of course. Come to think of it, we don't have much more knowledge of the reactions of our own contemporaries. So we can forget about that, and concentrate instead on finding a blend that does justice to the old music, presenting it on its own terms, and at the same time satisfies our own tastes (at least, the tastes of some of us).

The Illusion of an Unbroken Performing Style from Mozart's Time to Ours

The æsthetics and ideologies of the Romantics have been brilliantly discussed for generations, and the issues—as they appear to us today—are pretty clear. On the other hand, how the Romantics actually made music has been little understood. This is because—for a long time—we assumed we knew; that is, since we never stopped playing Beethoven, it was assumed his performing tradition had been handed down to us intact. But listening to recordings of Mengelberg's or Furtwängler's Beethoven, already so different from ours, suggests the possibility that performances in the nineteenth century were very far from our current taste.

Even if the repertoire has remained the same, it seems a lot to expect (when you think about it) that a performing tradition could remain intact and unchanged. Certain physical aspects might not have changed dramatically; the basic designs and pitch of orchestral instruments, for instance, are little changed since Beethoven's time. But the early Romantic period began two centuries ago, and we know from early recordings made one hundred years ago how different the customs of performance can be. What then do we know about Nikisch's or Mendelssohn's Beethoven? Some of the practices that characterize Modern style (like continuous vibrato and exaggerated literalness) are, as we have seen, inventions of the twentieth century. Yet as recently as 1980, the *New Grove* was maintaining that "'there was no 'lost tradition' separating the modern performer from the music of Haydn, Mozart etc." and that "there has been no severance of contact with post-Baroque music as a whole, nor with the instruments used in performing it."[10] This was the common belief until recently. To quote Lowenthal, "People in so-called traditional societies confidently assert that things are (and should be) the way they always have been, for oral transmission accumulates actual alterations unconsciously, continually readjusting the past to fit the present." Having another, critical look at traditional Romantic performing protocol, as Period performers have done, resembles Lowenthal's "literate societies," that can "less easily sustain such fiction, for written—and especially printed—records reveal a past unlike the present: the archives show traditions eroded by time and corrupted by novelty."[11]

Within a decade of the appearance of that *Grove* article, the musical world had already witnessed a series of recordings and performances of late eighteenth-century music in a species of Period style and on Period instruments. Surprised, it seems, by the speed and depth of this development, the new writers of this section in the latest *Grove* in 2001 give the subject a very different spin: "It had become increasingly apparent by the end of the 20th century that the idea of continuity of tradition even from the 19th century into the 20th was problematic."[12] Tradition, as Taruskin suggested, may be nothing more than "a cosmic game of 'telephone.'"[13]

Beethoven Lite and Manifest Destiny

When HIP began playing the symphonies of Beethoven, it was not without its irony. Not that the process of rediscovering a style for Beethoven was in any essential way different from what it had been for Bach. But for decades, HIP's "announced purpose has been to wipe the distortions of Romanticism from the face of the pre-Romantic repertory."[14] The Movement had originally begun as a rejection of Romantic style. To accomplish that, it was necessary to know what Romantic style was. But the Movement started with the same fallacious assumption that had led the *New Grove* in 1980 to state that "there has been no severance of contact with post-Baroque music as a whole, nor with the instruments used in performing it." How could anyone have hoped to recover authentic performing protocols of the nineteenth-century starting with misinformation like this?

With this new branch of the Period movement dashing energetically off on a false trail, the Establishment, embodied in the symphony orchestra, meanwhile found itself once again in an embattled position, in barely the space of a generation. Up until the 1980s, the Romantic repertoire had been reserved turf, owned and controlled by Modern style, which had inherited it from Romantic style. No longer was it a matter of giving up Bach and Handel, or even Mozart. HIP was in the core of the Romantic stronghold: Beethoven, Schubert, and Brahms were being played in "authentic style."

As time goes on, and the Movement asserts its right to perform all the music of the past, symphony orchestras and opera companies are gradually appearing in their real form as a glorious anachronism, an expensive and obsolete relic, maintaining the fiction of an unbroken performing tradition to Romantic times. The reality is, as we have seen, that Modern style lacks the logic of history, and although it is now the mainstream performing style, there is a good chance that with time it will gradually recede, and become an endangered species in need of artificial help. Meanwhile, if we continue to love the Romantic repertoire, we may well find ourselves reviving the performing style that originally went with that music: Romantic style. The irony is that it will be the Period music movement (already at work on this project as we speak) that will reawaken Romanticist practices, and lift its former arch-enemy from its early and undeserved grave. Fantastic as it now sounds, I believe this is a reasonable prediction. "Early music" will have come full circle, from a Movement devoted to finding an alternative to Romantic performing style to one that revives that very style.

In the meantime, things are rather confused. The present situation is that there are three Beethovens:

- Ludwig on early twentieth-century recordings, which may (or may not) preserve the last vestiges of nineteenth-century tradition;
- Ludwig in Modern style, currently mainstream but potentially in danger; and
- Ludwig in Period Romantic style, indistinguishable at the moment from Period eighteenth-century style.

As for the early twentieth-century recordings, it's difficult to put them in context. Some writers like Philip and Brown believe they represent a style not yet far from Beethoven's own. Philip ventures that

> The basic evidence . . . leads to the conclusion that much of the style of the early 20th century, which now sounds old-fashioned, represents the end of a long tradition of performance extending back to Beethoven and beyond. . . . in fundamental ways, musicians of the early 20th century were closer to the traditions of Beethoven's day than we are now.[15]

One wonders what this "basic evidence" can be, and why it should indicate something as unlikely as that performing style stood still during the turmoil and changes in the music of the nineteenth century. Recordings like those of Joachim, Mengelberg, and Furtwängler include practices like flexible tempo, rubato, portamento, beat hierarchy, and controlled use of vibrato. These last two traits are the only ones that are part of the original documented Romantic style.

What we may be hearing on those recordings are echoes of a number of nineteenth-century styles, not least the one developed by Wagner and his followers. To play Beethoven in the style of early twentieth-century recordings is probably to play it similarly to how they did in the second half of the nineteenth century. That may have been a far cry from Beethoven's own style; Bowen thinks, for instance, that both Mendelssohn and Berlioz preferred fast and steady tempos, like musicians do nowadays. Early twentieth-century musicians, by contrast, played slowly, with lots of rubato.

The second style, Modern style, is in denial about history. Like the old Romantic style, it participates in the custom of "continually readjusting the past to fit the present." In fact, it has the least ties to historical tradition, being stripped down, regularized, and clarified. Dulak characterized it this way, "In terms of the favourite metaphor of the early-music movement, they [late nineteenth-century repertoire] are not paintings buried under layers of grime, but rather works marred by a careless restorer [Modern style], who in the process of cleaning them has mistakenly stripped off the top layers of paint."[16] Yet again, Modernism throws the baby out with the bathwater.

What has the third style, Period style, added to the mix? The Movement seemed to move naturally and easily into the nineteenth century, led by some of the same musicians who had been central in establishing Period style for Baroque music. But there was—and is—an awkward fact. The new performances, in a style that is supposed to be historical and Romantic, don't resemble the recordings of Beethoven from the early twentieth century. The "Historical-Romantic" style of Norrington, Gardiner, Harnoncourt, Kuijken, and Brüggen resembles that of the Romantic recordings of the early twentieth century "about as much as Bermuda resembles the surface of the moon," as Dulak puts it.[17] Robert Philip comments, "The underlying æsthetic assumptions of the [Period] musicians venturing into this territory [the nineteenth century] appear to have changed not at all: the goal is still to lighten, quicken, clarify."[18]

Modern style and Period style versions of Beethoven share certain features that contrast to Romantic style. Neither Modern style nor Period style use portamento, phrasing is unanimously crystal clear in both, rhythm is predictable, tempo fluctuation subtle or absent, the seriousness and intense vehemence of Romantic performances replaced by a detached serenity, and ensemble and intonation are impeccable.

We know it is impossible to be certain we have successfully achieved a historical style. Here again, our own accent is the one that is most difficult for us to hear. Hill comments that we are unable "to see our own standards of good taste as culturally relative . . . in our revivals of extinct performance traditions[. W]e probably have been reconstructing selectively . . . aspects . . . that suit our own values and expectations while ignoring discrepancies between our reconstructions and the evidence."[19] And yet again, the carousel comes round.

"Perpetual Revolution" and Changing Taste

We tend to talk about taste as if it were permanent. But, although we don't always notice, our tastes do change. We learn to like new things. Our listening vocabulary has been regularly extended. Recordings document how the Period style of two generations ago, or even one, is not the Period style of today. Joshua Rifkin used the cheerful term "perpetual revolution" to describe a HIP that remains meaningful.[20]

It also true, as Dreyfus writes, that "intuitively, we understand a great deal about Bach's music and do not find the culture in which he worked especially mystifying. While this statement does not admit of any proof, it seems a good place to begin."[21]

We live in a culture where it is possible to hear music of many periods, and in order to make sense of it, we "adjust to its pastness, bringing into play modes of discrimination and patterns of expectation which are relevant to the style of the work. That is, we attune our minds to the viewpoints, conventions, and normative procedures which the artist had and which he presumed his audience to have."[22] We are able to listen to many Period styles on their own terms, and even notice when there are stylistic solecisms. John Butt argues that "just as humans can learn to express themselves in more than one language they can pick up the essentials of any particular historical style." Rameau's harmonies and voice leading sound decidedly daring, for instance—how could we sense something like that, unless we automatically placed him in his historical and geographical context, attributing to him a plausible horizon of expectations for his era (as we understand it)?

As Butt observes, "To suggest that a later norm automatically negates an earlier surprise is ultimately to suggest that we cannot appreciate the historical difference between Bach, Beethoven and Berlioz." He suggests that to recapture the original effect of the beginning of Beethoven's first symphony "we'd have to use 20th-century harmonies."[23] He concludes that "it may well be a specific feature of our age that we are able to appreciate stylistic and linguistic differences better than ever before."

Just as we can take seriously the reality of a dramatic situation even though we know it is being acted, "following its unfolding and responding to its surprises as if it were being revealed for the first time, even though we have seen it before and know what will take place," we can appreciate the meaning of earlier music on its own terms, even though its language seems limited or predictable next to later music.[24]

Speaking of plays, there is the Shakespeare analogy. How authentic should our Shakespeare be? Some people draw the line at Period costumes or at altering the geography of the plays. The theater is not terribly interested in authentic Shakespeare these days. They are afraid of turning off audiences, and their answer is to emulate and modernize. That's not my answer because I think most people appreciate the historical dimension and are more interested in replication (but I'm biased).

If the "past is a foreign country," what about music from other contemporary cultures, foreign countries to us? Do cultural differences prevent or hinder us from sharing the effects of other musics? Some kinds of "foreign" music we appreciate and even intuitively understand, like Ozarks Bluegrass, Indian flute, and Balinese gamelan. Others may seem incomprehensible, such as Chinese opera and Iranian love songs, where we do not benefit from understanding the words, but Europeans can learn to perform them. Music, the universal language: if it crosses cultural barriers, it may cross time as well.

Fabian asks another relevant question. Why, if we worry about being able to hear with the ears of Bach's contemporaries, do we not worry about seeing with the eyes of Rembrandt's contemporaries?[25]

HIP Is Anti-Classical

By every standard indication, "Early" music is a kind of Classical music. The two categories "share the same sections of record-review journals, many of the same concert halls, and the same Classical-music radio stations."[26] "Early" music is found in the "Classical" department not only in Grout's standard *History of Western Music* but in record stores anywhere in the world. It's played in the same venues, the musicians wear the same anachronistic costumes, Allegro and Adagio are the names of the movements. If you look up Bach on Amazon.com, they seem to think he's "Classical."

And yet, "Early" music is no more "Classical" than it is early; we keep trying to stuff it in the box, and it keeps popping back out.

Taruskin points out one of the paradoxes of trying to turn Rhetorical (that is, non-Canonic) music into Canon. He writes of the criticisms that Robert Levin has inspired by improvising cadenzas while performing Mozart concertos. The objection is that no mere modern should pretend to add to the work of a genius of the past. Adding a cadenza, as Mozart would have done, threatens "our most cherished concepts of repertory and canon. To admit a performance practice that exalts spontaneous creativity over work-preservation, and that when exercised at the highest level can actually threaten work-identity, would violate the most fundamental tenet of our classical music culture, that of *Werktreue.*"[27]

Historically speaking, Rhetorical music didn't place much value on many of the attributes of music of the nineteenth and twentieth centuries: the shortlist of "Masterpieces" that it plays over and over, repeatability and ritualized performance, active discouragement of improvisation, genius-personality and the pedestal mentality, the egotistical sublime, music as transcendent revelation, *Absolute Tonkunst,* music as autobiography in notes, ceremonial concert behavior, and pedagogical lineage.

On the contrary, Rhetorical music flourished in an atmosphere with very different assumptions: that pieces were recently composed and for contemporary events, that they were unlikely to be heard again (or if they were, not in quite the same way), that surface details were left to performers, that composers were performers and valued as craftsmen rather than celebrities, that music was meant to be touching and moving and to enhance the meaning of poetry, that the personal feelings of the composer/performer as an individual were not relevant to public performances of their music, and that audiences behaved in a relaxed and natural way. In fact, a musical event before about 1800 was different in almost every important way from that of a Canonic/Romantic concert.

Default Style

In a new book, Robert Philip observes with apparent relief that "period orchestras not only sound better than they used to, they sound more like conventional orchestras than they used to."[28] And commenting on Norrington's success in getting symphony orchestras to temporarily go without vibrato, he writes, "The startling thing is how a modern orchestra of conventional players can instantly be converted into an orchestra with period-sounding strings, even though they are all playing on 'wrong' instruments."[29] As I understand it, Philip is suggesting here that achieving a Period orchestra sound is as simple as "holding the vibrato" (like holding the mayonnaise); he also seems to be saying that in any case, getting a sound too far away from the modern is undesirable.

I've no doubt it's a relief to get rid of the constant vibrating. But what about other differences that divide Period style—and sound—from the usual style of a modern orchestra, like the seamless legato, climax phrasing, lack of beat hierarchy, unyielding tempos, and unstressed dissonances? These modern stylistic traits are deeply ingrained, many of them learned along with basic playing techniques when the musicians were young, and, whatever their attitude, they are not easily or quickly changed.[30]

I have discussed the growing realization that style doesn't come with the instruments, except in a few instances where technical effects like *flattement* are easier without keys. But certainly we hear Period styles occasionally emanating from instruments that are anachronistic. I repeat: this is great, but it doesn't mean many musicians are about to do it. In fact, it's a pretty rare occurrence.

Going back a half-generation, Richard Taruskin seems to have been announcing the end of the revolution in 1991 (not the first time that has occurred). "Why," he asked, "has historical performance been improving so spectacularly over the last decade? Why do we hear so much less self-conscious downbeat bashing than we used to, so much less distracting *messa di voce*?"[31] Things seemed, for him, to be getting back to normal. "The [HIP] movement has spawned a viable oral tradition. . . . A hardy social practice has been growing up that obeys its own dictates, has its own momentum, is becoming more and more eclectic, contaminated, suggestible. . . . Can we just stand back and let tradition have its way?"[32] Taruskin seemed to be asking, "At what point do we stop consulting history, at what point do we give up on the ideal of historical Authenticity, and just 'play it by ear?'" ("Eclectic" is code for mixing styles, losing focus.) Several years before, he had written what he thought would happen if we "just stand back and let tradition have its way": "If you are a trained musician," he wrote, "what you will find if you scratch your intuition will be the unexamined mainstream, your most ingrained responses, treacherously masquerading as imagination."[33] Whether he's right or not, this, too, is a shoddy kind of "end" of Early music: "default style," with superficial cosmetics—trills from the upper note, perhaps, or a little less vibrato.

Philips and Taruskin are both willing to settle for too little, too soon.

Speak for yourselves, gentlemen. Many of us think we're just getting started; "downbeat bashing" and *messa di voce* are just the beginning. If you can't stand the heat, get out of the kitchen. There are plenty of musicians you can listen to who perform Rhetorical period music but scrupulously avoid the Eloquent style. I don't myself have time for that, but am glad we are fortunate enough to be able to choose from a variety of approaches.

Historians of Necessity

Eugène Green wrote in *La Parole baroque* (2001) that his goal had been to do for Baroque theater what musicians have done for the Grand Siècle.

The idea seems worth considering that HIP is nothing less than an example and an affirmation of a complete theory of art, that of Rhetoric, the art of communication.

Though it may not seem so to us who are living now, the values of Romanticism are very young when measured against the twenty-five-hundred-year history of the Western theory of art, dominated by the principles of Rhetoric. Romanticism's emergence as a comprehensive approach to art, shared by a large number of critics, dates back not much more than two centuries.[34] No wonder many of its values seem as close to us as our back-pockets.

Seen most broadly, it's possible that the restoration of Rhetoric could do for all the performing arts what HIP has done in music. Romanticism discredited and replaced Rhetoric in the nineteenth century, so it could be that restoring Rhetoric as an underlying principle in the arts would offer an alternative to Romanticism. History offers us Rhetoric as a rationale for a general style. In that sense, Judy Tarling put it very well when she called the Classical sources on declamation "the ultimate performance practice manuals."[35]

Trying to See over the Horizon of Time

For musicians, consciously choosing a lost performing protocol is like actors trying to speak a foreign language well enough that the audience is convinced they are native speakers. "You can learn to pronounce the words, but your performance will be wooden if you do not learn what they mean and also how they mean it. . . . A good accent is not sufficient. Even imitating all the nuances of a previous great performance is not enough. A direct imitation of the external sound is hollow, and misses the point."[36] As José Bowen writes, the bulk of modern performance practice research deals with outsides: superficial text-focused subjects like editions and guides to gracing, "which far outnumber studies on contemporary aesthetics and what was considered beautiful playing."[37] There is more to authentic performance than simply plugging in an isolated technique, as these old recordings make immediately obvious. "It is not as if players simply had 'rules' which they applied, and which we could decide to apply too." "To slide like a string player of Elgar's day, one would have to abandon the modern notion that 'clean' playing is tasteful playing."[38]

Robert Philip gloomily commented about old recordings:

> If an attempt to reconstruct early 20th-century performance practice is doomed to failure, imagine how much worse the situation would be if there were no recordings from the period, but we had to rely on written sources as we do for earlier periods. . . . In fact with all of these [twentieth-century practices: vibrato, portamento, flexibility of tempo, rubato, overdotting], even the most widely described, we would be left to guess how they were really applied in performance, and we would certainly guess wrong.[39]

Philip shows how impossible it would have been without recordings to understand the nature of Elgar's tempos, Joachim's portamento, Bartók's rhythmic lightness, or Rachmaninoff's rubato.

This is all true, but it doesn't take into account the way music is actually made. There are other ways to discover these things: by trying them out and getting them to work. "Hum a few bars, and I'll fake it." Music is never resurrected solely out of books.[40] It doesn't take much to create much, when the musicians involved are good.

The Pursuit of Authenticity

I'd like to finish with a last idea from R. G. Collingwood:

> Historical thinking means nothing else than interpreting all the available evidence with the maximum degree of critical skill. It does not mean discovering what really happened, if "what really happened" is anything other than "what the evidence indicates." If there once happened an event concerning which no shred of evidence now survives, that event is no part of any historian's universe; it is no historian's business to discover it; it is no gap in any historian's knowledge that he does not know it.[41]

If the historians take such a detached view, we musicians hardly need aspire to finding "the way it really was." Of course it is simple common sense to doubt whether we are capable of achieving complete stylistic conformity with the past. The fact that we would have no way to know if we had done so proves that—in itself—it is a pointless exercise. But then, real historical performing is not our ultimate concern.

Our ultimate concern is *trying* to approach historical performing. We can never know how close we get. But we can know if we have tried. "A goal," as Bernard Sherman writes, "might still be worth seeking even if it's impossible to attain."[42]

"It is, of course, impossible to exactly re-create the sounds Bach would have had in his orchestra," as Barthold Kuijken writes, "but this doesn't mean that we can't try. It has become fashionable now to say that since you can't know, why bother? To this objection I'd answer that the way is more interesting than the goal."[43]

Paradoxically, just as the inventors of Seconda Pratica at the end of the sixteenth century had no realistic hope of actually reviving the music of antiquity, the process of trying in all seriousness to achieve Authenticity changes us, and the familiar world around us, and generates something new, beautiful, and interesting. After recording with the Amsterdam Baroque Orchestra, Yo-Yo Ma made a similar observation (he had had to change his 1712 Stradivarius cello for the recording back to its original setup): "Whenever you have gone beyond the world that you know, and then go back to the familiar world, you find it changed. Whenever you move into a different world like that, it's not with a sense of losing something from our traditional music. You end up with greater freedom, not less."[44]

As we know, the end result of Seconda Pratica was not the music of antiquity (as originally intended) but a *nuove musiche* that had never existed before. In striving for Authenticity, we are creating something of our own, modern through and through. And something impossible to achieve, incidentally, by continuing to use received tradition. With time, Authenticity has found its most useful role as a paradigm, an ideal and an inspiration that may or may not actually exist. It is not the realization of Authenticity that is important to us as musicians; it is rather the pursuit of it. Harry Haskell's suggestion that Authenticity, like perfection or happiness, is "best conceived as an ideal to be pursued rather than as a goal to be attained"[45] seems eminently sensible. (Perfection tends to be a rather absolute concept, but in my experience, happiness is often mixed, momentary, and provisional. Authenticity may be like that too.)

Could it be that unconsciously we have been using HIP merely as a stratagem—or a mindset—to allow the creation of this new style we're now using? In our optimism and innocence, we call it "Period style." The inspiration comes from somewhere else (or somewhen else), but in reality we know it works because we make it work.

How could we do differently? We are too modest in ascribing this tradition to our ancestors. What we can be sure of, if we like it so much, is that it must be "our own."

Notes

Preface

1. Hawkins 1776:1:705, quoted in Weber 1992:217.
2. Roger North, ca. 1726, in Wilson 1959:283.
3. My thanks to Todd Barton for this quotation from *The Art-Crazy Old Man*.
4. 1906:8–9.
5. Wilson 1959:xxiv.

Acknowledgments

1. Mattheson 1739:3:26 § 33 (Harriss 1981:871).

List of Recorded Excerpts

1. Thanks to Teri Noel Towe for advice on this dating.

Introduction

1. Bailey 1992:98.
2. *Encyclopaedia Britannica*, "European history and culture," 18:689. See also Mattick 1993:1.
3. Finnegan 1986:77.
4. Collingwood 1946:321.
5. This is a paraphrase of the passage by David Boyden (1965:313) quoted at the beginning of ch. 4.

6. See the *Oxford English Dictionary* 2:492. The word was coined by Horace Walpole in 1754.

7. Taruskin 1995:79.

8. Ong 1971:1.

9. Dahlhaus 1983: ch. 6, "Hermeneutics in history."

10. Parakilas 1984:10.

11. Collingwood 1946:326.

12. That his picture was two-dimensional and oversimplified is something I'll discuss in ch. 3.

13. "Classical" music survives with the same kind of invidious comparison: it is the other kind from "popular"—it's "unpopular," in other words, or worse yet, "elitist."

14. Brad Lehmann in a candid discussion on articulation at the Bach Cantatas website.

15. For that matter, Brahms on a modern grand also has its problems, seeing how much the piano has evolved since Brahms's day.

16. Small 1998:back cover.

1. *When You Say Something Differently, You Say Something Different*

1. Small 1998:145.

2. Jay Bernfeld, personal communication.

3. Burney 1771:197; see also 1771:208.

4. Mattheson 1739:1:10 § 105.

5. Mattheson 1739:2:14 § 50–51.

6. Butt 1994:17.

7. North 1728:255.

8. Weber 1992: 92, 161, 171.

9. Avison 1753 :46–47.

10. Harnoncourt 1988:198.

11. This phrase was used by Gerber (*Lexikon*, 1790) and cited in *NG1:*4: 450 (for a list of abbreviations used in the notes and bibliography, see the bibliographic abbreviations preceding the bibliography).

12. Burney 1773:263.

13. See Small 1998; Mellers 1992:921.

14. Harnoncourt 1989:32.

15. Hewitt 1966:2:9.

16. This is Leopold Stokowski, 1957. Bach: Geistliche lied "Komm, süsser Tod," BWV 478, arr. Stokowski.

17. Parakilas 1984:11.

18. Bowen 1993a:164.

19. Marais 1711. "Les plus belles pièces [perdent] infiniment de leur agrément, Si elles ne sont exécuttées dans le goût qui leur est propre."

20. Mattheson 1739, last paragraph; translation based on Robin Stowell, *The early violin and viola* (Cambridge, 2001), p. xiii.

21. Quoted in Ranum 2001:430.

22. Quantz 1752:11 § 5.

23. Harnoncourt 1989:78.

24. Parakilas 1984:9.

25. Parakilas 1984:9.

26. Restout 1964:356.

27. Diderot 1773:111.

28. Dahlhaus 1983:63.

29. See Harnoncourt 1988:14. Danuser 1996:1057–59 discusses chronocentrism as "aktualisierender Modus," making several interesting observations. It is unclear why he distinguishes it from Modern Style, which he calls "traditioneller Modus." Chronocentrism has also been called a "continuity of tradition" (Golomb 2004:39–40) and "cultural imperialism" (Erauw 1998:114).

30. Lowenthal 1985:xvi.

31. Mellers 1992:925.

32. Brown 1999:30ff.

33. Taruskin 1995:151.

34. Walls 2003: 115.

35. Brown 1999:163.

36. Landowska (1909)1924:96.

37. Haskell 2001:831.

38. Harnoncourt 1989:186–87.

39. Wagner did think carefully about the changes he made and explained them in print; see Wagner 1873.

40. Parakilas 1984:10.

41. Dahlhaus 1983: ch. 6, "Hermeneutics in history."

42. Collingwood 1946:289, 326. See also "Authenticity as a Statement of Intent" in the introduction.

43. Bowen 1999:438.

44. Goehr 1992:246.

45. Harnoncourt 1988:73.

46. I'm comparing here the Triébert système 6 with Types A, B, C, D, and F. See Haynes 2001:78–89.

47. Harnoncourt 1988:87.

48. This is Nietzsche's "alienation," discussed in Dahlhaus 1983:55, 57.

49. Godlovitch 1988:262.

50. On Prima and Seconda Pratica, see ch. 10 and Carter 1992:187.

2. Mind the Gap

1. Tosi 1743:112.

2. After working with these three categories for several years, I ran across the same ones in an article by Jacques Handschin written in 1927and cited in Hill 1994. Hermann Danuser's three "modes of musical interpretation" in his article "Interpretation" in *MGG* is also helpful.

3. I'm aware of other names and time-lines for these categories (see, for instance, Butt 2002: ch. 5). The names are not important, but the changes described here are.

4. Dulak 1993:46.

5. Wagner 1873:247.

6. The transcriptions were called "Bachowski" by snobs when they first came out in 1957–58. Van den Toorn 2000:6.

7. The "phonautograph" was invented by Léon Scott in 1857 but did not apparently record music.

8. Day 2000:147–48. See Joachim 1903.

9. Brown 1999:449. The transcription is on pp. 450–54.

10. Holoman, Winter, and Page 2001:19:375.

11. Hill 1994:40.

12. Brown 1999:428. A CD featuring Moreschi at the Vatican is presently available from Opal 9823.

13. Gould 1965, quoted in Payzant 1978:44.

14. Landowska published *Musique ancienne* in 1909; Dolmetsch's *The interpretation of the music of the XVII and XVIII centuries* appeared in 1915.

15. This is Treitler's phrase (1989:116).

16. Haskell 1988:43.

17. See Haskell 1988.

18. See the portrait in *NG* 2:7:434. According to Haskell 1988:29, Morris was one of Dolmetsch's earliest admirers and persuaded him to build his first harpsichord in 1896.

19. Campbell 1975: p. xi.

20. Haskell 1988:53, quoting Alice Ehlers.

21. Ralph Kirkpatrick, quoted in Haskell 1988:39.

22. Campbell 1975:166 n. 7.

23. Hindemith 1950.

24. Walter 1957:180–82.

25. Fabian 2003:232.

26. Fabian 2003:233.

27. Fabian 2003:57, 95.

28. Their windways were usually bigger, they had little flexibility of tone or dynamics, and of course were at A-440, all of which changed their character and sound. For a comparison of the two types, see Haynes 1969.

29. See Haynes 1969.

30. I considered it a symbolic moment when in 1969 I convinced the Boston local of the American Federation of Musicians to put my name in a specially created new section for "Baroque Oboe" in its member listings.

31. Fabian 2003:92.

32. Notes to Harnoncourt's recording of the *St. John* (Telefunken).

33. Golomb 2004:118.

34. Harnoncourt 1989:132.

35. Fabian 2003:167–68.

36. Fabian 2003:166.

37. Fabian 2003:91, 220.

38. Fabian 2003 describes the paradigm shift that occurred in the 1960s on pp. 13, 22, 39, 57, and 95.

39. In *Tijdschrift voor Oude Muziek*, 1986/5, quoted in Vester 1999:11.

40. Bowen 1993a:164.

3. Mainstream Style

1. Hill 1994:42.

2. Botstein 2001:870.

3. Hill 1994:40.

4. Hill 1994:41.

5. Brown 1999:415; Philip 1994:195–96.

6. Salonen also recorded the arrangement by Mahler of the "Air on the G string" (BWV 1068).

7. Golomb 2004:43

8. Fabian 2003:165.

9. Brown 1999:558ff.; Walls 2003:90.

10. Boult 1977. Used courtesy of Teri Noel Towe.

11. Quantz 1752:7 § 10.

12. Brown 1999:172.

13. Keller 1955:33.

14. Quantz 1752:7 § 10.

15. The long-line or climax phrase is not discussed as such by Brown 1999.

16. See Burgess 2003:41 and Potter 1998:49.

17. In language, grammar is the study of the classes of words, their inflections, and their functions and relations in the sentence. In music, grammar is the study of the classes of notes, figures and gestures, their inflections, and their functions and relations in phrases.

18. This is frequently heard in the orchestras conducted by M. Suzuki and T. Hengelbrock.

19. Philip 1992:92.

20. Philip 2003:362.

21. Brown 1999:415, 426.

22. For a discussion of this idea, see Harnoncourt 1988:33–34 and 40.

23. Duffin 1995:2.

24. See Stokowski 1957, track 8 (Air on the G string).

25. Restout 1964:54.

26. Restout 1964:86–87.

27. Discussed by Brown 2003:64ff.

28. See Haynes 1991.

29. Philip 1992:139.

30. This is Marga Höffgen (b. 1921).

31. Brown 1999:8, 9, 11, 625.

32. Fabian 2003:192, 225 calls this the "baroque slur."

33. Quantz 1752:11 § 12.

34. Hill 1994:42.

35. Cited in Hill 1994:46.

36. Dulak 1993:47.

37. Babitz 1974:8; Taruskin 1989:104, 167ff.

38. Hill 1994:44, quoting *A Virgil Thomson reader* (1981), 197.

39. Taruskin 1995:129.

40. Taruskin 1995:129. Taruskin, a specialist on Stravinsky, makes a number of very effective quotations (pp. 129–30) from Stravinsky's *Poetics of music* (1939).

41. Day 2000:187.

42. Quoted by Philip 1992:10, citing Ernest Newman.

43. That's my idea, not his.

44. Bijlsma 1998:83.

45. Restout 1964:401.

46. Philip 1994:198–99.
47. Horowitz 1987:221–22, quoting David Ewen, *The man with the baton* (1936), 114–16.
48. Philip 1992:7, 37.
49. Philip 1992:93.
50. Taruskin 1995:168 and 136.
51. Quantz 1752:11 § 21.
52. Mattheson 1739:1:6 § 18–19.
53. Mace 1676:147, quoted in Dolmetsch 1915:14.
54. Mason 1748:12.
55. Taruskin 1995:317.
56. Taruskin 1995:316ff.
57. Taruskin 1995:167.
58. Butt 2002:102.

4. *Classical Music's Coarse Caress*

1. Restout 1964:54.
2. Gay 1995:99, quoting Johanna Schopenhauer (1839).
3. Dreyfus 1996:30.
4. Philip 1992:238–39.
5. Ross 2004:152.
6. Harnoncourt 1988:73.
7. Samson 2001:7.
8. Weber 2001:227.
9. Small 1998:89.
10. Spitzer 1983:248.
11. Sparshott 1998: ch. 1.
12. Harnoncourt 1988:69.
13. Small 1998:118.
14. Avison 1753:98.
15. Kerman 1985:33. Kerman adds, "Exception must be made for Gregorian chant and some other kinds of liturgical music."
16. Burney 1771:2.
17. Burney 1773:2:259.
18. Burney 1771:34.
19. Weber 1977:16.
20. Phillipe-Joseph Caffiaux, a Benedictine monk, had produced a systematic history of music from pre-history to contemporary times in seven volumes in 1756; the book was never published and is now in the Bibliothèque nationale, Paris. Padre Martini's *Storia della musica* had also begun appearing, starting in 1757.
21. Burney 1771:13.
22. Burney 1771:6–7.
23. Johann Friedrich Agricola [1773:2:91], Carl Philipp Emanuel Bach [1773:2:251], Claude-Bénigne Balbastre [1771:38], Franz Benda [1773:2:129], Armand-Louis Couperin [1771:41], Denis Diderot [1771:405], Farinelli (Carlo Broschi) [1771:204], Christoph Willibald Gluck [1773:1:228, 1:264–65, 1:290], Johann Adolf Hasse [1773:1:228, 1:280, 1:348, 1:351], Friedrich Wilhelm Marpurg [1773:2:107], Padre Giovanni Martini [1771:200], Pietro Metastasio [1773:

1:228, 1:300], Leopold and Wolfgang Amadeus Mozart [1771:236, 255], Johann Joachim Quantz [1773:2:157], Voltaire [1771:60ff.], and Georg Christoph Wagenseil [1773:1:329].

24. Burney 1771:13.

25. Burney 1771:34–35. In a later notebook, Burney went even further in a private message to himself: "I dare not say what I have long thought. That it is our reverence for old authors and bigotry to Handel, that has prevented us from keeping pace with the rest of Europe in the cultivation of Music" (Hogwood 1984:245). See Weber 1992.

26. Duckles 1980:12:839.

27. The idea of contemporary music as controversial was an invention of the Wagnerians; see Weber 1984:63.

28. Burney 1771:3.

29. Boyden 1965:313.

30. Weber 1992:170.

31. Weber 1992:194, 204–5.

32. Wagner, *Über das Dirigieren* (1869), 162, quoted in Bowen 1993b:88.

33. Kingsbury 1988:44–45.

34. Rosen 2000:214.

35. Lowenthal 1985:233.

36. Hoffmann, April/May 1810, in Hoffmann 1963:34–51. See Gay 1995: 16–17.

37. Abrams 1953:94.

38. Combarieu 1895, quoted in Dahlhaus 1989:3.

39. Dahlhaus 1985:58.

40. Lustig in Dahlhaus 1989:vii.

41. Le Cerf de la Viéville 1704, 3d Discours:143.

42. Burney 1773:2:159.

43. Babbitt 1966:242.

44. Goehr 1992:186.

45. Quantz 1752:10 § 21.

46. Weber 1999:337.

47. Dahlhaus 1983:147.

48. See the interesting discussion of this phenomenon in Higgins 2004.

49. Dahlhaus 1983:75.

50. Barnett 1987:11. Barnett writes of acting, not composing.

51. North in Wilson 1959:142.

52. Spitzer 1983:415.

53. Spitzer 1983:429.

54. Finnegan 1986:77.

55. Spitzer 1983:17ff.

56. Spitzer 1983:428.

57. Spitzer 1983:429.

58. Spitzer 1983:457.

59. Dutton 1983:ix.

60. Kurz 1948:319.

61. Le Cerf de la Viéville 1704, 3d Discours:91 (tr. Ellison 1973:131).

62. Dahlhaus 1983:148.

63. Salmen 1983:272.

64. Leopold Mozart, letter of 28 May 1778.
65. Bailey 1992:41.
66. Parakilas 1984:10.
67. Dreyfus 1996:35.
68. Harnoncourt 1988:26-27.
69. Small 1998:160.
70. Lowenthal 1985:226, quoting Georg Lukács, *The historical novel* (1969), 22, 26.
71. Harnoncourt 1988:27.
72. Horowitz 1987:413.
73. Cook and Everist 1999:245.
74. Small 1998:187, 192. Harnoncourt 1988:27, also Taruskin 1995:205.
75. Burnham 1995:162–168.
76. Small 1998:192–93.
77. I have been told of recent instances where musicians playing *Messiah* and Brandenburg 4 (both Canonic by now) with a well-known Period orchestra in Toronto were instructed not to play any ornaments unless they were written in the parts.
78. North in Wilson 1959:177.

5. The Transparent Performer

1. Leech-Wilkinson 2002:253.
2. Godlovitch 1988:269.
3. Rosen 2000:202.
4. There is an enlightening discussion of it in Butt 2002:74ff. In theology, the parallel approach to reading scripture is known as "critical exegesis" and has been accepted as normal since the 1860s. See Steinmetz 1980.
5. Writers include Philip Alperson, John W. Bender, Lee B. Brown, David Carrier, Stephen Davies, Bengt Edlund, Stan Godlovitch, Lydia Goehr, Nelson Goodman, Timothy S. Hall, Peter Kivy, Jerrold Levinson, Thomas Carson Mark, Robert L. Martin, Aaron Ridley, James Ross, Francis Sparshott, Paul Thom, and J. O. Urmson.
6. Bowen 1993a:141.
7. Bowen 1999:428.
8. Bowen 1999:428.
9. Caswell 1964:2:68.
10. Bowen 1999:427.
11. Cook and Everist 1999:256.
12. Bailey 1992:98.
13. Small 1998:115.
14. Godlovitch 1988:270.
15. Restout 1964:401.
16. Mendel 1962:14.
17. Taruskin 1995:319.
18. Kingsbury 1988:88, 93.
19. Frisch 2003:278.

20. Frisch 2003:298.

21. Small 1998:118.

22. Small 1998:90.

23. Taruskin 1995:277.

24. Payzant 1978:38.

25. Kingsbury 1988:94.

26. Il s'est fait admirer sur tout du Signor Luiggi, qui pleuroit de joye de luy entendre executer ses Airs, Que dis-je executer ? Les orner & mesme y changer par-cy par-là des Notes pour mieux quadrer aux paroles Italiennes. Bacilly 1679:10.

27. Boorman 1999:420.

28. Brown 1999:417 and 427, quoting Domenico Corri, *A select collection* (ca. 1782), 2.

29. Bowen 1993b:84.

30. Bowen 1993b:78, quoting E. Polko, *Erinnerungen an Felix Mendelssohn-Bartholdy* (Leipzig, 1868).

31. Bowen 1993b:81–85.

32. Taruskin 1995:13. I don't mean to deliberately cast aspersions on the *NG 2*, which is a fine reference work. It is also a fat and unmoving target.

33. Harnoncourt 1989:203.

34. Potter 1998:52, citing C. Cairns (ed.), *The memoirs of Hector Berlioz* (1969), 212.

35. Mozart, letter of Jan. 17, 1778, quoted in Vester 1999:188.

36. Cited in Hunter 2005:364.

37. Translated in Schafer 1975:89.

38. Brown 1999:631.

39. Dupré, *Philosophie de la musique* (n.d.), 43, cited in Hill 1994:44.

40. Nordlinger 2004:6–7.

41. Brown 1999:391.

42. Small 1998:87.

43. Small 1998:89.

44. Davies 2001:211.

45. Elias Canetti, *Crowds and power* (1963), 394, quoted in Feld 1988: 94–95.

46. Personal communication, January 2006.

47. Small 1998:25.

48. From his *Mémoires*, 1:40, quoted in Spitzer and Zaslaw 2004:389.

49. See Horowitz 1987.

50. Horowitz 1987:403.

51. Horowitz 1987:403.

52. Houle 1987:34.

53. Interview, Aug. 1988, in Sherman 1997:327.

54. Tucker 2002:66.

55. Johann Samuel Petri (2/1782), *Anleitung zur praktischen Musik*, p.181, quoted in Spitzer and Zaslaw 2004:386. They quote a similar statement in I. F. C. Arnold (1806). *Der angehende Musikdirektor,* p.58.

56. Tucker 2002:14.

57. Tucker 2002:39, 75.

6. Changing Meanings, Permanent Symbols

1. Harnoncourt 1988:28.

2. The concept was discussed by Charles Seeger as early as 1958.

3. It was Nikolaus Harnoncourt who proposed this idea (1988:28–29). He calls the two forms "work-notation" and "performance-notation."

4. This is, of course, meant as a generalization, and Harnoncourt lists a number of exceptions (tablature, for instance, is essentially prescriptive, though it was commonly used long before the Romantic Revolution).

5. Goodman 1976:117.

6. If there are rehearsals, and repeat performances, this element of unpredictability disappears, of course.

7. Goehr 1992:188.

8. Maugars 1639.

9. Boorman 1999:410.

10. Boorman 1999:408.

11. Randel 1992:13.

12. As Boorman points out (1999:409 n. 19), trying to capture on paper the complex act of performing music has an interesting parallel in dance notation (which in the Baroque period did not even attempt to go further than recording foot placements).

13. Goodman 1976:186–87.

14. Bowen 1999:438.

15. Harnoncourt 1988:30.

16. This has been an issue with the *NBA* (the new Bach edition), which, in the modern spirit of consistency, adds articulations by analogy.

17. One of the best descriptions of a Romantic slur is the one by Franklin Taylor (in an early edition of *Grove's Dictionary* in the 1880s [!]): he wrote that "When the curved line is drawn over two notes of considerable length, or in slow tempo, it is not a slur, but merely a sign of legato." Cited in Brown 1999:34–35.

18. Brown 1999:30ff., 234.

19. See Harnoncourt 1988:44–45 and 1989:108–9; Brown 1999:35.

20. Taruskin 1995:71–72.

21. *HDM* 2003:648. Taruskin 1995:90–91 misinterprets the meaning of this phrase.

22. Jeffery 1992:69.

23. Walls 2003:87.

24. Houle 1987:190.

25. Brown 1999:29–30. Although there were many more articulation marks in composers' scores in the generations succeeding the eighteenth-century, performers were still expected to add considerably to the composer's indications of accentuation and phrasing.

26. Brown 2003:62.

27. Goehr 1992:30.

28. Golomb 2004:138.

29. Rifkin in Sherman 1997:379. I have to say (except for the part about flawless), that that's often how we recorded the Bach cantatas for Teldec. No previous rehearsals except for big pieces, which got one. The arias were often recorded in 3–4 takes.

30. Abrams 1953:71, quoting Horace, *Ars poetica* II:99–103. He cites also Quintilian *Institutes* III:5:2 and 6/2:25–27: "the chief requisite for moving the feelings of others, is . . . that we ourselves be moved."

31. Interview in Sherman 1997:386.

32. Rosen 2000:212; Brown 1999:425.

33. Quoted in Goehr 1992:1.

34. Brown 1999:631.

35. See Taruskin 1995:167, who made this same point. Although a sense of composers guarding their professional reputation was in the air by the mid-eighteenth century (see Fabian 2003:163 n. 26), and Geminiani in 1751:6 wrote "Playing in good Taste doth not consist of frequent Passages, but in expressing with Strength and Delicacy the Intention of the Composer."

36. Mertin 1986:1.

37. Avison 1753:108.

38. Quantz 1752:11 § 15.

39. Walls 2003:109.

40. Mattheson 1739, last paragraph; translation from Robin Stowell, *The early violin and viola* (Cambridge, 2001), p. xiii. Already quoted in ch. 1.

41. Bovet 2003:12.

42. J. M. Gesner, 1738, quoted in David and Mendel 1945:231.

43. Adorno quoted in Taruskin 1995:138.

44. Butt 2002:80. See also Dreyfus 1983:301.

45. Adorno, captive on the carousel of his own time, no doubt preferred his Bach played in a different style than is in vogue nowadays—Furtwängler's, perhaps, or Landowska's?

46. See Kivy 1993:97ff.

47. See Donington 1989:122.

7. Original Ears

1. Lowenthal 1985:77.

2. Gombrich 1966:122.

3. Lowenthal 1985:152.

4. Skowroneck 2002.

5. Harnoncourt 1989:26.

6. Harnoncourt 1988:129.

7. This question is sensitively discussed in Bianconi 1987:161ff.

8. See Strunk 1950:33–55.

9. Dreyfus 1983:322.

10. Donington 1989:122.

11. Lang 1997:184.

12. North in Wilson 1959:111.

13. Weber 1992:24–25.

14. North, *Notes of comparison*, in Wilson 1959:283.

15. Weber 1992:56ff. Charles Avison's *Essay on musical expression* (1753: 39–42, 49ff.) makes a superficial attempt to rank Italian composers and talks of music as seeming, from the time of Palestrina, "rather to have gradually improved."

16. Weber 1992:161, 155.

17. North 1728:272.

18. Weber 1992:87-88.

19. See Haynes 2001:137.

20. See Wilson 2001 and Kolneder 1970.

21. Le Cerf de la Viéville (1704), 3d Discours, p. 100 (tr. Ellison 1973:141).

22. Wood 1981–2:26.

23. Le Cerf de la Viéville (1704), 1st Discours, p. 62 (tr. Ellison 1973:88).

24. Muller 1982:238, quoting Agucchi's *Trattato* (1607–15). This resembles *trompe l'oeil.*

25. Kurz 1948:317.

26. Werness 1983:50–51.

27. See Kilbracken 1967; Werness 1983. Ironically, just before van Meegeren started producing fake Vermeers, Friedländer wrote in 1942 in his chapter on fakes (265), "A picture by Vermeer is something exceptionally precious. Of this master the dealers are dreaming."

28. Werness 1983:50–51.

29. From Eric Wen, notes with *Kreisler plays Kreisler,* BMG CD 09026-61649-2.

30. Lochner 1951:295ff.

31. Newman also maintained—questionably—that "Anyone . . . could produce this sort of thing"; that "a vast amount of seventeenth and eighteenth century music was merely the exploitation of formulae" that any intelligent musician could imitate today.

32. Werness 1983:48–49.

33. Haskell 1988:74. Despite Nicotra's obvious talent and his clear historical interest, the *NG 2* has no entry for him.

34. Lessing 1983:58.

35. Le Cerf de la Viéville 1704: 4th Discours, page 58. Ellison 1973:197 translates this as: "By Jove," cried the Marquis, "stupidities in writing! It is they that last longest." My snide remarks on musicology are sanctioned, by the way (even encouraged), by my Ph.D. in the field.

36. Collingwood 1946:246, 204.

37. "The attempt to know what we have no means of knowing is an infallible way to generate illusions" (Collingwood 1946:327).

38. Treitler 1989:39.

39. See Treitler 1999:360.

40. North in Wilson 1959:4.

41. This approach is very well put in the quotation of Kenneth Cooper in Taruskin 1995:100–101.

42. Temperley 1984:18.

43. Leech-Wilkinson 2002:3.

44. Leech-Wilkinson 2002:111.

45. Page 1992.

46. Dolmetsch 1915:468.

47. Fabian 2003:245.

48. See Parrott 2000. Le Cerf de la Viéville, (1704), 2d Discours, p. 75, comments that, unlike French operas that have a chorus of 20–25 singers, "these marvelous opera companies of Venice, Naples, or Rome consist of seven or eight voices" made up of the role-playing actors.

49. The Teldec cantata series made an effort to have boy soloists on the so-

prano part, but had an adult male falsettist sing the alto solos. None of the other subsequent series uses boys.

50. North in Wilson 1959:135; see also 303 n. 49.
51. Hawkins 1776:2:676.
52. Small 1998:97.
53. See Gay 1995:16–17.
54. Gay 1995:19.
55. Johnson 1995:172.
56. Gay 1995:21.
57. Finnegan 1986:83.
58. Ross 2004:151, 155.
59. Small 1998:38.
60. Johnson 1995:13.
61. Small 1998:23, 25, 27.
62. Weber 1984:30.
63. Tucker 2002:41, 163.
64. Small 1998:155.
65. Bartel 1997:34.
66. Small 1998:43.
67. Gay 1995:15.
68. Philip 2003:366.
69. Weber 1997:681.
70. Johnson 1995:13.
71. Burney 1773:68.
72. Burney 1773:208.
73. Johnson 1995:29.
74. Beaussant 1992:538.
75. Le Cerf de la Viéville (1704), 2d Discours, p. 303, Eng. tr. from Strunk 1950:139–40.

8. Ways of Copying the Past

1. See Ackerman 2000. Another recommended article on this subject is Wittkower's "Imitation, eclecticism, and genius" (see bibliography).
2. Lowenthal 1985:75–77.
3. Muller 1982:244.
4. Harnoncourt 1988:124.
5. Restout 1964:356.
6. Fabian 2003:16.
7. This information was frequently inaccurate or out of date, at least in my case.
8. Lowenthal 1985:302–3.
9. Wittkower 1965:157.
10. Ackerman 2000:13.
11. Collingwood 1946:280–81.
12. That is why a table of trills and other *agréments* is not enough, and why they caused the ire of Antoine Geoffroy-Dechaume: "It is sufficient to be aware of the great variety of execution of which each *agrément* is susceptible to realize *the inanity of ornament tables* [l'inanité des tables], which offer only a single transcription for each *agrément* and one, to boot, that is mostly only a pattern without musical merit" (quoted and translated from "L'Appoggiature ancienne," p. 91, in Neumann 1978:3).

13. Wikipedia, http://en.wikipedia.org/wiki/Descriptive_linguistics.

14. Friedländer 1942:261–62.

15. Vries 1945:63, 65. See also Goodman 1976: ch. 3 and Goodman 1995.

16. Spitzer 1983:376.

17. Taruskin 1995:102.

18. Harnoncourt 1989:25.

19. Restout 1964:407.

20. Adams 2002–5: debate with John Shinners.

21. Fabian 2003:22.

22. Quoted in Fabian 2001:155–56. Butt (2002:139) calls Harnoncourt an "inspired antiquarian," apparently ignoring this very clear stance.

23. Dart 1954:167.

24. Harnoncourt 1989:73.

25. Restout 1964:356. This is one of Fabian's points, that many of the subjects raised in English discourse in the 1980s had already been discussed in German.

26. Sherman 1997:3.

27. Adams 2002–5:7.

28. This example comes from Peter Schubert's interesting article (1994).

29. Heyerdahl 1951:35.

30. See Fabian 2003:19 reviewing Finscher's 1968 article.

31. Walls 2003:74.

32. Leech-Wilkinson 2002:223.

33. Harnoncourt 1989:8.

34. Treitler (1989:310 n. 26) points out that the way most of us use this phrase was not how it was intended by Ranke when he first wrote it.

35. Goldstein 1970:15, citing R.G. Collingwood (1965), *Essays in the philosophy of history*, ed. William Debbins, p.101.

36. Goldstein 1970:27.

37. Mink 1968:34.

38. Goldstein 1970:18.

39. Goldstein 1970:15, citing R. G. Collingwood (1965), *Essays in the philosophy of history*, ed. William Debbins, p. 53.

40. Leech-Wilkinson 2002:220.

41. Golomb 2003.

42. Philip 1992:238–39.

43. Fuller 1979:14. Fuller's article comes with a fascinating recording of a half-dozen instruments dating from 1640 to around 1830. Another excellent discussion of this subject is in Houle 1987:110–23.

44. Schmitz and Ord-Hume 2001:8:247.

45. Philip 1992:1.

46. See South 1937 (recorded excerpts, number 53).

47. Sorrell 1992:781.

48. Collingwood 1946:108.

9. The Medium Is the Message

1. Harnoncourt 1988:17.

2. Owen Jorgensen has described the basic philosophy of twentieth-century equal temperament as "to promote atonality with a neutral homogenized sound

that has no color contrasts and no variety among the keys." Jorgensen, *Tuning* (1991), p. 9, quoted in Lehman 2005:21 n. 52.

3. Fabian 2003:247.

4. Vény ca. 1828:30.

5. This depends on the instrument. Of course, there is a difference in sound and sometimes in technique, but we are talking about performing style.

6. Taruskin 1995:305.

7. Schmied 2000.

8. Quoted in Taruskin 1995:130.

9. An effect like flattement is possible, but the sound is different when keys are involved.

10. In fact, a whole tone higher than the Magnificat in Eb (BWV 243a).

11. Butt 2002:65.

12. Walls 2003:142.

13. Davies 2001:70–71. Although I agree with Davies's main point, he goes on to say "Because music does not have a semantic content, its message resides entirely in its accent and inflection." I look forward to discussing this idea in a future publication.

14. Site "Paul Verlaine-poèmes," http://www.pierdelune.com/verlaine1.htm, accessed 28 December 2006.

15. Bilson 1980:161.

16. Rosen 2000:211.

17. Fabian 2003:46 n.

18. Walls 2003:140.

19. Payzant 1978:155; Bazzana 1997:11.

20. I'm grateful to John Black of the Music Library at McGill University for telling me about this recording.

21. Skowroneck 2003:264.

22. Skowroneck 2003:263, 267–68.

23. Skowroneck 2003:267.

24. On an hautboy, for instance, the low c1 is usually tuned high, probably so c#1 can also be played with that fingering, and a largish and well-undercut 5th hole allows for the original f#1 fingering that works only in meantone. The use of these tuning ambiguities was not immediately evident when the hautboy was revived, so they seemed at first to be mistakes.

25. Collingwood 1946:200.

26. Skowroneck 2002.

27. Skowroneck 2002:12–13.

10. Baroque Expression and Romantic Expression Compared

1. Quantz 1752:11 § 1.

2. Buelow 2001:21:260.

3. Bartel 1997:57 n. 1 defends the application of Rhetoric to music from the criticisms of Brian Vickers. Vickers (1984) has no justification for claiming that Rhetoric is limited to languages, but his critical comparison of how Baroque musicians adopted the concepts to music is useful and interesting.

4. Tarling 2004:ii.

5. *OED*, "Affection."

6. North, in Wilson 1959:139–40. See also Hill and Ploger 2005.

7. Keith Hill, e-mail message to Skip Sempé.

8. Neubauer 1986:50.

9. Neubauer 1986:50.

10. "Mimesis in theatre," *EB* 28:523.

11. Bovet 2003:35.

12. Small 1998:145.

13. His best-known passages on affective expression are actually summaries of Descartes's influential treatise on Affections, *De passionibus animae (The Passions of the Soul)*, written in 1649. Buelow thinks that, from the context, *Affektenlehre* was meant to be a concept parallel to another science that appears in Descartes's book, *Natur-Lehre* (physics).

14. Buelow 2001:21:263, Buelow 1983.

15. Mattheson 1739:1:10 § 63.

16. Quantz 1752:11 § 16.

17. Neubauer 1986:42. See also Bartel 1997:31.

18. Mellers 1992:922.

19. Bartel 1997:34.

20. Burney 1771:294.

21. Sherman 1997:197.

22. Johnson 1995:60.

23. Richard Aldrich describing Josef Lhévinne's playing, 1908. Cited in Hill 1994:49.

24. Bekker 1922:297ff., cited and tr. in Hill 1994:58.

25. Fénelon, *Dialogues concerning eloquence* (tr. Wm. Stevenson London, 1722), cited on p. 113 of Vickers 1981.

26. Small 1998:120.

27. Bacilly 1668:253.

28. Quantz 1752: ch. 11, Bach ch. 3.

29. Quantz 1752: introduction, § 16.

30. See Tucker 2002:30 and Chaouche 2001.

31. I find several of the regular singers in the different series of recorded Bach cantatas quite unbearable, while others (I am told) love them.

32. Tarling 2004:239–40.

33. Shakespeare, *Hamlet,* Act I, scene iii; Polonius's advice to his son.

34. Poisson, *Reflexions sur l'art de parler en publique,* 1717:36, cited in Barnett 1987:14.

35. Quantz 1752:14 § 5.

36. Abrams 1953:71, quoting Cicero *De oratore* II: xxviii, xlv.

37. North 1728:271.

38. Collingwood 1938:110–11.

39. Quantz 1752:11 § 21, 11 § 1, 10 § 22.

40. Carroll (1998:64) calls it "the sincerity condition."

41. Quantz 1752:10 § 22. In German, it was "Das Singen der Seele, oder die innerliche Empfindung," and in French, it was "Ce chant de l'ame & ce sentiment interieur."

42. Bach 1753:1:119.

43. Bach 1753:1:122.

44. Burney 1773:2:270.

45. Hawkins 1776:2:675.
46. Le Cerf de la Viéville (1704), 2d Dialogue, p. 61 (tr. Ellison 1973:87).
47. Mattheson 1739:1:6 § 18–19.
48. Avison 1753:88.
49. Mason 1748:8.
50. Mason 1748:31, quoting Quintilian.
51. Abrams 1953:25.
52. Abrams 1953:3.
53. Carroll 1998:61.
54. Hunter 2005:384.
55. Hunter 2005:369.
56. Quoted in Salmen 1983:270–71.
57. Dahlhaus 1983:76.
58. Bartel 1997:79–80.
59. David and Mendel 1945:291.
60. See Gay 1995:37–42.
61. Collingwood 1938:110.
62. Quoted in Hunter 2005:366.
63. Quantz 1752:11 § 1.
64. Scruton 2001:8:466.
65. Abrams gives a similar example on his p. 152.
66. Small 1998:6.
67. Quoted in Dahlhaus 1989:69.
68. Avison 1753:127.
69. Treitler 1989:183.
70. Baker, Paddison, Scruton 2001:8:464.
71. Abrams 1953:15.
72. Mill, *Early Essays* (1897), 208–9, quoted in Abrams 1953:25; see also Abrams 1953:321.
73. Abrams 1953:25.
74. Day 2000:160.
75. Dreyfus 1996:2.
76. Collingwood 1938:37.
77. Wilson 1959:118 and Plate V.
78. January 1738. *Bach Dokumente* 2:304.
79. Taruskin 2005:364.

11. The Rainbow and the Kaleidoscope

1. Bijlsma 1998:17.
2. Harnoncourt 1988:25.
3. Haynes 2001:223–36 and Burgess 2003:41–44.
4. Burney 1773:158.
5. Harnoncourt 1988:41.
6. Butt 1990:17, 19ff., 113, 114, 140, 192ff.
7. Butt 1990:19ff., 116, 192ff., 208.
8. Butt 1990:23.
9. Mattheson 1739:2:14 § 48.
10. Vickers 1981:109.

11. In his published writings of 1599 to 1606, Burmeister uses none of the figures of melodic and harmonic ornamentation. Exhaustive lists of figures are given in Bartel. On figures, see Harnoncourt 1988:55,133; Ratner 1991; and Fabian 2003:160ff.

12. Bartel 1997:176.

13. Bartel 1997:192.

14. Bartel 1997:216.

15. Bartel 1997:234.

16. Bartel 1997:290.

17. Butt 1990:21; Bartel 1997:394.

18. Bartel 1997:409.

19. Bartel 1997:427ff.

20. Lamy 1675:218.

21. Prescott, *Mexico* (1843), 98, cited in *OED* 1:1136.

22. I take musical "meaning" here as what the music is trying to convey; why the composer wrote those notes and not others; what (as Laurence Dreyfus put it) the piece—at least this part of it—is "about," as music.

23. Drabkin 2001:17:227. In his magnificent study of Bach's compositional process, Marshall uses the term "motif" for a "fully formed melodic idea." Marshall 1972:119, 125, 126.

24. Kirkendale 1980:131.

25. Dreyfus 1996:27.

26. At least, those of us who like puns can call it that!

27. Quantz 1752:11 § 14.

28. Quantz 1752:11 § 15.

29. Harnoncourt 1988:41ff.

30. Quantz 1752:14 § 11.

31. Agricola 1757:48.

32. Mozart 1756:103, tr. Boyden 1965:393.

33. In a letter written in 1760 and quoted in Boyden 1965:393.

34. Fabian 2003:131–32.

35. Quantz 1752:11 § 14.

36. Butt 1994:86, citing Mattheson 1739:2:1 § 20, tr. Harriss 1981:244.

37. See Donington 1989:125.

38. Taruskin 1995:194.

39. Fuller 1989:138.

12. Passive and Active Musicking

1. Adams 2002–5: debate with John Shinners.

2. Birnbaum 1738 in *Bach Dokumente* II:299.

3. Small 1998:110.

4. Ong 1982.

5. Bailey 1992:10.

6. Preface to *Euridice*, quoted in Neumann 1978:10.

7. Bacilly's colleague Jacques de Gouÿ—on the advice of fellow-composers Lambert and Moulinié—actually removed graces he had notated in an edition of 1650.

8. See Neumann 1978:31–36.

9. Rameau, *Code de musique pratique* (1760), 13, quoted in Neumann 1978:11.

10. This little section is not meant to describe the whole subject, merely some aspects that have to do with our modern response to them. A good short summary of historical gracing is Fuller 1989:124–30, and two excellent books of practical instruction in gracing and passages are Mather 1973 and Mather and Lasocki 1976.

11. *Troisième Livre* (1722).

12. Goehr 1992:232.

13. Rosen 2000:212; Brown 1999:425.

14. Hunter 2005:367.

15. 1893, I:vii, quoted in Haskell 1988:33.

16. North in Wilson 1959:149.

17. Quantz 1752:14 § 2–3.

18. Bailey 1992:66.

19. Baird 1995:28.

20. Cited by R. Osborne in *NG* dictionary of opera 1:311, and quoted in Brown 1999:420.

21. Libby 1989:16.

22. Brett 1988:107 (quoting Reinhard Strohm, "Towards an understanding of the opera seria," *Essays on Handel and Italian opera* (Cambridge, 1985), 94–98).

23. Kivy 1995:163.

24. Bailey 1992:19.

25. Golomb 2003.

26. Lochner 1951:298ff.

27. North 1728:258.

28. Burney 1773:1:312.

29. North 1728:257.

30. Quoted in Dahlhaus 1989:69.

31. Quoted in Michel 1982. It should be noted that these remarks are evidence of the modesty of a great musician, who has on occasion gone as far into composition as to make very convincing transcriptions of several of Bach's pieces for solo instruments. These include BWV 995, 996, 998, 1001, 1002, 1004, 1005, 1006, and 1012.

32. Michel 1982.

33. Published by Amadeus and Carus.

34. Lessing 1983:59.

35. Michel 1981: introduction.

36. Maute 2005: Vorwort.

37. Bowen 1996a:35.

13. Perpetual Revolution

1. Bowen 1996a:34.

2. Mellers 1992:930.

3. Collingwood 1946:218.

4. See Dahlhaus 1983:153.

5. Butt 2002:66–67.

6. Taruskin 1995:46.

7. Walls 2003:52.
8. North, *Notes of comparison*, ca. 1726, in Wilson 1959:283.
9. Philip 1992:238–39.
10. *NG* 1:14:388.
11. Lowenthal 1985:40–41.
12. Holoman, Winter, and Page (2001), *NG* 2:19:374.
13. Taruskin 1995:267.
14. Dulak 1993:45.
15. Philip 1994:203.
16. Dulak 1993:47.
17. Dulak 1993:46.
18. Philip 2004:222.
19. Hill 1994:41.
20. Golomb 2004:128.
21. Dreyfus 1996:29.
22. Meyer 1967:65–66.
23. Butt 2002:28.
24. This is a conflation of two ideas in Meyer 1967:46–50.
25. Fabian 2003:20.
26. Parakilas 1984:6.
27. Taruskin 1995:283.
28. Philip 2004:218.
29. Philip 2004:221.
30. Philip 2004: 226.
31. Taruskin 1995:194.
32. Taruskin 1995:194.
33. Taruskin 1995:78.
34. Based on Abrams 1953:3.
35. Tarling 2004:iii.
36. Bowen 1996a:34.
37. Bowen 1996a:27.
38. Philip 1992:235.
39. Philip 1992:235.
40. Roger North, ca. 1726, in Wilson 1959:283.
41. Quoted in Goldstein 1970:15 from Collingwood, *Essays in the philosophy of history,* ed. W. Debbins (1965), 99.
42. Sherman 1997:10.
43. Barthold Kuijken in Kuijken and Hook 2004:33.
44. Liner notes to "Simply Baroque."
45. Haskell 1988/1996:188.

Bibliographic Abbreviations

AM	*Acta Musicologica*
AMZ	*Allgemeine musikalische Zeitung*
BJHM	*Basler Jahrbuch für historische Musikpraxis*
EB	*Encyclopedia Britannica*
EM	*Early Music*
EML Bulletin	*Early Music Laboratory Bulletin*
GPS	*Grazer Philosophische Studien*
GSJ	*Galpin Society Journal*
HDM	*The Harvard Dictionary of Music*
ICMPC	*International Conference on Music Perception and Cognition*
IRASM	*International Review of the Aesthetics and Sociology of Music*
JAAC	*Journal of Aesthetics and Art Criticism*
JAE	*Journal of Aesthetic Education*
JAMS	*Journal of the American Musicological Society*
JIDRS	*Journal of the International Double-Reed Society*
JM	*Journal of Musicology*
JMM	*The Refereed On-Line Journal for Multi-Disciplinary Research on Music and Meaning*
MGG	*Die Musik in Geschichte und Gegenwart*
MQ	*Musical Quarterly*
NBA	*Neue Bach Ausgabe*

NG 1	*New Grove Dictionary, 1980*
NG 2	*New Grove Dictionary, 2001*
PhPR	*Philosophy and Phenomenological Research*
PPR	*Performance Practice Review*
PRMA	*Proceedings of the Royal Musical Association*
RMM	*Recorder and Music Magazine*

Bibliography

Abrams, M. H. (1953). *The mirror and the lamp: Romantic theory and the critical tradition.* Oxford University Press.

Ackerman, James (2000). "Imitation." In *Antiquity and its interpreters,* ed. A. Payne, A. Kuttner, and R. Smick, 9–16. Cambridge University Press.

Adams, Piers (2002–5). "Artist vs. Critic." Debate with J. Shinners / Interview with A. Mayes / Source quotations on the ensemble Red Priest.

Agricola, Johann Friedrich (1757). *Anleitung zur Singkunst.* [In Baird 1995]. Reprinted 1966.

Alperson, Philip (1984). "On musical improvisation." *JAAC* 43:17–30.

Arnheim, Rudolf (1983). "On duplication." In *The forger's art: Forgery and the philosophy of art,* ed. D. Dutton, 232–45. University of California Press.

Avison, Charles (1753). *An essay on musical expression.* Reprinted 1967.

Babbitt, Milton (1966). "Who cares if you listen?" *The American composer speaks: A historical anthology, 1770–1965,* ed. G. Chase (orig. appeared in 1958 in *High Fidelity*), 234–44. Louisiana State University Press.

Babitz, Sol (1952). "A problem of rhythm in baroque music." *MQ* 38:533–65.

—— (1967). "Concerning the length of time that every note must be held." *Music Review* 28:21–37.

—— (1974). "Rhythmic freedom: A historical table in the light of wind instrument tonguing." *EML Bulletin* 11 (entire issue).

Bach, C. P. E. (1753–62). *Versuch über die wahre Art das Clavier zu spielen.* Reprinted 1969.

Bach-Dokumente (1963, 1969, 1972). *Supplement to Neue Bach Ausgabe,* ed. W. Neumann and H.-J. Schulze. 3 vols.

Bacilly, Bénigne de (1668 2/1679). *L'Art de bien chanter.* Reprinted, 1971.

Bailey, Derek (1992). *Improvisation: Its nature and practice in music.* Da Capo.

Baird, Julianne C. (1995). *Introduction to the art of singing by Johann Friedrich Agricola* [annotated translation]. Cambridge University Press.

Baker, David (1983). *Jazz improvisation: A comprehensive method of study for all players,* 2d ed. Alfred.

Baker, Nancy Kovaleff, Max Halle Paddison, and Roger Scruton (2001). "Expression." *NG 2,* 8:463–72.

Barnett, Dene (1978). "Non-uniform slurring in eighteenth-century music: Accident or design?" *Haydn Yearbook* 10:179–99.

———— (1987). *The art of gesture: The practices and principles of 18th century acting* (with the assistance of Jeanette Massy-Westropp). Winter.

Bartel, Dietrich (1997). Musica Poetica: Musical-rhetorical figures in German baroque music. University of Nebraska Press.

Bazzana, Kevin (1997). *Glenn Gould: The performer in the work, a study in performance practice.* Oxford University Press.

Beaussant, Philippe (1992). *Lully ou le musicien du soleil.* Gallimard.

Bekker, Paul (1922). *Klang und Eros.*

Bergeron, Katherine, and Philip V. Bohlman (eds.) (1992). *Disciplining music: Musicology and its canons.* University of Chicago Press.

Bianconi, Lorenzo (1987). *Music in the seventeenth century,* trans. D. Bryant. Cambridge University Press.

Bijlsma, Anner (1998). *Bach, the fencing master: Reading aloud from the first three cello suites.*

Bilson, Malcolm (1980). "The Viennese fortepiano of the late 18th century." *EM* 8/2:158–62.

Blyth, R. H. (1942). *Zen in English literature and oriental classics.* Dover.

Bollioud de Mermet, Louis (1746). *De la corruption du goust dans la musique françoise.* Reprinted 1978, AMS.

Bonds, Mark Evan (1991). *Wordless rhetoric: Musical form and the metaphor of the oration.* Harvard University Press.

Boorman, Stanley (1999). "The musical text." In *Rethinking music,* ed. N. Cook and M. Everist, 403–23. Oxford University Press.

Borges, Jorge Luis (1962). "Pierre Menard, author of Don Quixote" (1939). In *Ficciones,* 45–55. Grove.

Botstein, Leon (2001). "Modernism." *NG 2,* 16:870.

Boult, Sir Adrian (1977). "Peter Wadland interviews Sir Adrian C. Boult." April 11, 1977. Private interview (never broadcast or circulated). Courtesy of Teri Noel Towe.

Bovet, Jeanne (2003). *Les Poétiques de la voix dans le théâtre classique.* Ph.D. diss., Université de Montréal.

Bowen, José A. (1993a). "The history of remembered innovation: Tradition and its role in the relationship between musical works and their performances." *JM* 11/2:139–73.

———— (1993b). "Mendelssohn, Berlioz and Wagner as conductors: The origins of the ideal of 'fidelity to the composer.'" *PPR* 6:77–88.

———— (1996). "Performance practice versus performance analysis: Why should performers study performance?" *PPR* 9/1:16–35.

———— (1999). "Finding the music in musicology: Performance history and musical works." In *Rethinking music,* ed. N. Cook and M. Everist, 424–51. Oxford University Press.

—— (2003a). "The rise of conducting." In *The Cambridge companion to conducting*, ed. J. A. Bowen, 93–113. Cambridge University Press.

Bowie, A., S. Davies, L. Goehr, and F. E. Sparshott (2001). "Philosophy of music." *NG 2*, 19:601–31.

Boyd, Malcolm (1980). "Arrangement." *NG 1*, 1:630.

Boyden, David D. (1965). *The history of violin playing*. Oxford University Press.

Braatz, Thomas (2003). "Matthäus-Passion BWV 244 conducted by Günther Ramin." *Bach Cantatas Website* http://www.bach-cantatas.com. Accessed 1 May 2006.

Brauner, Charles S. (1992). "The Seconda Pratica, or the imperfections of the composer's voice." In *Musical humanism and its legacy: Essays in honor of Claude V. Palisca*, ed. N. K. Baker and B. R. Hanning, 195–212. Pendragon.

Brett, Philip (1988). "Text, context, and the early music editor." In *Authenticity and early music*, ed. N. Kenyon, 83–114. Oxford University Press.

Brown, Clive (1999). *Classical and Romantic performing practice*. Oxford University Press.

—— (2001). "Articulation marks." *NG 2*, 2:89–92.

—— (2003). "Joachim's violin playing and the performance of Brahms's string music." In *Performing Brahms: Early evidence of performance style*, ed. M. Musgrave and B. D. Sherman, 48–98. Cambridge University Press.

Brown, Howard Mayer (1988). "Pedantry or Liberation? A sketch of the historical performance movement." In *Authenticity and early music*, ed. N. Kenyon, 27–56. Oxford University Press.

Buelow, George J. (1983). "Johann Mattheson and the invention of the Affektenlehre." In *New Mattheson studies*, ed. by G. J. Buelow and H. J. Marx, 393–407. Cambridge University Press.

Buelow, George J., and Peter A. Hoyt (2002). "Rhetoric and music." *NG 2*, 21:260–75.

Burgess, Geoffrey V. (2003). *"The premier oboist of Europe": A portrait of Gustave Vogt*. Scarecrow.

Burmeister, Joachim (1606). *Musica poetica*. Reprinted in English trans., 1993.

Burney, Charles (1771). *The present state of music in France and Italy; or, the journal of a tour through those countries*.

—— (1773). *The present state of music in Germany, the Netherlands, and the United Provinces*, 2 vols.

Burnham, Scott (1995). *Beethoven hero*. Princeton University Press.

—— (1999). "How music matters: Poetic content revisited." In *Rethinking music*, ed. N. Cook and M. Everist, 193–216. Oxford University Press.

Burstyn, Shai (1997). "In quest of the period ear." *EM* 692–701.

Butt, John (1990). *Bach interpretation.: Articulation marks in primary sources of J. S. Bach*. Cambridge University Press.

—— (1994). *Music education and the art of performance in the German baroque*. Cambridge University Press.

—— (1999a). "Bach recordings since 1980: A mirror of historical performance." In *Bach perspectives* 4, ed. David Schulenberg, 181–98.

—— (1999b). Review of Bartel 1997, *Early Music History* 18:398–404.

—— (2002). *Playing with history*. Cambridge University Press.

Caccini, Giulio (1601). *Le nuove musiche*.

Campbell, Margaret (1975). *Dolmetsch: The man and his work*. University of Washington Press.

——— (2001). "Arnold Dolmetsch," *NG 2*, 7:433–35.

Carrier, David (1983). "Interpreting musical performances." *Monist* 66:202–12.

Carroll, Noël (1998). *A philosophy of mass art*. Oxford University Press.

Carter, T. (1992). "Artusi, Monteverdi, and the poetics of modern music." In *Musical humanism and its legacy: Essays in honor of Claude Palisca*, ed. N. K. Baker and B. R. Hanning, 171–94. Pendragon.

Caswell, Austin B. (1964). *The development of seventeenth-century French vocal ornamentation and its influence upon late Baroque ornamentation-practice*. Ph.D. diss., University of Minnesota.

Chan, Mary, and Jamie C. Kassler (1990). *Roger North's* The musical grammarian 1728. Cambridge University Press.

Chaouche, Sabine (2001). *L'Art du comédien: Déclamation et jeu scénique en France à l'age classique*.

Chua, Daniel K. L. (1999). *Absolute music and the construction of meaning*. Cambridge University Press.

Cohen, Joel, and Herb Snitzer (1985). *Reprise: The extraordinary revival of early music.* Little, Brown.

Collingwood, R. G. (1938). *The principles of art*. Oxford University Press.

——— (1946). *The idea of history*. Clarendon Press.

——— (1978). *An autobiography*. Oxford University Press.

Collins, Michael, et al. (2001). "Improvisation: The Baroque period." *NG 2*, 12:102–17.

Cook, Nicholas, and Mark Everist (eds.) (1999). "Analysing performance and performing analysis." In *Rethinking music*, ed. N. Cook and M. Everist, 239–61. Oxford University Press.

Couperin, François (1717). *L'Art de toucher le clavecin*.

Cudworth, Charles (1957). "'Baptist's Vein'—French orchestral music and its influence, from 1650 to 1750." *PRMA* 83:29–47.

Dadelsen, Georg von (1980). "'Es gibt keine schlechte Musik, es gibt nur schlechte Interpreten'." In *Musik, edition, interpretation: Gedenkschrift für Günter Henle*, ed. M. Bente, 125–32. Henle.

Dahlhaus, Carl (1983/1977). *Foundations of music history (Grundlagen der Musikgeschichte)*. Cambridge University Press.

——— ed. (1985). *Die Musik des 18. Jahrhunderts*. Laaber-Verlag.

——— (1989). *The idea of absolute music*. University of Chicago Press.

Dannreuther, Edward (1893). *Musical ornamentation*.

Danuser, Hermann (1996). "Interpretation." *MGG* 4:1053–69.

——— (1998). "Vortrag." *MGG* 9:1817–36.

Darbellay, Étienne (1985). "Tradition and notation in baroque music." In *The oral and the literate in music*, ed. Y. Tokumaru and O. Yamaguti, 57–68. Academia Music.

——— (1988). "C. P. E. Bach's aesthetic as reflected in his notation." In *C. P. E. Bach Studies*, ed. Stephen L. Clark, 43–63. Oxford University Press.

Dart, Thurston (1954). *The interpretation of music*. Hutchinson's University Library.

David, Hans T., and Arthur Mendel, eds. (1945). *The Bach reader*. 2nd ed., rev., 1966, Norton.

David, Werner (1951). *Johann Sebastian Bach's Orgeln*. Wiedereröffnung der Berliner Musikinstrumenten-Sammlung.

Davies, Stephen (2001). *Musical works and performances: A philosophical exploration.*Oxford University Press

Day, Timothy (2000). *A century of recorded music: Listening to musical history.* Yale University Press

Descartes, René (1649). *The passions of the soul* [tr. of *Les passions de l'âme* by Stephen Voss].

Diderot, Denis (1773). *Paradoxe sur le comédien* [introduction and notes by Jean M. Goulemot].

Dolmetsch, Arnold (1915). *The interpretation of the music of the XVII and XVIII centuries.* Novello.

Donington, Robert (1963). *The interpretation of early music.* Faber and Faber.

——— (1989). "The present position of authenticity." *PPR* 2:117–25.

Douglas-Home, Jessica (1996). *Violet: The life and loves of Violet Gordon Woodhouse.* Harvill Press.

Drabkin, William (2001). "Motif." *NG* 2, 17:227–28.

Dreyfus, Laurence (1983). "Early music defended against its devotees: A theory of historical performance in the twentieth century." *MQ* 69:297–322.

——— (1996). *Bach and the patterns of invention.* Harvard University Press.

Druce, Duncan (1992). "Historical approaches to violin playing." In *Companion to contemporary musical thought*, ed. J. Paynter et al., 2:993–1019. Routledge.

Duckles, Vincent, et al. (1980). "Musicology." *NG 1*, 12:836–62.

Duckles, Vincent, with Janet Page and Lydia Goehr (2001). "Musicology: Performance practice, aesthetics and criticism." *NG* 2, 17:503–4.

Duffin, Ross W. (1995). "Performance practice: que me veux-tu? (What do you want from me?)." Online article at http://music.cwru.edu/duffin/EMPP/ppqmvt/p1.html. Accessed 1 November 2004.

Dulak, Michelle (1993). "The quiet metamorphosis of 'Early Music.'" *Repercussions* 2:2, 39–61.

Dunsby, Jonathan (2001). "Performance." *NG* 2, 19:346–49.

Dürr, Alfred (1955). Kritischer Bericht for the *Magnificat, NBA* 2/3.

Dutton, Denis (ed.) (1983). *The forger's art: Forgery and the philosophy of art.* University of California Press.

Edidin, Aron (1998). "Playing Bach his way: Historical authenticity, personal authenticity, and the performance of classical music." *JAE* 32/4:79–91.

Ellis, Alexander J. (1880 /R. 1968). "On the history of musical pitch." *Journal of the Society of Arts* (5 Mar 1880):293–336.

Ellison, Mary B. (1973). The *Comparaison de la musique Italienne et de la musique françoise* of Lecerf de la Vieville: An annotated translation of the first four dialogues. Ph.D. diss., University of Miami.

Encyclopaedia Britannica (*EB*) (1768–71, 2nd ed., 1790–97, 3rd ed., 1803).

Encyclopedia Britannica (1974). 15th ed.

Engramelle, M. D. J. (1775). *La Tonotechnie.*

Erauw, Willem (1998). "Canon formation: Some more reflections on Lydia Goehr's *Imaginary museum of musical works*," *AM* 70:109–15.

Everist, Mark (1999). "Reception theories, canonic discourses, and musical value." In *Rethinking music*, ed. N. Cook and M. Everist, 378–402. Oxford University Press.

Fabian, Dorottya (2001). "The meaning of authenticity and the Early Music movement—a historical review." *International Review of the Aesthetics and Sociology of Music* 32:153–67.

—— (2003). *Bach performance practice, 1945–1975: A comprehensive review of sound recordings and literature.* Ashgate.

Fabian, Dorottya, and Emery Schubert (2002). "Is there only one way of being expressive?" *ICMPC* 7:112–15.

Feld, Steven (1988). "Aesthetics as iconicity of style, or 'lift-up-over sounding': Getting into the Kaluli groove." *Yearbook for Traditional Music* 20:74–113.

Finnegan, R. (1986). "The relation between composition and performance: Three alternative modes." In *The oral and the literate in music,* ed. Y. Tokumaru and O. Yamaguti, 73–87. Academia Music.

Finscher, Ludwig. (1968). "Historisch getreue Interpretation—Möglichkeiten und Probleme." In *Alte Musik in unsere Zeit,* ed. W. Wiora, 25–34. Kassel.

Fisher, John Andrew, and Jason Potter (1997). "Technology, appreciation, and the historical view of art." *JAAC* 55:169–85.

Forchert, Arno (1985–86). "Musik und Rhetorik im Barock." *Schütz Jahrbuch* 7–8:5–21.

Fortune, Nigel (2001a). "Sprezzatura." *NG 2,* 24:223–24.

—— (2001b). "Air." *NG 2,* 1:252–53.

Frescobaldi, Girolamo (1615). Preface, *Toccate e partite d'intavolatura di cimbalo.*

Fried, Michael (1990). *Courbet's realism.* University of Chicago Press.

Friedländer, M. J. (1942). *On art and connoisseurship.* Cassirer.

Frisch, Walter (2003). "In search of Brahms's First Symphony: Steinbach, the Meiningen tradition, and the recordings." In *Performing Brahms: Early evidence of performance style,* ed. M. Musgrave and B. D. Sherman, 277–301. Cambridge University Press.

Fuller, David (1977). "Dotting, the 'French style' and Frederick Neumann's counter-reformation." *EM* 5/4:517–43.

—— (1979). "Mechanical musical instruments as a source for the study of 'notes inégales.'" *Bulletin of the Musical Box Society International,* Summer 1974 (reprint includes recording).

—— (1989). "The performer as composer." In *Performance practice: Music after 1600,* ed. H. M. Brown and S. Sadie, 117–46. Norton.

Gay, Peter (1995). *The naked heart.* Volume 4 in *The bourgeois experience: Victoria to Freud.* Oxford University Press.

Geminiani, Francesco (1751). *The art of playing on the violin.*

Godlovitch, Stan (1988). "Authentic performance." *Monist* 71:258–77.

Goehr, Lydia (1992). *The imaginary museum of musical works: An essay in the philosophy of music.* Oxford University Press.

Goehr, L., and F. Sparshott (2001). "Philosophy of music." *NG 2,* 19:601–31.

Goldstein, Leon J. (1970). "Collingwood's theory of historical knowing." *History and Theory* 9:3–36.

Golomb, Uri (1991–93). "The spectrum of authenticism" (unpublished manuscript).

—— (1998). "Modernism, rhetoric and (de-)personalisation in the early music movement." Seminar paper, King's College, London, August 1998.

—— (2003). "Interview with Ton Koopman." *Goldberg Magazine,* www.goldbergweb.com. Accessed 31 March 2004.

—— (2004). "Expression and meaning in Bach performance and reception: An examination of the B minor mass on record." Ph.D. diss., King's College,

Cambridge. Available online at http://edocs.ub.uni-frankfurt.de/volltexte/ 2005/3077/ (links to page with dissertation abstract and to PDF file with complete text of dissertation).

——— (2005). "Rhetoric and gesture in performances of the First Kyrie from Bach's Mass in B minor (BWV 232)." *JMM: The Refereed On-Line Journal for Multi-Disciplinary Research on Music and Meaning*, http://www .musicandmeaning.net/issues/showArticle.php?artID=3.4. Accessed January 2005.

Gombrich, E. H. (1966). "The style all'antica: imitation and assimilation." In *Norm and form: Studies in the art of the Renaissance*. University of Chicago Press.

Goodman, Nelson (1976). *Languages of art: An approach to a theory of symbols*. Bobbs-Merrill.

——— (1983). "Art and authenticity." In *The forger's art: Forgery and the philosophy of art*, ed. D. Dutton, 93–114. University of California Press.

——— (1995). "Authenticity." *The dictionary of art*, 2:834–35.

Grant, Pat (2003). "Identification vs. transcription in cataloguing" (unpublished commentary).

Green, Eugène (2001). *La Parole baroque*. Descle'e de Brouwer.

Hailperin, Paul. (1997). "Copy—reconstruction—musical instrument." In *A time of questioning: Proceedings of the international early double-reed symposium*, Utrecht, 1994, ed. D. Lasocki, 183–86.

Handschin, Jacques (1927). "Die alte Musik als Gegenwartsproblem." In *Gedenkschrift Jacques Handschin: Aufsätze und Bibliographie*, ed. Hans Oesch, Haupt, 1957, 338–41.

Hanning, Barbara Russano (1992). "Monteverdi's three genera: A study in terminology." In *Musical humanism and its legacy: Essays in honor of Claude V. Palisca*, edited by N. K. Baker and B. R. Hanning, 145–70. Pendragon.

Harnoncourt, Nikolaus (1988). *Baroque music today: Music as speech* (trans. of *Musik als Klangrede*, Salzburg, 1982). Amadeus Press.

——— (1989). *The musical dialogue: Thoughts on Monteverdi, Bach and Mozart*. Amadeus Press.

Harris, Ellen T. (1989). "Voices." In *Performance practice: Music after 1600*, ed. H. M. Brown and S. Sadie, 97–116. Norton.

Harriss, Ernest C. (1981). *Johann Mattheson's Der Vollkommene Capellmeister: A revised translation with critical commentary*. University Microfilms.

Haskell, Harry (1988/1996). *The early music revival: A history*. Dover.

——— (2001). "Early music." *NG 2*, 7:831–34.

Haspels, J. J. L. (1987). *Automatic musical instruments: Their mechanics and their music, 1580–1820*. Zwolle, Netherlands.

Hatten, Robert S. (2004). *Interpreting musical gestures, topics, and tropes: Mozart, Beethoven, Schubert*. Indiana University Press.

Hawkins, Sir John (1776). *A general history of the science and practice of music*. Reprinted 1875, 1963, 1969, Dover.

Haynes, Bruce (1968). "'The decline of the recorder in the 18th century': A further scrutiny." *RMM* 2:240–42.

——— (1969). "The baroque recorder: A comparison with its modern counterpart." *American Recorder*, 11:3–8.

——— (1991). "Beyond temperament: Non-keyboard intonation in the 17th and 18th centuries." *EM* 19:357–81.

——— (1997a). "Das Fingervibrato (Flattement) auf Holzblasinstrumenten im 17., 18. und 19. Jahrhundert" [2 parts]. *Tibia* 2/97:401–407, 3/97:481–87.

——— (1997b). "Playing 'short' high notes on the hautboy." *JIDRS* 25:115–18.

——— (2001). *The eloquent oboe: A history of the hautboy, 1640–1760.* Oxford University Press.

——— (2002). *A history of performing pitch: The story of "A."*

Hewitt, Stevens (1966). *Method for oboe.* Self-published.

Heyerdahl, Thor (1951). *Kon-Tiki:* Across the Pacific by raft. Rand McNally.

Higgins, Paula (2004). "The Apotheosis of Josquin des Prez and other mythologies of musical genius." *JAMS* 57/3:443–510.

Hill, Keith, and Marianne Ploger (2005). "The craft of musical communication, Part 2." Online at http://www.musicalratio.com/onaffect.html. Accessed 31 December 2006.

Hill, Robert (1994). "Overcoming Romanticism: On the modernization of 20th century performance practice." In *Music and performance during the Weimar Republic,* ed. B. R. Gilliam, 37–58. Cambridge University Press.

——— (2000). "Spohr in Berlin oder: Musikgeschichte als Aufführungspraxisgeschichte." In *Jahrbuch des Staatlichen Instituts für Musikforschung Preussischer Kulturbesitz,* 46–56.

Hindemith, Paul (1950). *Johann Sebastian Bach. Ein verpflichtendes Erbe.* Privately printed.

Hobsbawm, Eric (1983). "Inventing traditions." In *The invention of tradition,* ed. E. Hobsbawm and T. Ranger, 1–14. Cambridge University Press.

Hoffmann, E. T. A. (1963). *Schriften zur Musik: Nachlese,* ed. F. Schnapp. Winkler-Verlag.

Hogwood, Christopher (1984). *Handel.* Thames & Hudson.

Holoman, K., R. Winter, and J. Page (2001). "Performing practice, the 19th century." *NG 2,* 19:374–77.

Horowitz, Joseph (1987). *Understanding Toscanini: How he became an American culture-god and helped create a new audience for old music.* Knopf.

——— (1995). *The Post-classical predicament: Essays on music and society.* Northwestern University Press

Hospers, John (1974). "Philosophy of art." In *The new Encyclopaedia Britannica,* 15th ed., 25:694–710.

Houle, George (1987). *Meter in music, 1600–1800.* Indiana University Press

Howlett, Alan J. (2000). "Das Utrechter Festival. Alte Musik—Die Bedrohung von innen—Die Philister vor den Toren." *Musik & Ästhetik,* 13:104–13.

Hunter, Mary (2005). "'To play as if from the soul of the composer': The idea of the performer in early Romantic aesthetics." *JAMS* 58/2:357–98.

Huray, Peter le, and James Day (1981). *Music and aesthetics in the eighteenth and early-nineteenth centuries.* Cambridge University Press

Jeffery, Peter (1992). *Re-envisioning past musical cultures: Ethnomusicology in the study of Gregorian chant.* University of Chicago Press

Jeppson, Lawrence (1970). *Fabulous frauds: A study of great art forgeries.* Weybright and Talley.

Johnson, James H. (1995). *Listening in Paris, a cultural history.* University of California Press.

Kakuzo, Okakura (1906). *The Book of Tea.* Fox Duffield.

Keller, Hermann (1955). *Phrasing and articulation: A contribution to a rhetoric of music*. Norton.

Kenyon, Nicholas (ed.) (1988). *Authenticity and early music*. Oxford University Press.

Kerman, Joseph (1985). *Contemplating music*. Harvard University Press

Kier, Herfrid (1968). *Raphael Georg Kiesewetter (1773–1850), Wegbereiter des musikalischen Historismus*.

Kiesewetter, R. G. (1820). *Über den Umfang der Singstimmen in den Werken der alten Meister, in Absicht auf deren Aufführung in unserer Zeit; gelegentlich auch Etwas über die mit dem Stimmtone auf den Orgeln und in den Orchestern nach und nach vorgegangenen*.

―――― (1827). "Wiens musikalische Kunst-Schätze." *AMZ* 29:145–56.

Kilbracken, Lord (1967). *Van Meegeren: A case history*. Scribner's.

King, Martin Luther, Jr. (1963). "I have a dream." http://www.americanrhetoric.com/lspeeches/Ihaveadream.htm. Accessed 22 October 2004.

Kingsbury, Henry (1988). *Music, talent, and performance: A conservatory cultural system*. Temple University Press.

Kirkendale, Ursula (1980). "The source for Bach's 'Musical Offering': The 'Institutio oratoria' of Quintilian." *JAMS* 33:88–141.

Kirshnit, Fred (2005). "The problem with conservatories." *New York Sun*, Arts & Letters, Sept. 12:11.

Kivy, Peter (1983). "Platonism in music: A kind of defense." *GPS* 19:109–29.

―――― (1993). *The Fine Art of Repetition: Essays in the Philosophy of Music*. Cambridge University Press

―――― (1995). *Authenticities: Philosophical reflections on musical performance*. Cornell University Press.

Kolneder, Walter (1970). *Georg Muffat zur Aufführungspraxis*, 50. Heitz.

Kuhn, Thomas (1962). *The structure of scientific revolutions*. University of Chicago Press.

Kurz, Otto (1948). *Fakes: A handbook for collectors and students*. Yale University Press.

Kuijken, Barthold (2003). "Early music in this period and how it should be played" (talk given at Seoul, Oct. 18, 2003).

Kuijken, Barthold, and Sara Anne Hook (2004). "Barthold Kuijken: Confessions of an autodidact." *Early Music America*, 10/1:31.

La Gorce, Jérôme de (1989). "Some notes on Lully's orchestra." In *Jean-Baptiste Lully and the music of the French baroque*, ed. J. H. Heyer, 99–112. Cambridge University Press.

Lambert, Constant (1934). *Music Ho! A study of music in decline*. Pelican.

Lamy, P. Bernard (1675). *La Rhétorique ou L'art de parler*, ed. Timmermans.

Landowska, Wanda (1909). *Musique ancienne*. Published as *Music of the past* (1924), tr. W. A. Bradley. Knopf.

Lang, Paul Henry (1997). *Musicology and performance*. Yale University Press.

Lawson, Colin (1994). "Beethoven and the development of wind instruments." In *Performing Beethoven*, ed. R. Stowell, 70–88. Cambridge University Press.

Lawson, Colin, and Robin Stowell (1999). *The historical performance of music: An introduction*. Cambridge University Press.

Le Cerf de la Viéville, Jean Laurent (1704–6). *Comparaison de la musique italienne et de la musique francoise.* Pages cited apply to 2-vol. ed. pub. Graz, 1966.

Leech-Wilkinson, Daniel (1984). "The limits of authenticity: A discussion." *EM* 12/1:13–16.

———— (2002). *The modern invention of medieval music: Scholarship, ideology, performance.* Cambridge University Press.

Leedy, Douglas (1991). "Communication," *PPR* 4/2:221–23.

Lehman, Bradley (2000). "Decoro, sprezzatura, grazia." Available from Bradley Lehman's home page. http://www-personal.umich.edu/~bpl/sprezza.htm. Accessed 1 July 2005.

———— (2002, 2004). "What does a musical performer think about?" [section "Gestural performance manner"]. Available from Bradley Lehman's Home Page. http://www-personal.umich.edu/~bpl/sprezza.htm Accessed 1 July 2005.

———— (2005). "Bach' extraordinary temperament: Our Rosetta Stone [Parts 1 and 2]," *EM* 33/1:3–23 and 33/2:211–26.

Leppard, Raymond (1988). *Authenticity in music.* Amadeus Press

Lessing, Alfred (1983). "What is wrong with a forgery?" In *The forger's art: Forgery and the philosophy of art,* ed. D. Dutton, 58-76. University of California Press.

Levinson, Jerrold (1990). *Music, Art, & Metaphysics: Essays in philosophical aesthetics.* Cornell University Press, 1990

Levy, Janet M. (1995). "Beginning–ending ambiguity: Consequences of performance choices." In *The practice of performance: Studies in musical interpretation,* ed. J. Rink, 150–69. Cambridge University Press.

Libby, Dennis (1989). "Italy: Two opera centres." In *The Classical era,* ed. N. Zaslaw, 15–60. Prentice-Hall.

Lochner, Louis (1951). *Fritz Kreisler.* Macmillan

Locke, Ralph P. (1999). "Musicology and/as social concern: Imagining the relevant musicologist." In *Rethinking music,* ed. N. Cook and M. Everist, 499–530. Oxford University Press.

López Cano, Rúben (2000). *Música y retórica en el barroco.* UNAM.

Lowenthal, David (1985). *The past is a foreign country.* Cambridge University Press.

Lowinsky, Edward (1964). "Musical genius—evolution and origins of a concept." *MQ* 476–95.

Marais, Marin (1711). "Avertissement," *Pièces de viole* [book 3].

———— (1717). "Avertissement," *Pièces de viole* [book 4].

Mark, Thomas Carson (1981). "Philosophy of piano playing: Reflections on the concept of performance." *PhPR* 41:299–324.

Marshall, Robert L. (1972). *The compositional process of J. S. Bach.* Princeton University Press.

Martin, Anthony (2004). "I'm all wound up about the strings we use." *Early Music America* Summer:56.

Mason, John (1748). *An essay on elocution and pronunciation.*

Massip, Catherine (1999). *L'Art de bien chanter: Michel Lambert (1610–1696).* Societe Francaise de Musicologie.

Mather, Betty Bang (1973). *Interpretation of French music from 1675 to 1775: For woodwind and other performers.* McGinnis & Marx.

Mather, Betty Bang, and David Lasocki (1976). *Free ornamentation in woodwind music, 1700–1775.* McGinnis & Marx.

———— (1984). *The art of preluding 1700–1830 for flutists, oboists, clarinettists and other performers.* McGinnis & Marx.

Mattheson, Johann (1713). *Das neu-eröffnete Orchestre.* Reprinted 1993.

———— (1737). *Kern melodischer Wissenschaft.*

———— (1739). *Der vollkommene Capellmeister.* In Harriss 1981.

Mattick, Paul, Jr. (ed.) (1993). *Eighteenth-century aesthetics and the reconstruction of art.* Cambridge University Press.

Maugars, A. (1639). *Response faite à un curieux sur le sentiment de la musique d'Italie.*

Maute, Matthias (2005). *Blockflöte & Improvisation: Formen und Stile durch die Jahrhunderte.* Breitkopf und Härtel.

McClure, Theron (1988). "Making the music speak: Silences d'articulation." *American Recorder,* 53–55.

Mealy, Robert (2005). "A note about the performance." Program notes to St. Matthew Passion, New York Collegium, Mar. 2005.

Mellers, Wilfrid (1992). "Present and past: Intermediaries and interpreters." In *Companion to contemporary musical thought,* ed. J. Paynter et al., 2:920–30. Routledge.

Mendel, Arthur (1962). "Evidence and explanation." *Report of the eighth congress of the International Musicological Society, New York, 1961* 2:2–18.

Mersenne, Marin (1636–7). *Harmonie universelle.* Reprinted 1963.

Mertin, Josef (1986; orig. 1978). *Early music: Approaches to performance practice* (tr. S. Levarie). Da Capo Press.

Meyer, Leonard B. (1967). *Music, the arts, and ideas: Patterns and predictions in twentieth-century culture.* University of Chicago Press.

———— (1989). *Style and music.* University of Chicago Press.

Michel, Winfried (1981). Giovanni Paolo Simonetti: Sechs Sonaten für zwei Altblockflöten und Basso continuo, Op.2. Composed and edited by Winfried Michel. Amadeus.

———— (1982). Simonetti-Manifest.

Middleton, Richard (2001). "Popular Music, §1, Popular music in the West." *NG* 2, 20:128–53.

Mink, Louis O. (1968). "Collingwood's dialectic of history." *History and Theory* 7:3–37.

Mitchell, William J. (tr.) (1949). C. P. E. Bach's *Versuch,* as *Essay on the true art of playing keyboard instruments.* Norton.

Morgan, Robert P. (1988). "Tradition, anxiety, and the current musical scene." In *Authenticity and early music,* ed. N. Kenyon, 57–82. Oxford University Press.

Mozart, Leopold (1756; 3/1787). *Versuch einer gründlichen Violinschule.* Reprinted 1976, 3 Reprinted 1956.

Muffat, Georg (1695). Foreword to *Suavioris harmoniae instrumentalis hyporchematicae florilegium primum.* Reprinted 1894 DTÖ.

———— (1698). Introduction to *Florilegium secundum.*

———— (1701). Introduction to *Auserlesene Instrumental-Music.* Reprinted 1904 (DTÖ).

Muller, Jeffrey M. (1982). "Rubens's theory and practice of the imitation of art." *Art Bulletin* 64:229–47.

Nagel, Thomas (1974). "What is it like to be a bat?" *Philosophical Review* 83: 435–50.

Nettl, Bruno (1999). "The institutionalization of musicology: Perspectives of a North American ethnomusicologist." In *Rethinking music*, ed. N. Cook and M. Everist, 287–310. Oxford University Press.

Neubauer, John (1986). *The emancipation of music from language: Departure from mimesis in eighteenth-century aesthetics.* Yale University Press.

Neumann, Frederick (1978). *Ornamentation in Baroque and Post-Baroque music, with special emphasis on J. S. Bach.* Princeton University Press.

Newman, Anthony (1995). *Bach and the baroque*, 2d ed. Pendragon.

Nordlinger, Jay (2004). "Who cares what critics say?" *The New Criterion.* Feb. 22. Available online at http://www.newcriterion.com/archive/22/feb04/Nov6 .htm, Accessed 24 February 2004.

North, Roger (1728). *The musical grammarian*, ed. M. Chan and J. C. Kassler, 1990, 315–59. Cambridge University Press.

——— (1959). Mss c1710–28, including *Theory of sounds, Memoires of Musick, Musical grammarian*, etc. In *Roger North on music*, ed. John Wilson, 1–360. Novello.

Ong, Walter J. (1971). *Rhetoric, Romance, and Technology.* Cornell University Press.

——— (1982). *Orality and literacy: The technologizing of the word.* Routledge.

Ord-Hume, Arthur W. J. G. (1973). *Clockwork Music: An illustrated history of mechanical musical instruments.* Crown.

Orton, Richard (1992). "From improvisation to composition." In *Companion to contemporary musical thought*, ed. J. Paynter et al., 2:762–75. Routledge.

Page, Christopher (1992). "Going beyond the limits: Experiments with vocalization in the French chanson, 1340–1440." *EM* 22/3:447–59.

Palisca, Claude V. (2001). "Prima pratica." *NG 2*, 20:320.

Parakilas, J. (1984). "Classical music as popular music." *JM* 3:1–18.

Parrott, Andrew (2000). *The essential Bach choir.* Boydell Press.

Pascall, Robert, and Philip Weller (2003). "Flexible tempo and nuancing in orchestral music: Understanding Brahms's view of interpretation in his Second Piano Concerto and Fourth Symphony." In *Performing Brahms: Early evidence of performance style*, ed. M. Musgrave and B. D. Sherman, 220–43. Cambridge University Press.

Payzant, Geoffrey (1978). *Glenn Gould: Music & mind. Journal of Aesthetics and Art Criticism* 37/4:513–514

Penin, Jean-Paul (2000). *Les Baroqueux ou le musicalement correct.* Gründ.

Philip, Robert (1992). *Early recordings and musical style.* Cambridge University Press.

——— (1994). "Traditional habits of performance in early-twentieth-century recordings of Beethoven." In *Performing Beethoven*, ed. R. Stowell, 195–204. Cambridge University Press.

——— (2003). "Brahms's musical world: Balancing the evidence." In *Performing Brahms: Early evidence of performance style*, ed. M. Musgrave and B. D. Sherman, 349–72. Cambridge University Press.

——— (2004). *Performing music in the age of recording.* Yale University Press 2004

Playford, John (1654). *A Breefe Introduction to the Skill of Musick.*

Potter, John (1998). *Vocal authority: Singing style and ideology.* Cambridge University Press.

Powell, Newman (1958). "Rhythmic freedom in the performance of French music from 1650 to 1735." Ph.D. diss., Stanford University.

Praetorius, Michael (1618/2 1619 /R. 1958). [Volume 3], *Syntagmatis musici tomus tertius.*

Printz, Wolfgang Caspar (1696). *Phrynis Mitelenaeus, oder Satyrischer Componist.*

Quantz, Johann Joachim (1752). *Essai d'une méthode pour apprendre à jouer de la Flûte Traversière / Versuch einer Anweisung die Flöte traversiere zu Spielen.* Voss.

Randel, Don Michael (1992). "The canons in the musicological toolbox." In *Disciplining music: Musicology and its canons,* ed. K. Bergeron and P. V. Bohlman, 10–22. University of Chicago Press.

Ranum, Patricia M. (2001). *The harmonic orator: The phrasing and rhetoric of the melody in French Baroque airs.* Pendragon.

Ratner, Leonard G. (1991). "Topical content in Mozart's keyboard sonatas." *EM* 19/4:615–19.

Reidemeister, Peter (1996). "Einführung." *BJHM* 20:6–19.

Restout, Denise (1964). *Landowska on music.* Stein and Day.

Riccoboni, Louis (1738). *Pensées sur la déclamation.*

Riemann, Hugo (1884). *Musikalische Dynamik und Agogik; Lehrbuch d. musikalischen Phrasirung.*

Rilling, Helmuth (1985). "The significance of Bach" (tr. Gordon Paine). Speech delivered at a reception in Stuttgart; available online from The Oregon Bach Festival site, http://bachfest.uoregon.edu/bachground/bachbits/significance .shtml. Accessed 1 February 2004.

Rooley, A. (1992). "Renaissance attitudes to performance: A contemporary application." In *Companion to contemporary musical thought,* ed. J. Paynter et al., 2:948–60. Routledge.

Rosen, Charles (2000). 'The Benefits of Authenticity', *Critical Entertainments* 200–21. Harvard University Press

Ross, Alex (Nov. 3, 2003). "Escaping the museum." *New Yorker,* 100–1.

——— (2004). "Listen to this." *New Yorker,* Feb. 16 and 23:146–55.

Rousseau, Jean-Jacques (1768). *Dictionnaire de musique.*

Salmen, Walter, ed. (1971). *Der Socialstatus des Berufsmusikers vom 17. bis 19. Jahrhundert.* Eng. tr. 1983 as *The social status of the professional musician from the middle ages to the 19th century.* Pendragon.

Salter, Lionel (2001). "Landowska, Wanda." *NG* 2, 14:225–26.

Samson, Jim (2001). "Canon (iii)." *NG* 2, 5:6–7.

Schafer, R. Murray (1975). *E. T. A. Hoffmann and music.* University of Toronto Press.

Schmied, Ernesto (2000). "Interview with Frans Brüggen, 12 January 2000." *Goldberg Magazine* (http://www.goldbergweb.com/en/magazine/interviews/ 2000/06/512_print.php). Accessed 15 November 2005.

Schmitz, Hans-Peter (1949). "Jazz und Alte Musik." Stimmen 16; reprinted in *Tibia* 4/98:257–61.

——— (1951). *Über die Wiedergabe der Musik Johann Sebastian Bachs.* Knauer.

——— (1973). *Die Kunst der Verzierung im 18.Jahrhundert.* Bärenreiter.

———— (n.d.). *Prinzipien der Aufführungspraxis Alter Musik*. Knauer.
Schmitz, Hans-Peter, and Arthur W. J. G. Ord-Hume (2001). "Engramelle, Marie Dominique Joseph." *NG2* 8:247–48.
Schubert, Peter (1994). "Authentic analysis." *JM* 12/1:3–18.
Schulenberg, David (2001). Music of the Baroque. Oxford University Press.
Schweitzer, Albert (1905). *J. S. Bach*. Eng. tr. 1911 by E. Newman. Breitkopf & Hartel.
Scruton, Roger (1982). *Kant, a very short introduction*. Oxford University Press.
———— (2001). "Expression." *NG 2*, 8:466.
Seedorf, Thomas (1994). ". . . Per imitar la voce." *Tibia* 4/1994:288–92.
Shelemay, Kay Kaufman (2001). "Toward an ethnomusicology of the early music movement: Thoughts on bridging disciplines and musical worlds." *Ethnomusicology* 45/1:1–29.
Shepherd, J., and P. Wicke (1997). *Music and cultural theory*. Polity Press.
Sherman, Bernard D. (1997). *Inside early music: Conversations with performers*. Oxford University Press.
———— (2003). "How different was Brahms's playing style from our own?" In *Performing Brahms: Early evidence of performance style*, ed. M. Musgrave and B. D. Sherman, 1–10. Cambridge University Press
Skowroneck, Martin (2002). "'The harpsichord of Nicholas Lefebvre 1755': The story of a forgery without intent to defraud." *GSJ* 55:4–14.
———— (2003). *Cembalobau / Harpsichord construction*. Bochinsky.
Small, Christopher (1998). *Musicking: The meanings of performing and listening*. Wesleyan University Press
Smith, Robert (1749/2 1759). *Harmonics, or the philosophy of musical sounds*. Reprinted 1966.
Sorrell, Neil (1992). "Improvisation." In *Companion to contemporary musical thought*, ed. J. Paynter et al., 2:776–86. Routledge.
Sparshott, Francis Edward (1998). *The future of aesthetics: The 1996 Ryle lectures*. University of Toronto Press.
Spitzer, John (1983). "Authorship and attribution in western art music." Ph.D. diss., Cornell.
Spitzer, John, and Neal Zaslaw (2004). *The birth of the orchestra: History of an institution, 1650–1815*. Oxford University Press
Steinmetz, David C. (1980). "The superiority of pre-critical exegesis." *Theology Today* 37/1:27–38.
Stevens, Denis (1997). *Early music*.
Strunk, Oliver (1950). *Source readings in music history*. Norton.
Tarling, Judy (2004). *The weapons of rhetoric*. Corda Music Publications.
Taruskin, Richard (1989). "The pastness of the present and the presence of the past." In *Authenticity and early music*, ed. N. Kenyon, 137–207. Oxford University Press.
———— (1995). *Text and act: Essays on music and performance*. Oxford University Press.
———— (2005). *The Oxford history of western music*. Oxford University Press.
Temperley, Nicholas (1984). "The limits of authenticity: A discussion." *EM* 12/1: 16–20.
Thiemel, Matthias (2001). "Accentuation." *NG 2*, 1:49.

Thom, Paul (1983). "The corded shell strikes back." *GPS* 19:93–108.

——— (1993). *For an audience: A philosophy of the performing arts.* Temple University Press.

Toft, R. (1994). "The expressive pause: Punctuation, rests, and breathing in England, 1770–1850." *PPR* 7:1–32, 199–232.

Tokumaru Yoshihiko and Yamaguti Osamu (1985). *The oral and the literate in music.* Academia Music.

Tomlinson, G. (1987). *Monteverdi and the end of the Renaissance.* University of California Press.

Tosi, Pier Francesco (1723). *Opinioni de' cantori antichi e moderni.* Reprinted 1968.

——— (1743). *Observations on the Florid Song* (tr. Eng. by Galliard).

Treitler, Leo (1989). *Music and the historical imagination.* Harvard University Press.

——— (1999). "The historiography of music: Issues of past and present." In *Rethinking music*, ed. N. Cook and M. Everist, 356–77. Oxford University Press.

Trilling, Lionel (1972). *Sincerity and authenticity.* Harvard University Press.

Tucker, Patrick (2002). *Secrets of acting Shakespeare: The original approach.* Routledge.

Van den Toorn, Gregory (2000). Notes to CD "Bach Transcriptions," cond. E.-P. Salonen.

Vény, Louis-Auguste (1828/2 1844–55). *Méthode abrégée pour le hautbois* [later ed. titled *Méthode complète pour le hautbois*]. Pleyel et Cie.

Vester, Frans (1999). *W. A. Mozart: On the performance of the works for wind instruments.* Broekmans & Van Poppel.

Vickers, Brian (1981). "Rhetorical and anti-rhetorical tropes: On writing the history of elocutio." In *Comparative criticism*, ed. E. S. Shaffer, 105–32.

——— (1984). "Figures of rhetoric/figures of music?" *Rhetorica*, 1–44.

Vries, A. B. de (1945). *Jan Vermeer van Delft.* Batsford

Wagner, Richard (1869). *On Conducting [Ueber das Dirigieren]: A treatise on style in the execution of classical music*, tr. E. Dannreuther [1887/1989].

——— (1873). "The rendering of Beethoven's Ninth symphony." In *Richard Wagner's Prose Works*, tr. W. A. Ellis, 229–53.

Waitzman, Daniel (1989). "Up from authenticity, or how I learned to love the metal flute—a personal memoir." Online, Daniel Waitzman's Web page, http://home.sprynet.com/~danwaitz/memoir.htm. Accessed 1 October 2005.

Waleson, Heidi (2004). "Mainstream musicians performing in style." *Early Music America* 10/4:24–27, 39.

Wallfisch, Elizabeth (2003). *The art of playing 'chin-off' for the brave and the curious: A treatise on one technical aspect of Baroque violin playing.* King's Music.

Walls, Peter (2003). *History, imagination, and the performance of music.* Boydell and Brewer.

Walter, Bruno (1957). *Of music and music-making.* Norton [1961, trans. of *Von der Musik und von der Muzieren*].

Weber, William (1977). "Mass culture and the reshaping of European musical taste, 1770–1870." *IRASM* 8:5–21.

—— (1984). "Wagner, Wagnerism and musical idealism." In *Wagnerism in European culture and politics*, ed. D. C. Large and W. Weber, 28–71. Cornell University Press.

—— (1992). *The rise of musical classics in eighteenth-century England: A study in canon, ritual, and ideology.* Clarendon Press.

—— (1997). "Did people listen in the 18th century?" *EM* 25/4:678–91.

—— (1999). "The history of musical canon." In *Rethinking music*, ed. Nicholas Cook and Mark Everist, 336–55. Oxford University Press.

—— (2001). "Concert (ii)." Revised *NG 2*, 6:221–35.

Wentz, Jed (2000). "Freedom of expression: A right to 'mutilate the meter.'" *Traverso* 12/2:1–3.

Werness, Hope B. (1983). "Han van Meegeren fecit." In *The forger's art: Forgery and the philosophy of art*, ed. D. Dutton, 1–57. University of California Press.

White, Harry (1997). "'If it's baroque don't fix it': Reflections on Lydia Goehr's 'work-concept' and the historical integrity of musical composition." *AM* 69:94–104.

Williams, Peter (1992). "Performance practice studies: Some current approaches to the early music phenomenon." In *Companion to contemporary musical thought*, ed. J. Paynter et al., 2:931–47. Routledge.

Wilson, Blake, George J. Buelow, and Peter A. Hoyt (2001). "Rhetoric and music." *NG 2*, 21:260–75.

Wilson, David (2001). *Georg Muffat on performance practice.* Indiana University Press.

Wilson, John (ed.) (1959). *Roger North on music.* Novello.

Wittkower, Rudolf (1965). "Imitation, Eclecticism, and Genius." In *Aspects of the eighteenth century*, ed. E. R. Wasserman, 143–61. Johns Hopkins University Press.

Wood, Caroline (1981–2). "Orchestra and spectacle in the tragédie en musique 1673–1715 oracle, sommeil and tempête." *PRMA* 108: 25–46.

Wray, Alison (1992). "Authentic pronunciation for Early Music." In *Companion to contemporary musical thought*, ed. J. Paynter et al., 2:1051–64. Routledge.

Zender, Hans (1999). "A roadmap for Orpheus?" In *Theory into practice (collected writings of the Orpheus Institute)*, ed. P. Dejans, 103–16.

Index

Abrams, M. H., 77, 111, 174, 176–77, 180, 181, 225
Absolute music, 5, 28, 35, 76–78, 87, 155, 167, 180, 223. *See also* chronocentrism; performing as part of creative process; Romanticism
  as expressing what is inexpressible in other media, 77
  instrumental because wordless, 77
  and music analysis, 29
  as not combining with other arts, 76
  reverse of Rhetorical music, 77
Academy of Ancient Music, 123–24. *See also* Concert of Antient Music
  members included many performers, 124
Ackerman, James, 138, 141
Adams, Pierce, 144–45, 203
Adorno, Theodor, 115
Æsthetics, 181. *See also* Prima pratica
  beauty unconnected to art by ancient Greeks (Collingwood), 181
  defining art as exclusively "beautiful," 181
  modern tendency to look only for the Beautiful in Rhetorical art, 182
  possibly defining element of Romanticism, 183
  word invented at end of eighteenth century, 181

Affections, 8, 69, 166, 167–71, 174, 176, 178, 179, 181, 182. *See also* commitment of performer to Affection portrayed; declamation; delivery; persuasion, musical; Realism
  including unpleasant ones, 182
  instrumental pieces based on single Affection (Mattheson), 170
  Keith Hill's list of, 168
  meaningful categories of, ceased to exist in Romantic period, 170
  modern audience reaction to, 135
  multiple and changing, 170
  as musical meaning, 168
  need to function in a framework of familiarity, 169
  North's list of, 167
  not unlike movie tag music, 169
  and Schweitzer's association of gestural shapes with, 169
Affektenlehre (Doctrine of the Affections), 167, 169, 169n13
agogics, 13, 49, 52, 59, 109
  agogic accent, 57
  defined, 13
agréments (essential graces), 4, 14, 142n12
  defined, 13
Agricola, Johann Friedrich, 73, 196
Akademie für Alte Musik, 36

267